Modern German Literature

Cultural History of Literature

Ann Hallamore Caesar and Michael Caesar, *Modern Italian Literature*
Christopher Cannon, *Middle English Literature*
Sandra Clark, *Renaissance Drama*
Glenda Dicker/sun, *African American Theatre*
Alison Finch, *French Literature*
Roger Luckhurst, *Science Fiction*
Michael Minden, *Modern German Literature*
Katie Normington, *Medieval English Drama*
Lynne Pearce, *Romance Writing*
Charles J. Rzepka, *Detective Fiction*
Jason Scott-Warren, *Early Modern English Literature*
Charlotte Sussman, *Eighteenth Century English Literature*
Mary Trotter, *Modern Irish Theatre*
Andrew Baruch Wachtel and Ilya Vinitsky, *Russian Literature*
Andrew J. Webber, *The European Avant-Garde*
Tim Whitmarsh, *Ancient Greek Literature*

Modern German Literature

MICHAEL MINDEN

polity

First published in 2011 by Polity Press

Polity Press
65 Bridge Street
Cambridge CB2 1UR, UK

Polity Press
350 Main Street
Malden, MA 02148, USA

ISBN-13: 978-0-7456-2919-3
ISBN-13: 978-0-7456-2920-9(pb)

A catalogue record for this book is available from the British Library.

Typeset in 11.25 on 13 pt Dante
by Toppan Best-set Premedia Limited
Printed and bound in Great Britain by MPG Books Group Limited, Bodmin, Cornwall

The publisher has used its best endeavours to ensure that the URLs for external websites referred to in this book are correct and active at the time of going to press. However, the publisher has no responsibility for the websites and can make no guarantee that a site will remain live or that the content is or will remain appropriate.

Every effort has been made to trace all copyright holders, but if any have been inadvertently overlooked the publisher will be pleased to include any necessary credits in any subsequent reprint or edition.

For further information on Polity, visit our website: www.politybooks.com

For Mary and Joe

Contents

Acknowledgements

In writing this book I have often had cause to remember with fondness and gratitude the supervisions on German literature I had from Traudl Herbert in the 1960s. Many colleagues and friends have helped me with its actual composition. I should especially like to thank Anita Bunyan, Ian Cooper, Stephen Fennell and Andrew Plowman for reading parts of earlier drafts, and Nicholas Boyle, Paul Connerton, Peter Hutchinson, Hunter Steele and Jo Whaley for reading whole chapters in draft. James Bowman provided substantial help throughout, giving feedback, listing references and translating quotations. Finally, I should like to thank Sally-Ann Spencer and Andrea Drugan, the two editors I have worked with at Polity, who have been so patient and supportive, and the two anonymous readers who subjected an earlier draft to some salutary hard love. The idiosyncrasies and shortcomings of the finished book are my responsibility alone.

Michael Minden
Cambridge

Introduction: Cultural History
of Literature

This book is as much about literature as it is about Germany. As a 'cultural history' of German literature, it is a study of literature in German as a variety of social and artistic practices. It is neither literary criticism nor literary history but something in between. I ask what kind of resource many different kinds of writing in German from many different parts of Europe have been in the period one could roughly describe as 'modernity'. I understand this to mean the part of European history that goes from the high tide of the Enlightenment in the middle of the eighteenth century to the end of the Cold War in 1989, when it finally ceased to be possible to believe that capitalism meant freedom simply because it was not state controlled.

Of course, there are aspects of German literature that mark it out as German. Many of these will be highlighted in the pages that follow (and readers can find diverse accounts of the Germanness of German literature in the Further Reading section at the end of the book), but one particular complex of issues bears upon my method, and so it will be mentioned, briefly, here.

The Reformation began in Saxony in the early sixteenth century. Its extraordinarily rapid repercussions throughout the Holy Roman Empire were in part the effect of Gutenberg's invention around the middle of the previous century, elsewhere in Germany, of movable metal type (the basis of printing technology for the next three hundred years). The relevance of this to literature is manifold, not least in the importance Luther attached to reading the Bible and in the introduction of hymns in the vernacular, sung by the congregation, both of which encouraged a direct relationship between words and the experience of ordinary people, no longer mediated by priests. The breaking down of the strict boundary between ministers and their congregation, for instance in the abandonment of celibacy and the existence of households in which the spiritual and secular meshed, and from which children imprinted with this spiritual–secular coding issued, created the conditions for the emergence of a modern literature in German.

There are many reasons why the realization of this potential was delayed by three hundred years, for instance the wars of religion, the attitude of the German nobility to literature in German, and the Protestant distrust of pleasure. But the crucial factor is that the European Enlightenment unlocked it. As we shall see, it was theologians and the sons of pastors who made the new secular German literature of the 1770s, bringing to the Enlightenment carnival of emancipation remarkable powers of introspection and abstraction long held back by piety and political servitude.

These powers of thought, rooted in experience yet turned towards the absolute, liberated the diversity that dwells within the specific experience of individuals and collectives, and thus sanctioned a modern literature as a resource for secular society. Such is the contribution of the East Prussian Protestant minister and theologian Johann Gottfried Herder (1744–1803; see chapter 1). Furthermore, they delivered a power of abstraction that could *situate* this lived diversity between the human mind and the absolute truth, and such is the extraordinary contribution of the East Prussian Protestant philosopher Immanuel Kant (1724–1804).

The point for my method is that this remarkable culture of critical consciousness not only in effect created modern German literature but covered it up again. In the nineteenth century, post-Kantian Idealism – that is, the systematic power of ideas or the organizing power of human consciousness – was enlisted for the purposes of nation-building. In this vast project, the specificity of literature, with its links in modernity to complex individual pleasure and to the marketplace, was neglected in favour of the *ideas* that might dwell within it and require uncovering, especially if they served the purpose of constructing a usable national identity or adding to its prestige.

It is often said that German literature is more philosophical than other comparable modern literatures. This may or may not be true, but my aim has been to correct, as far as I am able, the 'philosophical' distortion suffered by specific works and writers in German resulting from the process I have just described. This is not to say that I make no use of social and other sorts of theory where they are helpful and relevant, but they, and I, are there to serve the literature, and not to make it mean anything other than what it says. For this reason also, my interest in questions of German national identity takes second place to my interest in what German literature was actually like, what was written, what was read, what mattered to it (which certainly was sometimes national identity) but, most importantly, what was and is great literature.

A word about the tension between literature and history. My guiding principle in writing has been to navigate a way between two competing contemporary perils. These are, on one side, the subordination of history to literature that I was brought up to regard as natural, to which I unfortunately incline personally, and that, on a sophisticated level, vitiates much theoretical discourse of recent decades. On the other side, there is the temptation to contextualize away the specificity of literary 'events', to fall victim to the delusion that the responsible and life-affirming duty of the scholar in the humanities can only be discharged by the kind of 'research' that in fact takes its template from the natural sciences (where it has an entirely different modality and function) because that is the template grant-awarding bodies most readily understand.

It comes down to a question of narrative, and here we may engage again in some specifics of German history. The first two chapters deal with literature as a more or less defined (if varied and changing) entity from about 1750 to about 1890. The third, on the transition between 1890 and 1916, begins to register how any seamless literature–history narrative would distort the true facts of the matter. The national narrative points, under Prussian leadership, towards European dominance, while culture, resonating with the cultural Modernism elsewhere in Europe (particularly in those parts of the German-speaking lands not following Prussia into the sunset), begins to dispute the ineluctable quality of this narrative and insist instead upon the need to think, feel, see and do otherwise. The last three chapters then abandon chronology – not, paradoxically, to downplay the importance of historical events, but on the contrary to give them their real due. The Great War revealed how precarious European institutions, both visible and invisible, both political and moral, were. In this context, the German experience was one of a story traumatically and incomprehensibly interrupted. These chapters – on the Literature of Negation, literature under totalitarian regimes, and literature under democratic capitalism – chart the fate of the oppositional tendency that became dominant in literature at the end of the nineteenth century. This tendency could do nothing tangible to prevent or correct the calamities consequent upon the hypertrophy of technology or value-neutral economic processes. Instead, literature was subordinated and scattered, but took new forms and continued to provide testimony to human resilience and to the will to live and make new values among the wreckage of the old.

1

A European German Literature

Towards the end of the nineteenth century, the best-selling novelist and theorist of realism Gustav Freytag described the earlier Golden Age of German literature as a soul without a body. He regarded it as miraculous that the writing of Johann Wolfgang von Goethe (1748–1832), Friedrich Schiller (1759–1805), and the whole ensuing cultural attitude that became famous in Europe by the name of 'Romanticism' could have come about before there was a definable Germany. It was surprising that this could have happened in advance of the subsequent political maturity of modern Germany with which Freytag and his colleagues identified themselves. Yet, despite the late feudalism of small duchies, bishoprics and principalities and the sclerotic institutions of the Holy Roman Empire (to which Napoleon finally put an end in 1806), there was a German cultural identity, based upon a shared language, that went back in various ways to the Middle Ages, and which had been particularly strong since the Protestant Reformation. The very social and political deficits of the German lands in relation to France and Great Britain were the strongest elements in a powerful desire for a public German culture that transcended random political and national boundaries.

The desire among educated Protestant Germans for a modern cultural identity realized through the resource of the German language coincided with the wider European interest of the late eighteenth century in individualism and interiority. This coincidence is behind the particularly intense and fertile symbiosis between German writers and European culture from the 1770s onwards. Several factors are at play here. First, there is the pressure-cooker effect of this urge for collective and personal identity, each intensifying the other, pushing up against social and political forms generally uncongenial to it. With the French Revolution and the Napoleonic wars, however, local allegiance to progressive states, of which Prussia and Weimar are different kinds of example, gave shelter from the storm, both politically and financially. They provided a base from which to rein back the alarming results of the revolution, aesthetically at least, without discarding the ideals that inspired the revolution in the first place.

At the same time, the efflorescence of German writing represented in successive waves by Friedrich Gottlieb Klopstock (1724–1803), Gotthold Ephraim Lessing (1729–1781), Herder, Goethe, Schiller, Heinrich von Kleist (1777–1811), Friedrich Hölderlin (1770–1843) and others, coincided more immediately than could be said to be the case with the original Golden Ages of France, Britain or Spain with the modernization of the publishing industry. A self-consciously aspirational literary culture there-fore sought to find an accommodation with the new market for literature. In this it was not entirely successful, yet this lack of success highlights a discrepancy between cultural values and pragmatic circumstances imma-nent in European cultural history to this day.

These factors make of the first great phase of German literature – before its 'soul' becomes 'embodied', to recall Freytag's simile, in modern German political nationalism – a magnification of the hopes, tensions and accom-modations within post-Enlightenment modernity more generally. Under the name of 'Romanticism', what one might term the first symbiosis of German literature with that of Spain, France and Britain offers the rest of Europe after 1815 not only a model for nationalism, but also an alternative to the rise of industrial culture and utilitarianism, which is paradoxically at the same time a sphere of activity and production – modern literature – admirably suited to capital exploitation.

Enlightenment identities

In the 1720s, the Leipzig university professor Johann Christoph Gottsched (1700–1766) launched a cultural campaign in support of the dignity of the German language. Leipzig at that time was the literary capital of the German lands, and from here Gottsched's campaign adumbrated the authority and set the terms of reference for a recognizably modern institu-tion of literature in German Protestant areas from East Prussia to Switzer-land. Gottsched's attention was particularly turned towards dramatic literature since the theatre is at once a tangible public event and a cultural medium. Gottsched and his wife, Luise Adelgunde Victorie, née Kulmus (1713–1762), wrote tragedies and comedies and, in cooperation with the first serious modern German theatre director Friederike Caroline Neuber and her husband Johann, laid the groundwork for the later cultural revolu-tion of the 1770s which was expressed largely in the forms of dramatic literature, taking its traditional literary historical name, the 'Sturm und Drang', from the title of a play published in 1776.

The symbiotic moment in the case of the Gottscheds and the Neubers in the earlier part of the century was one between German needs and French influence. Gottsched, in converting a relatively modest local organization of German-language poets into the *Deutsche Gesellschaft*, wanted to emulate the *Académie française*. The plays he and his wife produced were largely based on classical models in the French manner, while his reform of German literature followed Boileau's *Art poétique*, that is to say a regular and prescriptive model for the 'kinds', the forms and themes, of literature, such as to make them an appropriate vehicle for the civilizing ideals of reason and order emanating from the French Enlightenment.

Luise Gottsched's most famous play, *Die Pietisterey im Fischbein-Rocke* [*Pietism in a Whalebone Skirt*, 1736], was a rationalist satire upon the gullibility, hypocrisy and bigotry of Pietists. The second wave of symbiosis that enriched German literature was intimately bound up with precisely the area of experience the rationalist dramatist had controversially lampooned.

Pietism was a development within the Protestant persuasion away from dogmatic Lutheran orthodoxy in the direction of the practical cultivation of good works, collective immersion in scripture, and personal worship. Despite its emphasis upon private devotion and its aversion to the official Protestant establishment, its influence spread throughout the Lutheran parts of the German-speaking world, sometimes with official state approval. In the early decades of the eighteenth century, Philipp Jacob Spener and August Hermann Franke introduced Pietist pedagogical initiatives at the University of Halle, and Nikolaus Graf von Zinzendorf founded what became a famous religious community at Herrnhut in Saxony. Pietism came to be associated with deep, life-denying introspection in the later part of the century and was in itself opposed to modern secular literature.

Despite this puritanical remoteness from secular life, the importance that Pietism attached to reading and to individual experience (in the heart of which revelation was sought) and its opposition to cold authoritarian dogma from which it sprang as a movement were congenial to the psychological formation of individuals who contributed decisively to a new sort of literature.

This literature provided the common ground upon which personal and national identity came together. In the widely read writing of Klopstock (*Der Messias* [*The Messiah*], first three cantos 1748; *Oden*, 1771), religious feeling, at once highly personal in the Pietistic inflection and something with which all Protestant Germans could identify collectively (Herder called *Der Messias* the first classical German book since Luther's Bible), fused with the noisy rebuttal of rule-bound literary dogma. It was at once specific to German identity and another point of symbiosis, since Klopstock's main model was Milton's *Paradise Lost*.

Eschewing rhyme as trivial and using the then unfashionable hexameter in his epic and free rhythms in his lyric poetry (of which 'Die Frühlingsfeyer' ['Spring Celebration'] of 1759 is a good example), Klopstock identified literature as something other than a bourgeois version of courtly refinement or public entertainment. It became a medium in which serious issues – the big questions in life – and a broad swathe of *das Volk*, in other words 'the nation', could be addressed. It was the portal through which the 'soul' of Protestant affect entered German literature.

The confluence of religious sensibility with personal affect in lyric poetry is a chief characteristic of German literature from Klopstock onwards. It reflects the popularity of Pietist hymns and resonates in the extraordinary suggestive power that the famous *Lieder* of nineteenth-century Romantic composers add to the words of lyric poems. Modern German lyric poetry not only carries the range of reference from small to sublimely large ('Staub, und auch ewig' ['dust and yet eternal'], as Klopstock wrote of the nature of man in the ode 'An Gott'), but it retains the range of appeal from popular to hermetic, often in the work of the same poet.

Lessing combined a rationalist impulse to reform public culture with indigenous German Protestant individualism. In 1767, by then already famous as a playwright and critic, he agreed to become the dramatic critic (*Dramaturg*) of a project for a national theatre launched by a consortium of leading citizens of the free city of Hamburg. This project took up the initiative of the Gottscheds and the Neubers to create at the institutional level a focus for a German culture to rival that of other European countries, but failed to sustain itself for more than three years, largely due to the reluctance of the government of Hamburg to subsidize it. It is entirely consistent with Freytag's image of disembodiment that Lessing's actual writings for the Hamburg theatre grew more and more remote from their original function as part of a planned national institution, becoming instead founding theoretical documents of a new dramatic literature.

In these and other writings, Lessing developed his ideas about what the theatre should be in contemporary Germany. Less rationalist and dogmatic than the Gottscheds, he was more empirically focused upon realism as a pragmatic and social value. He took Shakespeare as the polemical counter to French neoclassicism. He wanted to encourage and facilitate an attitude of moral progress without overt didacticism and by fashioning an appeal to the expectations and experience of the contemporary audience. His plays and aesthetic writings explored the possibilities of dramatic literature as a testing ground for practical morality, in which the pleasure of the spectator fused with an increase in his or her sensitivity for others and for the complexities of the competing value systems, both moral and aesthetic, of the time.

Hence with *Minna von Barnhelm* (1767), which became the most performed piece in the repertoire of the Hamburg theatre (and remains popular to this day), Lessing wrote a comedy in which familiar comedy types were nuanced into socially and psychologically differentiated characters, and the traditional comic intrigue, the function of which was to unmask delusion or vice, became a means of investigating the competing and equally valid claims of honour and love. Both in this play and the tragedy *Emilia Galotti* (1772), to which we return below, a realism not only of dialogue, character and plot motivation but also of social and political topicality coexists with the commitment to create serious drama along more or less traditional lines. They are plays in which the given tensions of the time, between Enlightenment and absolutism, empiricism and rationalism, debate and authority, faith and scepticism are inscribed on every level to create complex modern works of art.

While Lessing opposed arbitrary authority wherever he encountered it, in state, church or theatre, he nevertheless assumed, along with his generation, and indeed the next one, that a coherent account of the universe and of man's place in it would be the ultimate outcome of every emancipated investigation. Hence behind his famous demolition of Gottsched's rationalist imitation of French classical tragedy (in the seventeenth of his *Letters* on contemporary literature, 1759), there stands a belief in the timeless authority of Aristotle, just so long as he has been properly understood. Likewise, it is the calling of reason to discern behind the vicissitudes and accidents of empirical experience the work of divine providence. His contribution to German literature resides in the fact, therefore, that his concessions to contemporary reality and rhetorical informality, and his commitment to moral improvement through emotional engagement, rest upon an authority all the more unchallengeable for being ultimately invisible behind the masks of Aristotle, Shakespeare, God: the authority of 'art' as a modern alternative to the dogmas of church and state. This in turn rests upon the assumption of the time that the universe was coherent in relation to human identity in history, even as the evident dubiousness of this assumption was bound to leave questions unanswered.

The case of Karl Philipp Moritz (1756–1793) provides an especially rich and multi-faceted insight into the cultural pattern that underlies the narrative of German literary history in these decisive decades of the eighteenth century. In his psychological novel, which is also an autobiography, *Anton Reiser* (1785–1790), Moritz provides an account of what it was like for an individual socialized in the pre-modern world to experience the impact of the new culture. Goethe's *Die Leiden des jungen Werthers* [*The Sorrows of Young Werther*, 1774] was a public discourse of private anguish, a kind of legitimation of inwardness as a reality rather than as a sphere in need of subordination to explicit moral or religious regimens. When he reads it, Moritz/Reiser recognizes his own hitherto inchoate inner life portrayed in public. This felt like an infinitely more authentic externalization and staging of his sense of self than the sermons the young man, brought up in a strict Pietist household but shaped by a modern education, had once so fervently aspired to preach. These could have only ever been a rhetorical performance, a kind of morally sanctioned dissimulation, rather than what now seemed to a young generation to be a public projection of *genuine* personal feelings.

Yet Moritz's autobiographical novel does not just provide an account of this impact which in the 1770s was called the moment of the *Genie* (the word 'genius' used to describe an individual rather than a quality), denoting the discovery of an inner creativity that replaced the need for external authority. It is rather an empirical account of this impact and a diagnosis of it as a psychological and moral shortcoming. It puts the *Genie* back in the bottle. What makes Moritz representative is both an awareness of the power of this emancipatory moment, in which private and collective identities merge and confirm one another, and of the need for it to be contained.

Under Goethe's influence, Moritz was the first to propose in theoretical terms the idea of art as autonomous. This conception of art was brought into the mainstream of aesthetic thought by Kant in his *Critique of Judgement* in 1790 and by Schiller in his wake. In propounding his theory, Moritz is providing the positive to the negative he had given in *Anton Reiser*. Reiser, his (former) self, was someone who emerged from the grim ordinariness of eighteenth-century Germany into the artificial light of the new reading and writing. He was seduced by it into inventing a false self, a bogus authenticity not just symbolized by, but actually historically embodied in, the exaggerated expectations for the theatre among the generation of the

1770s. The categorical distinctions Moritz devised correct this failing. He argued that the poet as an artist (as opposed to the hack or dilettante) must *not* write with an effect in mind but must achieve a representation of the indwelling (ultimately divine) truth of the original reality or experience. Real poets are also categorically distinguished from those who may aspire to a state of attention in which art can be appreciated but should not confuse this with the ability to create it. Poets are inhabited by a 'Tatkraft' or 'Bildungskraft' ('vigour or formative [creative] energy') that enables them to present the self-contained fullness required of real art. Consumers have the ability to *receive* the autonomous work of art but not to create it.

Yet Moritz held faith with his own experience over *Werther*. It was clearly vital to him to distinguish the *work*, which he always revered, from his bad reaction to it, which he turned into a cautionary tale. There is a similar process of rationalist discrimination when Moritz distinguishes his own literary prose work, the 'psychological novel' *Anton Reiser*, from *Werther*, which he calls poetry or art. This is because it achieves in its central moment the artistic miracle of *portraying* the desire to display without violating the autonomy of art by being the *result* or *effect* of that desire. The legitimation for *Anton Reiser* is not artistic at all but, on the one hand, moral, and, on the other, empirical-scientific.

The case of Moritz thus focuses the following: first, the difficulty for Germans to find a perspective from which to value the modern novel. Moritz had written a superb example of one, but denied it the dignity of art, while his life had been changed by another, but this he idealized. The plays of the *Sturm und Drang* superimposed upon a utopian dream of cultured public institutions the new realism of the empirical and rational Enlightenment. There is a creative mismatch between the aspiration to make a national culture, in which context a national theatre is attractive, and the surging print culture and book market, in which prose literature was at home.

The subsequent development of the serious modern German drama bears out its origin in utopian containment of potentially destructive emancipatory forces. The direction was set in Lessing's last play, *Nathan der Weise* (1779), in which a public theological debate, brought to an end by the combined forces of orthodox Lutheranism and local state power, was diverted into the realm of dramatic literature (written to be read rather than performed), in which an ideal accommodation between the Jewish, Christian and Islamic faiths and a rebuttal of benighted religious dogma is embodied in characters and blank verse rather than in direct polemic. After his debut as a revolutionary realist in the 1770s, Goethe's dramas, such as *Iphigenie auf Tauris* (1779–1787) and *Torquato Tasso* (1790), are artificial cultural constructs, highly stylized and remote from popular appeal. In the case of his most famous work *Faust*, on which he worked all his life, we have a sort of monstrous development beyond the popular dramatic form in which it originated in the 1770s in the direction of what Franco Moretti has termed 'modern epic'. By this, Moretti meant a compendious literary work, hybrid as regards genre, undertaking the impossible task of giving a unified artistic account of modernity. For Moretti, the category of modern epic also includes such works as Wagner's Ring cycle, in which the history of nineteenth-century German (indeed European) drama culminated, Joyce's *Ulysses* and Márquez's *One Hundred Years of Solitude*. This is a long way from popular improving entertainment.

Moritz was also representative of the time in that he occupied a position between the popular and the learned. The possibility of making a living as a writer was just beginning for Germans, although this required a tremendous struggle for survival. Moritz retained something of the *Genie* long after it was fashionable and exploited it in the service of his efforts to educate the public. If we add to this the connection he made between poetry and the indivisible unity of the divinity which was theological in origin, he provides a conduit from the source of the German literary revival in a secularized Protestant inwardness, through the defence of this against the threat of vulgarization, to the formulation of something, namely art, that could make sense in the modern world of rationalization, manufacture, trade and the need for distraction. In this he foreshadowed the Romantic movement.

The virtue of sexuality

The case of Moritz illustrates the context of the stirrings of modern German literature but one essential component is missing. It is the projection on the screen of public culture of what Friedrich Nietzsche (1844–1900) would later call the Dionysian.

When Goethe began to work on the new version of the novel that was to become *Wilhelm Meisters Lehrjahre* (*Wilhelm Meister's Apprenticeship*, 1796), he developed in it a figure, Laertes, whose unfortunate erotic experiences had made a depressive character of him. Goethe was paying secret tribute to his friend, Moritz, who had only recently died at the age of 36 (see Schings 1983). Moritz's documentary account of subjective partialness in *Anton Reiser* thereby becomes an implied complement to Goethe's novel.

In the former, sexuality is one of the traps besetting the protagonist, simply another potential pathology which it is the business both of moral/aesthetic reason and of empirical psychology to recognize and contain. For the mature Goethe of the *Lehrjahre*, things are quite different. Here, sexuality (that is, the figures of the desire of the subject-hero, Wilhelm Meister) is an absolutely integral part of the shape of the work. The novel begins with a pathological reaction to the power of sexual jealousy, certainly, but develops from Book to Book in fuller and more balanced relationships with women characters in which this first pathology is overcome and redeemed (albeit not without having left scars). What is one to make of this contrast between Moritz/Laertes' inept-farcical sexual lives and the redemption of sexuality in the *Lehrjahre*? In marking this contrast Goethe is, I think, pointing up the profound difference between the eighteenth-century and Enlightenment *materials* of the beginnings of modern German literature and the more incendiary sexual fuel that set them on fire.

The 'virtue' of the eighteenth-century European middle classes, upon which their literature was built, was a rebuttal of the corrupt leisure habits of the aristocracy. In the work of Christoph Martin Wieland (1733–1813), an exemplary exponent of the founding symbiosis of German with wider European literature and for a while the most famous living German author, this polemical preoccupation with virtue is tempered with an eroticism deriving from the rococo taste of contemporary small-time courts. The modern enlightened mind allied with the grace of courtly manners modified excessively arid subscription to the letter of virtue. The didactic poem *Musarion* (1768) exemplified the claim that wisdom is more effective when it emerges from graceful and attractive lips. Wieland's attempt to merge courtly Francophile eroticism (as in his *Comische Erzählungen* [*Comic Tales*], of 1765) with Enlightenment common sense brought him a bad reputation in religious quarters.

Yet for Wieland sexuality, however beguiling, was not the meaning of life but the refinement of a virtuous one. This is apparent from the contrast between the representation of women in Wieland's Fieldingesque novel *Geschichte des Agathon* (*The History of Agathon*, 1766–7) and Goethe's in *Wilhelm Meister*. Wieland's hero suffers from an addiction to abstract virtue and is cured of this by the attention of a beautiful courtesan, Danae. However, Danae is able to help Agathon because she understands the reality, and thus also the limits, of sex. The end of the novel is not a happy marriage, which would imply that the erotic trajectory was in some complex sense the right one (not only for the characters, but more profoundly, for the readers, whose simpler desires would thereby be gratified, as they would have been in a more popular kind of novel), but instead renunciation and companionship. Wieland used sexuality to explore the interiority of his protagonist, an exploration that was felt to be path-breaking by Lessing and Christian Friedrich von Blanckenburg, author of the first German 'Theory of the Novel' (*Versuch über den Roman*, 1774). But Wieland also saw the interior space as one in which moral values (virtue) must juggle perpetually with appetite in order to maintain the kind of civilized, but pragmatic, balance he proposes.

The plot of Lessing's *Emilia Galotti* (1772) requires for its tragic denouement that a father should kill his daughter to save her from dishonour. It is taken from the story of Virginius and his daughter Virginia, as told by Livy. In the original plot there is an explicitly political dimension which Lessing removes because he wishes his tragic catastrophe to be motivated by psychology. Emilia Galotti persuades her father to kill her because she is not sure that she will be able to resist the attraction she feels for the Prince, in whose physical and judicial power she finds herself. Her own sexuality is stressed by the importance accorded to it in the chain of circumstances leading to the tragic denouement.

Neither Wieland nor Lessing accord sexuality the kind of role it had acquired for the mature Goethe. Both writers are perfectly frank about the sexual element in human affairs and, indeed, about its place in literature. Wieland thinks a kind of erotic grace is important in civilized behaviour, and Lessing uses the dichotomy of sex and virtue to drive his German domestic tragedy. Sexuality as a source of pleasure remains in the end the preserve of the corrupt courts and a component of the critique levelled against them, while the pleasure for the implied (and presumably actual) audience comes from the intimate portrait of moral interiority.

So where did this mutation in the role of sexuality come from? In Goethe's fiction it began with a text to which we have already referred: *Die Leiden des jungen Werthers*. Sexual passion bursts through the familiar language of *Empfindsamkeit* ('sentimentalism'), recolouring the conventional (epistolary) representation of authenticity in a deeper, and more dangerous hue. Moral feeling and libido collapse into each other, destroying the protagonist's balance of mind and causing a suicide so graphically described as to be still shocking today.

The book left lying open on Werther's desk after his suicide is *Emilia Galotti*. Many interpretations have been placed upon this circumstance (which incidentally Goethe took from the actual account of Karl Wilhelm Jerusalem's suicide upon which Book Two of *Werther* is based). But one thing is clear: Emilia's assisted suicide is in the name of religious belief and moral purity, while Werther takes his own life because eros has got out of control.

This is manifest not only on the level of the plot but on that of the text also. Claudia, Emilia's mother, had explained to her in Act II, Scene 6, how an erotic discourse (the *Galanterie* associated with aristocratic amorousness) fatally undermines the distinction between moral feeling and appetite. Lessing's play is written against this kind of *galant* discourse. *Werther* is certainly no more *galant* than *Emilia Galotti*. But it is more subversive than any *Galanterie* because the sex in it is unsocialized. The power of unacknowledged sexuality in the mind is represented with immediate impact, and without any explicit or implicit moral corrective. Pastor Goeze, the chief Lutheran pastor of Hamburg, and Lessing's opponent in the theological debate that gave rise to *Nathan der Weise*, was in a way quite right when he said disapprovingly in 1775 that the message Goethe's text was sending to the youth of the day was the intolerable one that 'you should follow your natural urges' (quoted in Grimminger 1980: 710).

But, in another way, he was quite wrong – because what set readers alight was not an encouragement to actual immoral acts. The aristocratic hedonism upon which the Prince in *Emila Galotti* falls back could hardly have been farther from the point. Something much more portentous is being announced between the texts: the triumph of a particular kind of mental pleasure that is the condition of both Romanticism and modern consumerism. Strip away the moral component from Richardson and Lessing – although it is important to understand how much pleasure readers will have derived from identifying with that morality – and you find yourself in a world in which personal desire has been miraculously dignified.

Werther's story is pathological and, on the face of it, it is hard to understand why Goethe felt compelled to warn readers of the later edition against emulating his unfortunate hero. But we have first-hand testimony from Moritz, and others, as to why they liked it. It spoke more directly to them, to themselves as their own centres of feeling, as desiring, appetite-driven, imperfect real beings, than public discourse had done before. And as such it did more than any other text (certainly in German) to stake out an area for private pleasure, removed from the surveillance of either priests or enlightened rationalists (and, indeed, from the control of conscientious authors), but was spectacularly irresistible to publishers. It is no surprise that the publisher of *Werther*, C. F. Weygand of Leipzig, quickly followed it up with *Siegwart* in 1776, which was nearly as successful. Its author, J. M. Miller, was explicitly aiming to fill the gap in the market that Friedrich

Nicolai, a leading Berlin man of letters and publisher-bookseller, had identified in the early 1770s between the learned reading public and the popular end of the market.

What separates Wieland and Lessing, therefore, from *Werther* and after is that their writing is about, and subject to, the interplay of public values and private concerns, while the incipient culture, whatever it is about, is not. Releasing sexuality into the hidden heart of literature has the effect of dynamizing it to an unprecedented degree and of establishing poetry as a linguistic space no longer publicly answerable in traditional recognized ways. Yet, this same development makes the products of the imagination more vulnerable to co-optation by the objective forces of history outside them, commercial, political or a mixture of both. As we shall see, this has its most significant effects in the German literature of the post-Napoleonic period. Both the philosophical category of the 'aesthetic' and the attitude of Romanticism are projects whose function, whether explicitly or not, is to secure a public identity for this differentiated poetic space, to defend it against appropriation by making it 'autonomous'. The first symbiosis of German literature reflects a heroic effort in the cause of creating a public identity for what Nicholas Boyle has called 'the poetry of desire'.

The German idea of literature

Dionysos arrived as a 'virus' with the new ideas of Johann Gottfried Herder. The burden of Herder's contributions to the theory of language and to historiography are not reducible to sex, but they don't make sense without it. The implied importance of sexuality in Herder's organicism was more explicit in the religious thought of his guru, Johann Georg Hamann (1730–1788). In Hamann's writing, nothing was of greater importance than the divinely given unity of body and spirit, from which all energy flowed, and to the fracturing of which (for instance by abstract, disembodied thought) the evils of modern civilization could be attributed. From here, an explicitly sexual theme in writing can be traced through Wilhelm Heinse's influential novel *Ardinghello* (1787), in which an island utopia of free love is proposed, and Friedrich Schlegel's novel *Lucinde* (1799), in which an ideal of relationship is proposed in which body and soul are equally integrated, to Gutzkow's *Wally die Zweiflerin* (1835), Heine's *Neue Gedichte* (1844), and Nietzsche's Dionysianism (see Berlin 1994: 99–101, and chapters 2 and 3 below).

The example of Moritz showed, however, that the more typical reaction was less straightforward than an affirmation of the senses. Beyond the intimation of unbounded subjective potential, and leaving to one side the complexity of guilt feelings, it involved the need for a *Gestalt* ('form') in which this energy might expend itself productively ('creatively').

Herder argued that energy, shape, truth, come from within, and are not imposed by calculation or measurement upon living phenomena, be they individuals or collectivities. The great significance of these ideas for modern German literature was basically twofold. First, they provided the framework in which the general individualism of the European eighteenth century fused with the thirst for cultural identity that was a specifically German preoccupation. In Herder's intensification of them, both these things are driven from within. What is more, the latter provides the defining context for the former. This is by virtue of the significance Herder attached to language, in which we discern his second decisive contribution. Language was for him the indwelling *Gestalt* of distinct human entities, whether individual or collective. This was called *das Charakteristische*. The creative genius fulfils himself by working in his own native language which is also the spontaneous life of his language culture. It is, therefore, in language that identity comes about because it is common to both individual and culture. It is the dimension within which each recognizes, and, in recognizing, constitutes the other. Until Wagner read Schopenhauer some sixty years later, it is hard to imagine artists receiving a more empowering endorsement from philosophy: language, the medium of literature, is in this view the cornerstone of cultural value. Literature is a living force, carrying within it the creative drive of humanity, not constrained by externalities of any description but simply seeking to be and become itself.

The implications of this 'thinking from within' are enormous because they open the royal road to the modern understanding of history. Gone is the cultural hierarchy which, still for Wieland and Lessing, accorded Greek and Latin models an unassailable position, which wit and skill could imitate, emulate, even adapt, but never replace. Now each culture has its own voice and its own shape. Significant historical difference is born. However, there are huge unanswered questions. How, for instance, to avoid debilitating (Nietzsche will say 'decadent') relativism? Or, again, how to produce a spontaneous culture consciously? But before these problems can lengthen into solutions or evasions, they were first of all the 'stuff' of Goethe's generation of young authors.

Inspired by the organicism of Herder, with its fusion of individualist and national-cultural implications, the effects of symbiosis between the specifically German and the European context become spectacular. If we recall our earlier question about the difference between Laertes/Moritz and

Meister/Goethe, then this is the answer to it; this is the specifically German contribution to eighteenth-century European literary culture.

The celebrated historian Friedrich Meinecke gives a good explanation of this, summing it up under the name of *Historismus* ('historicism'; Meinecke 1946). Elements of eighteenth-century middle-class culture which, without betraying the Enlightenment, reflected the need for a diversity of gratifying distraction not catered for by strict intellectual rationalism modulate, in the minds of German cultural leaders, into what is virtually a new existential programme. The interest in Gothic (that is, medieval) architecture, for instance, which grew in England from the fashion for asymmetrical landscape gardening as an alternative to neoclassical taste, became in Goethe's ecstatic essay on Strasbourg Cathedral (1772) a polemic on behalf of the 'characteristic' in architecture. Goethe's essay, 'Von deutscher Baukunst' ('On German Architecture'), reflected an enthusiasm not shared by Herder, who nevertheless included it in the manifesto of the new cultural enthusiasm *Von deutscher Art und Kunst* (*Of German Character and Art*) of 1773. The 'characteristic', coming from within, cannot be governed or explained by neoclassical rules and conventions, and, in the case of the magnificent medieval cathedral at Strasbourg, expresses simultaneously the genius of the (German) architect, Erwin von Steinbach, and that of the German spirit. (In fact, neither of these claims has an objective basis.)

Von deutscher Art und Kunst also established a paradoxical link between folk (i.e. anonymous) poetry and the revolution in the contemporary lyric. Herder, arguing for the authenticity of folk poetry, published Goethe's then unknown love lyric 'Heidenröslein' ('Moorland Rose') as an example. The enthusiasm for spontaneous national literature and the expression of authentic affect in lyric poetry unbound by rules fuse nowhere more intimately than in the realm of the lyric poem. Goethe's poems from 1771 about Friederike Brion, for instance 'Mailied' ('May Song'), are excellent examples. This is also the point in German literature at which a surprising confluence of Pietistic poetry and sentiment (as in Klopstock) and secular eroticism (as in the early Goethe's love lyrics, embedded in a sense and a vocabulary of reciprocity with all creation) occurs, betraying a common element in the quasi-mystical holism of Hamann. In this there is further explanation of the tendency of the German lyric to span the range from individual experience to the transcendental horizon.

Edward Young's *Conjectures on Original Composition* (1759; German 1760) found a much greater resonance in Germany than it had in its native England. What in its original context was a contribution to literary criticism, expressing reservations about the principle of imitating the ancients, in Germany found itself central to the workings of a new philosophy. For Hamann and Herder and others, it confirmed the idea of the *Genie* as the source of creativity, with the corollary rejection of imitation. This rejection resonated strongly with the German urge for cultural self-assertion. It sanctioned the rejection of French taste and dominance and provided the inspiring model of Shakespeare, who was regarded, by Young as well as by his German appropriators, as the great model of an original genius.

A German Shakespeare

Goethe's *Götz von Berlichingen* (1773) derived its dynamic character from the uncertainty with which it relates private to public concerns. For there to be an interplay between these things, as had still been the case with Lessing and Wieland, they need to be defined against each other. With the new claims of individual eros, this is not given. On the level of the choice of motif, this is manifest in the figure of the independent feudal lord at war with the 'modernizing' episcopacy of Bamberg. An episode in German history assumes the form of a dramatic opposition between individualism and impersonal authority. This dramatizes Herder's opposition to schematic rationalism (with which he associated the efficient modern state of Prussia) from an 'organic' position, while on a deeper level validating German history, within which the significant antagonism is subsumed.

The indistinct line between the private and public spheres is likewise manifest on the structural level. The extensive subplot concerning the character of Weislingen is marked both by autobiographical elements and by the kind of domestic–moral conflict familiar in Lessing. It is as though one leading character represents practical, objective independence, something imagined as objectively German, and the other modern interiority. The play tracks indecisively the contamination of each by the other.

The ending of the play is also inconclusive. Götz, the character who seems intended to elicit the approbation of an audience, is morally compromised and defeated. But this happens in the name of a 'freedom' which links the charismatic licence of lords within the feudal system with a – different and undefined – claim on behalf of the present generation.

On the level of style, however, the victory is on the other side. The polemically 'Shakespearean' nature of the play, which is to say its identification as a product of German sensibility, historical, individual and free, was a clear and eloquent act of defiance against French neoclassicism, Enlightenment morality and all forms of abstract regulation.

Götz exemplifies the proto-realism of the German drama of the 1770s. The plays of the *Sturm und Drang* are in some sense only for reading, a 'virtual' theatre, a *Lesedrama*. The collective experience implied by this revolutionary piece is not the tangible social event of a theatrical production but rather that of the abstract sort of community made possible by print capitalism, the one aspect of modernity in which Germany was not lagging behind ('Shakespeare', at least until 1776 when an important production of *Hamlet* was staged in Hamburg, was first a reading experience for this generation). In this context, a multitude of private reading events (moments of mental pleasure) conduce to the formation of a sense of an 'imagined community', in Benedict Anderson's term, which was the most important condition for the modern consciousness of 'the nation'.

The specific case of *Götz* is not completely clear-cut, since it was successfully premiered soon after its publication (in 1774, in the Königliches Schauspielhaus [Royal Theatre] in Berlin of all places, by one of the pioneers of established theatre in Germany, G. H. Koch). Yet it appears to have made its substantial impact in print form first; initially privately published by Goethe and J. H. Merck, and pirated in two editions soon thereafter. Indeed, the performance was the result of the lively demand from enthused readers. That *Götz* is best understood as a *Lesedrama*, belonging in important senses to novel realism and to the world of commercial print culture, rather than to the theatre, is strongly suggested by the influence it had on Sir Walter Scott who translated it and, it is said, was inspired by it to write his historical novels – the most widely read novels in Europe in the first decades of the following century.

After Goethe, the second most innovative young dramatist of the 1770s was Jakob Michael Reinhold Lenz (1751–1792). For him, the Enlightenment view of the world was unshakable and he therefore felt able to oppose it without restraint. In essays on *Götz* and *Werther* (1773, 1775) and in an enthusiastic account of the theatre of which his generation dreamt, 'Anmerkungen über das Theater' ('Notes on the Theatre', 1774), which Lessing dismissed as 'hogwash', Lenz argued for a subjective aesthetic in which the fundamentally erotic force of the individual is adequate to grasp and realize the surrounding forces of nature. (This erotic component caused the guilt-ridden son of a strict Pietist minister perplexity and suffering.) Typically, Shakespeare is the model for this. What Lenz proposed was a state of 'natural' identity, such that, if one properly understood the self (Götz, Werther), then one also embodied, not the constructed moral system of rational thought, but the indwelling 'Moralität' ('moral-ness') of the rational universe itself.

This 'heroic' theory is pitched against the difficulty of its realization, a difficulty that eventually overcame the unfortunate empirical Lenz. His case illustrates important aspects of the situation of the 1770s generation, particularly the instability of their bid for a new, authentic, personal and national identity. Lenz is second to none in the passion of his denunciation of rules and in his advocacy of Shakespeare and nature. Yet there is a big fissure through the middle of his work, separating the energy of his essays from the practice of his writing for the (half-imagined) theatre. In the latter you will search in vain for the *Kraftkerl* ('titan') or the richness of Shakespeare or the abundance of nature: what you find is plays uncertain how to frame their narratives of the failure of individuals to identify with the possibilities of selfhood offered them by their social circumstances. Discourses of inner nature (sexuality) and outer nature (social realism) collide to create drama. What comes about in this representation of disappointment and the impossibility of fulfilment has rightly been described as proto-realism. The raging of an unconscious, unbounded sexual energy is objectified in the story of the ruin of a shopkeeper's young daughter as a result of her seduction by soldiers (*Die Soldaten* [*Soldiers*], 1776), or, even more tellingly, in the self-castration of a poor scholar who makes his pupil pregnant (*Der Hofmeister* [*The Private Tutor*], 1774).

Lenz was too unstable to fit in at Weimar and he died in obscurity, but he was rediscovered once the dream of natural moral fulfilment had faded. Testimony to the historical representativeness of his mental suffering came from Georg Büchner in his Novelle *Lenz* (1836; see chapter 2) and in the form of adaptations of his plays by Max Reinhardt, Bertolt Brecht and Heinar Kipphardt in the twentieth century.

It seems odd at first that, with *Die Räuber* (*The Brigands*, 1781), Friedrich Schiller's contribution to this neo-Shakespearean German realism comes along nearly ten years after the first high tide. Yet this lateness is exactly the point. Just as *Werther* informed the conventional expression of authenticity, *Empfindsamkeit*, with the new affective vigour of sexuality, thus refreshing it at the same time as bringing out a moral dilemma at its heart, so Schiller refreshes fervent insubordination with a sense of its own tragic impossibility, which in turn entails a political urgency. (Schiller came from the state of Württemberg which had had a relatively strong republican element since the sixteenth century.) In *Die Räuber*, undisciplined, incoherent but theatrically and humanly engaging excesses are bound into what is effectively a dramatic structure.

In a preface later suppressed, probably on the advice of a bookseller, Schiller actually promoted his rebellious text as a *Lesedrama* (he called it a 'dramatischer Roman' ['dramatic novel']). It thus recognizably falls into the same category as the dramas of Goethe, Lenz and others as a kind of wish-fulfilment in relation to the reality of contemporary theatre. Schiller appeals – or pretends to – to those who can *read* the complex moral seriousness of what to the actual theatregoing 'Pöbel' ('rabble') of all classes (as he puts it) would appear immoral and therefore elicit either disapprobation or emulation. Yet after nearly ten years of extreme German drama, the infrastructure for a stabilized modern theatre, able to recognize, assimilate and domesticate it, was more developed. The Mannheim bookseller to whom Schiller's inflammatory text was smuggled out would not print it (Schiller then had it privately printed) but recognized in it the kind of thing that would appeal to Reichsfreiherr Wolfgang Heribert von Dalberg, the noble director of the Mannheim theatre which had become a 'court *and* national theatre' in 1778. Under Dalberg, the Mannheim theatre became one of the most successful new permanent theatres in Germany. Its reconception as a 'national' theatre (which by now was code for 'modern') followed the founding in 1776 by Joseph II of Austria of the Teutsches Nationaltheater (German National Theatre), later the famous Burgtheater, in Vienna, and reflected the willingness among the rulers of German states to adapt to (or appropriate) developing trends. In return, Schiller's play was depoliticized by being put back in time, such that it felt a bit more like the sort of medievalizing piece made popular by *Götz*, and subjected to further very significant changes, bowdlerizations of a sort that would make even Hollywood blush carried out by Schiller himself, so keen was he (despite his polemic pose in the preface) to have his play performed.

The question of identity is engaged here concretely because Schiller, on the strength of the written, read and performed success of his play, threw over the career mapped out for him by Karl Eugen, Duke of Württemberg, as a doctor in the modernized national army and struck out for the life of a professional author. He certainly had the talent to write for the stage, but he was mistaken in thinking that he could earn his living by it, even in the improving conditions for the practical theatre. Domesticating his play was one thing, sacrificing his entire gift to the demands of a paying public turned out to be another. Schiller knew what you had to do, but couldn't do it, nor did he wish to compromise his gifts to that degree. This was left to the new generation of influential and competent playwright-actor-directors, of whom Iffland, Moritz's schoolfriend and a success as the first Franz Moor in the Mannheim production, was the most famous, and then to the prolific and genuinely popular August von Kotzebue (1761–1819), whose plays were performed everywhere in the German-speaking lands (and abroad – he was the author of *Lovers' Vows*, performed in *Mansfield Park*). In these practitioners the literary and theatrical excitement of the first wave of modern German literature was domesticated in the establishment of a flourishing bourgeois theatre in Germany, subsidized by modernizing dynastic rulers.

Greece comes to Germany

Schiller, like Moritz, and Goethe himself, who was identified from the 1780s with the culturally progressive court and theatre at Weimar, sought a more elevated development for the new German literature. If the dramatists of the 1770s had dreamt of a theatre that did not really exist, Schiller and Goethe collaborated from the mid-1780s on a modern German art, more idealist than realist, in order to redeem the commercial proliferation of bourgeois culture around them.

The decisive support in this search came from what must be the most influential piece of sublimation in art history. In 1755, Johann Joachim Winckelmann (1717–1768) had published a remarkable short book, *Gedancken über die Nachahmung der griechischen Wercke in der Mahlerei und Bildhauer-Kunst* (*Reflections upon the Imitation of Greek Works in Painting and Sculpture*). In it, he opposed the rococo and baroque taste in art in favour around him at the court of Dresden with a passionate exposition of Greek art, especially sculpture. Inspired by his natural enthusiasm for the male form, Winckelmann wrote the founding text of that other symbiotic moment, alongside the symbiotic identification with Shakespeare, through which a Germany determined to force cultural self-consciousness defined itself.

In his account of the specific qualities and context of Greek art, Winckelmann was stressing a creative, organic, ancient culture quite distinct from the associations of Latin: clerical authority, scholarly opacity, rote learning. This is why his tremendous scholarly yet thoroughly humanist enthusiasm for Greece could anticipate a synthesis between Herder's emphasis upon original creativity and the sophisticated neoclassical French version of the doctrine of imitation; elements which not long after became polarized in the hysterical proclamations of the 1770s. This is really the model that enabled Goethe and Schiller to attempt an idealizing, stylized form of German literary and dramatic art that could also lay claim to being modern.

When it comes to the argument about originality and imitation in literature or the arts in general, a peculiar dialectic comes into play. In this instance it worked as follows: first, the Germans had to develop the ambition to be like the French (for instance in Gottsched, or in the very aspiration to have a cultural identity at all, the 'national' theatres that were founded in the 1770s went back to the foundation of the *Comédie française* in 1680), in order to develop the ambition to be different from them (Lessing). Winckelmann himself is touching the same point when he argues in the *Gedancken* that the only path to inimitable greatness is by imitating the ancients.

In Winckelmann's account, the perfection of Greek art is explained not by reference to an abstract philosophical ideal, but by the delight it causes, and in relation to the background against which it had come about. It was the human perfection of the Greeks' lifestyle that made it possible for them to represent, in terms of 'eine edle Einfalt und eine stille Grösse' ('a noble simplicity and calm greatness') the ideal formal perfection that is always potential, but not yet present, in nature herself. The Greek imitation of nature is proclaimed to be an imitation that nature herself requires from humans as its completion. In imitating this, as the above quotation suggests, the Germans will transcend imitation.

This is not far from the way Shakespeare was read slightly later. What matters is less the specific historical precedent that is being evoked – the art of Greece, as opposed to that of Rome and the Italo-French stylization of antiquity, the plays of Shakespeare, rather than those of Voltaire and Gottsched – than the way in which Germans can make an impressive entry into cultural history.

Winckelmann's Greece provided the intellectual context within which Goethe and Schiller could think about 'form' as a social appearance, at once rationally explicable, and turn towards the irreducible immediacy of lived experience. The pleasure of this form, the sublime sublimation of Winckelmann, was as far from aristocratic licentiousness as it was from commercial vulgarity. The pleasure it promised was aesthetic and moral too, since it spoke for the ideal of humanity as it had once been lived by the Greeks.

The particular moment of Goethe and Schiller's conscious effort to reshape German literary culture in the last years of the eighteenth century was expressed in a range of texts, shared enterprises and mutual encouragement. What they had in common was less the ambition to formulate a new national culture than the desire to embody the idea of significant form. They aspired to bear witness to that point at which universal truth and historical or individual specificity meet, a point which they feared, with some justification, had been buried in the carnage of the French

Revolution. In different ways, Schiller's stylized history plays, such as *Wallenstein* (1798–99) or *Maria Stuart* (1800), or the middle phase of Goethe's lifelong labour upon the theme of Faust (1790, 1808), test the metaphysical edge of empirical experience, in Schiller's case by seeking to represent moral truth in tragic action, in that of *Faust Erster Teil* by embedding a tragic love story in a dramatic structure that brings with it, in the character of Mephistopheles, the necessity of asking what evil means in the secular world.

A closer look at two works can typify their efforts: Goethe's *Italienische Reise* (*Italian Journey*, published 1816–17) and Schiller's *Über die ästhetische Erziehung des Menschen in einer Reihe von Briefen* (*On the Aesthetic Education of Man in a Series of Letters*, 1795).

When we refer to Goethe's 'Italian Journey', we refer to two distinct things with many gradations between them. The first is the journey itself which took place between 1786 and 1788. Goethe displaced himself from his life at the court of Weimar and went to study art and to deepen his experience of the cultures of antiquity and the Renaissance in Rome and elsewhere in Italy. The second is an autobiographical text that became a literary composition only thirty years later, the purpose of which was to represent the life-changing significance of the journey for its author.

If this journey was a literal displacement, it was a psychological one, a matter of identity, also. Goethe went without servants and as incognito as his celebrity would allow, and he devoted himself less to literature, upon which that celebrity rested, than to the study and practice of art. His declared aim, as he explained under the entry for 17 September 1786, was not to 'delude', or perhaps escape, himself, but to 'discover' himself in the objects he saw.

The differences between the kind of culture implied by the later Goethe, constructed gradually in the literary representations of the journey itself, and that of the 1770s are: first, a rediscovery of rules, but rules which regulate nature as well as art, providing a rigorous rationale for the way nature can be understood as sanctioning the 'translations' of artists; and, second, a conscious acknowledgement of sexuality as part of the continuum of human experience. Indiscriminate libidinal excitement, over-lighting everything it touches, is replaced by an even sunlight, an affirmation of the sensual aspects of human experience as compatible with – indeed indispensable to – a sense of order in the relation between the individual, nature and social forms. Gone is the enthusiasm for the 'characteristic' Gothic and, in its place, there is passionate testimony to (not dogmatic assertion of) the significance of form that owes much to Winckelmann.

This self-discovery, however, is neither in itself complete nor already an interaction with the real historical or social circumstances of Goethe's time. On the face of it, the opposite seems to be the case: there is an escape from these circumstances, now experienced as oppressive, into another cultural domain. The interaction only begins to happen in reality, once this experience is reflected back to the public realm through writing.

This escape was indeed from the start also conceived as a report back to the very world from which it had been an escape. Goethe was at pains retrospectively to gain approval for his unofficially taken sabbatical. This was no desertion: it was courageous self-assertion, but still bounded by respect for social and professional obligations. It was immediate experience, managed through a range of texts. There was a conventional template. Journeys to Italy were part of the education of young Germans of Goethe's social background, and his father had undertaken one himself and produced a written account. The discursive account of the experience was part of the experience. In Goethe's case, letters and diary drafts, some of them indistinguishable from one another, flowed back to Weimar, intended as drafts for later reworking. Herder and Charlotte von Stein, Goethe's favoured friend and confidante at Weimar, were among the recipients.

On his actual return from Italy, Goethe felt isolated and misunderstood. The material he had gathered during the time in Italy which seemed in later retrospect to have been for him the happiest and most decisive of his life – a kind of rebirth – was too personal to be adequately framed for his contemporaries. The social circumstances were unpropitious for a public account of Goethe's private Italy. Instead, fragments appeared anonymously in Wieland's *Teutscher Merkur* [*German Mercury*], a place of publication that underlines the aspiration to speak to the educated public. Discrete episodes were written up and published, such as the description of the Carnival in Rome, which became a well-known and influential piece. Goethe also embarked upon a series of biographical essays in which the quick of his cultural experiences in Italy was touched upon but bounded by the objective reference to another. He wrote about the Renaissance goldsmith and sculptor Benvenuto Cellini (1803), the landscape painter Philipp Hackert (1811) and Winckelmann himself (1805).

This was a protracted negotiation between travel literature and autobiography because what was at stake here was the deeply felt aspiration to keep personal experience and public values in touch with one another. What Goethe aspired to in working through these experiences, and in all the extensive autobiographical writing that became an important part of his output towards the end of his long life, was to write between self and world, such as to see and to show the continuity between them. The miracle of his literary *oeuvre* as a whole is that his greatest writing emerged from this contest between subjective experience and public discourse. Many individual works were formed by the Italian experience (*Römische Elegien* [*Roman Elegies*], 1795, to name only the most explicit).

Goethe did not trivialize the arduousness of this task. By the time he completed the text of *Italienische Reise*, Europe had been politically transformed by the international conflict following the French Revolution. This put strain upon the nature of his insights, which depended upon gradualness and process. The text could not but become a defence against volcanically destructive historical change and against the Romanticism that sought to redeem the effects of this change by means of a secularized religiosity and an alliance with popular culture to which Goethe was deeply opposed.

There is an irony in Goethe experiencing a personal rebirth in the years immediately preceding the events in France, which set the stage for the overwhelming acceleration of depersonalizing modernization in Europe. Schiller's great text of German classical aesthetics, *Über die ästhetische Erziehung des Menschen*, reflects more clearly how much harder it was to become, in the post-revolutionary era, to sustain the thought that self and world can interact within a genuine public sphere.

In 1795–6, Schiller published a famous essay in which he set up a distinction between the kind of writer he was and the kind Goethe was. 'Über naive und sentimentalische Dichtung' ('On Naive and Sentimental Poetry') contrasted a mode of writing that came from nature, unreflected and naive in that sense, with the writing, prevalent in modernity that was bound to take the route through self-conscious reflection in order to achieve the sort of composition and unity then required of works of art. That Goethe should attempt his classical displacement from the starting point of a personal experience (albeit, typically, a 'staged' one) is in conformity with Schiller's taxonomy. Indeed, Goethe himself said in 1796 that he felt his notes on the Italian journey were just too 'naive' to be offered to the public. It is equally in conformity with Schiller's scheme that he should himself start out from a philosophical position, that of the critical philosophy of Immanuel Kant, and attempt, from this angle, to set up a viable model for an interrelation between the Greek–German sense of selfhood and the modern European world as a whole.

The *Ästhetische Briefe* begin with a threnody on the integrated vision at stake in Winckelmann and Goethe's Italian journey and its rewritings.

Post-revolutionary Europe is polarized between desiccated, machine-like forms of social organization and unbounded animal disorder.

In the meticulous if labyrinthine argument that follows, Schiller sets up a complex model, according to which a Greek–German configuration of complete (though not static) selfhood is offered as the answer to the dehumanizing disassociation between individual faculties of the human subject and between individuals and modern social collectives.

The three components of this model represent in associated form those elements that have catastrophically fallen asunder in modern life. First, there is the Greek ideal itself, something that in its undivided oneness is difficult or impossible to express without tautology. Second, no less integral to Schiller's model of a configured self, is the sense of the lack of that fullness that accompanies the sense of the value of that which is lacking. Third, there is the Kantian apparatus that insists upon the differentiation between categories in order, not to divide them, but to understand them as perfectly as they may be understood.

The thrust of the argument is then that the first two must be able to combine in such a way as to recognize Kant's non-transcendable differentiation between the sphere of reason, or freedom, and that of determination, or the body, to recognize it, but also to facilitate their cooperation within an ideal of integrated personality. Like Winckelmann, Goethe and Moritz, Schiller looks to art for the key to this aim.

This Greek–German ideal combines within its complex economy those elements that must be made to cohere in the modern world. First, Greek plenitude is the positive 'nature' corresponding to the unbounded aggressive 'nature' that threatens with the break up of the *ancien régime*. Second, the recognition of the value of the Greek world, with the concomitant sense that it is not attainable in modern conditions, is a stabilized version of that dissociation of faculties, that division of labour, which Schiller so memorably articulated. Third, the Kantian apparatus that provides the philosophical framework is the benevolent equivalent of that machine-like instrumentalization that desiccates the modes and forms of modern government.

This complex, shifting configuration is the life of the *Aesthetic Letters*, expressing Schiller's concern to animate but not subvert Kant's formal categories. What must be distinguished in critical philosophy must not be divided in real social experience. The text is itself the bid for an act of identification, by means of which a Greek–German subject can speak to and be heard by post-revolutionary Europe.

Casualties of Idealism

Most of the writers who we will be mentioning in the context of Romanticism in the next section were born in the 1770s. The two writers of the same vintage (Hölderlin born in 1770, Kleist in 1777) who have achieved European status for their literature rather than their ideas cannot be subsumed under that heading. They both speak to later ages because their writings exhibit a certain anguish at loss or absence, pointing beyond the consolation of art towards the metaphysical spheres of, in Hölderlin's case, heaven, and in that of Kleist, politics, law and morality.

Why would one place Hölderlin's *oeuvre* – a poetic novel *Hyperion* (1797–9); an unfinished tragedy about the death of the pre-Socratic poet, philosopher and seer Empedocles; and a body of odes and hymns of extraordinary linguistic concentration, deep seriousness and ambitious scope – under the heading 'Casualties of Idealism'? The reason is that, while he was the co-founder with his contemporaries at the Tübingen seminary, G. W. F. Hegel (1770–1831) and F. W. J. von Schelling (1775–1854), of the mainstream of post-Kantian German philosophical Idealism, unlike them, he did not become a major academic Idealist philosopher. He became instead the poet of the suffering associated with Idealism in history.

His idealism, in the everyday sense, sprang from the hope that the French Revolution, which occurred while he was at the seminary, would sweep away the constriction of dynastic rule. The Idealism with which he failed to identify himself comfortably (but which he took as seriously as it could possibly be taken) was that which Hegel built upon Kant and the French Revolution to construct with brilliant ingenuity a system in which the spirit is immanent in history. What is meant by this can most readily be conveyed by the example of the Revolution itself which is seen as the inevitable unfolding in time and space, that is, in historical circumstances, of the Idea of Reason.

Hegel and Hölderlin felt that at other points also the presence of the divine spirit had been manifest in time and space, for instance in ancient Greece, or in the birth of Christ. Greece and Christianity would combine with the post-revolutionary modern world to reveal a progressive unfolding of *Geist*, the Spirit, which was Hegel's word for God. Yet, to construct an ingenious philosophical model according to which time and timelessness are ultimately unified is one thing; to experience the former as the absence in the present of the latter is another.

Hölderlin's strenuous efforts to bear witness in poetry (that is, in time and space) to absent gods – Greek and Christian – lays an immense burden upon the imagination and upon language itself, since both must function, as it were, without a safety net. They become charged in their very texture and operation with an insoluble problem. What is poetic about this is that it concentrates upon what is the only irreducibly and incontestably true thing about language and the figures of the imagination, namely that they are not true at all, since 'the thing in itself' is not directly knowable or therefore expressible.

Hölderlin can be situated in relation to the rest of contemporary German literature in the following ways: first, it will be evident that in his own practice of poetry he is following Klopstock in an idiom that can sustain the 'soul' of religious experience in literary language. Klopstock already fused German sensibility with Greek metres and structures (such as the hexameter), and Hölderlin exceeded Goethe and Schiller in the detail and enthusiasm in his use of ancient forms (such as the Pindaric ode). Hence, second, that his writing rests at a profound level upon the union of Greek and Christian spirituality is also a continuation of the forms of symbiosis we have already seen. Third, there is a dialectic that moves from the enlightened dignification of human individual experience to the need for a more-than-human context in which to evaluate that dignity. Hölderlin places the kind of individual experience that Goethe, in his early love lyrics and hymns (for instance 'Wandrers Sturmlied' ['The Wayfarer's Storm Song'], 1772), fuses in reciprocity with nature and the erotic other into the wider, post-revolutionary collective context of history. It is at this point that he makes a bid for a language that can manifest Idealism in words and comes up against the impossibility.

Fourth, however, in reaching this limit, Hölderlin calls the bluff of the new theorists of 'art', from Lessing onwards, who install it as placeholder for an invisible authority to replace and transform the defective authority of church and state. If Goethe and Schiller in their neoclassical post-Kantian period from the 1790s test the edges of empirical reality, Hölderlin wants the metaphysical results. In the long poem 'Patmos' (1801–3), he writes: 'Zu lang, zu lang schon ist / Die Ehre der Himmlischen unsichtbar' ('Too long, too long now / The honour of the Heavenly has been invisible'). If art really is to replace authority, rather than produce elaborate representations around its absence, then there must at its core be the hard truth of adversity. To this core, Hölderlin's language returns.

Finally, we can say that in Hölderlin that range within the German lyric mentioned above, from dust to eternity as it were, reaches its most attenuated form. The key moments are those at which the two extremes lose touch with each other entirely in the experience (or more particularly in the language) of the individual. The short poem 'Hälfte des Lebens' ('Half of Life', *c*.1803) encapsulates this significant disjuncture perfectly in its two strophes. It presents a sense of dichotomy between metaphorical language, with the power to convey metaphysical truth, and language that can express nothing beyond the literal. The mystery lies between them.

Hölderlin wrote poetry situated upon the margin of language and thus provided the model for 'raids on the inarticulate', as T. S. Eliot said in *East Coker*, of Modernist poetry a hundred years later. As such, his work has had a unique and defining influence on the finest questioning lyric poetry in German since his day: George, Trakl, Rilke, Celan all write in the presence, as it were, of Hölderlin.

Heinrich von Kleist came from a different sort of Germany. He wasn't a pastor's son, a theology student or a bourgeois, but the scion of a noble Prussian family with a tradition of military service and he spent his formative years in the army, during which time he witnessed the reality of warfare. He never visited the non-vocational sort of university that, as we shall see, fostered the Romantic movement. What he did have in common with many of the others was that he worked as a state official and was enthusiastic about progressive ideas (especially those of Rousseau). For a time, he worked in the department headed by the Prussian reformer Karl von Stein zum Altenstein on programmes of modernization and liberalization. As a writer, not unlike Moritz or Schiller, he tried to reconcile two historically diverging things: high aesthetic aspiration and writing as a profession.

Kleist was not able to identify with the kinds of role for which his birth and upbringing predestined him. Instead, he aspired to discharge his debt of honour to the family name on the field of the new German literature. He began with accordingly high aspirations. He wanted to adapt complex historical material, as Schiller had done in *Wallenstein* (Kleist used the story of the first-century Norman duke of Apulia, Robert Guiskard, about which he had read in Schiller's periodical for the new arts, *Die Horen*) to the pure analytic form of tragedy as exemplified by Sophocles' *Oedipus*. He wished, as a modern independent creative writer, to combine the ancient and the Romantic (the Greeks and Shakespeare; art and history) in a tragedy for the modern age and in so doing perform a spectacular and significant public act. This was his moment of attempted Idealist synthesis.

His failure to achieve it – he burnt the almost-complete manuscript in 1803 and had a psychotic breakdown – inaugurated the literary career that gave rise to the body of work for which Kleist is known. It consists of seven plays and eight stories (*Erzählungen*) written in the aftermath of this trauma.

In them, the world is represented as an impure mixture of empirical causality and moral substance. What is demonstrated repeatedly, like a lesson in pragmatism spiced with sadomasochism, is not, as with Hölderlin, the threat that the empirical and the metaphysical will separate absolutely but the conviction that they can never be separated cleanly.

Although there is no overarching metaphysic, the figure of the arch is an important one in Kleist's imagination. The arch is an architectural entity that stays up as a result of the common tendency of the stones in it to fall. In the story *Das Erdbeben in Chili* (*The Earthquake in Chile*, 1807), a character escapes destruction in an earthquake because stones form an impromptu arch. In Kleist's last play, *Prinz Friedrich von Homburg* (1810), the potentially tragic conflict between two flawed (that is, metaphorically, falling) authority figures ultimately issues in mutual support, such as to maintain the political and moral integrity of the state of Brandenburg. Significantly, the flaw of one of them, the Prince of the title, once he has overcome a creaturely fear of death and is perhaps stiffened by this experience, is to imagine that his personal fate has a tragic significance above or beyond the immediate circumstances. No character in Kleist is permitted such a certainty, even though sometimes it might be true (the possibility exists, for instance, in *Michael Kohlhaas* [1808–10] and *Der Zweikampf* [*The Duel*, 1811]).

Kleist's version of introspection, if he had one, was internalized from eighteenth-century philosophy about personal development. He had a strong, if warped, sense of public duty, and his writings are intended as, and have the internal character of, public acts. One of Kleist's favourite tenets was that it was impossible to communicate one's own thoughts or know those of others. A public utterance may or may not succeed in conveying the intention in which it originated. He refers to the writing of plays and stories as 'dice throws', and in one essay he describes how thoughts come about in the course of their formulation in language. The example he cites is that of Mirabeau, who destabilized the *ancien régime* and ushered in the French Revolution in a speech the core idea of which – that the authority of the representatives of the estates was inviolable – only emerged once he had got up and started to speak.

Kleist's works display the will to order and form, yet sardonically betray their awareness that, as acts like any other, they do not have absolute control over their results. They share with the practices of ritual that, in rehearsing the forms and shapes of the tragedy or the comedy, or of the moral story that goes back to Boccaccio and Cervantes, they perform raids on disorder in the service of order, repeating the founding acts of civilization because the order of the world may never be taken for granted. In *Penthesilea* (1808), for instance, the Amazon queen's love for the Homeric hero Achilles is distorted by circumstances in such a way as to lead her to murder and cannibalize him. If this act of savagery points back to primitive sacrificial origins behind the ritual of Holy Communion, Kleist's literary visits to the edge also lead him into areas that point forward in time. Beneath moral behaviour, he reveals unconscious motivation (what the psychoanalysts would later call 'overdetermination') and, in depicting the resistance on the part of empirical circumstances to categories of absolute right and wrong, he wrote the first historical novel in German, *Michael Kohlhaas*.

Infinity for all

As is usually the case with cultural history, if not with all history, the attempts made to contain a great change fail but have a decisive influence upon the shape things take after that change happens. 'Romanticism' begins at the points at which the efforts of Goethe and Schiller to bend the Dionysian energy of the 1770s and the French Revolution back into forms and values of the earlier eighteenth century gave way to the post-revolutionary world. They were recognized by the younger Romantic generation as significant national artists, but their attempt to adapt the Greek ideal to modern requirements was seen as arbitrary. German classicism was arbitrary because it was willed and chosen and not the spontaneous expression of a powerful polity, as had been the case with classicisms of the past. Yet this arbitrariness was also characteristically modern since it was a style choice promoted in journal and publication and, as an act of free cultural choice, the prototype for a practical infinity of cultural choices which have in common only their abstraction from, and thus vulnerability to, the very contingency they oppose.

The tone for the German Romantic turn in literature was set by the volume *Herzensergießungen eines kunstliebenden Klosterbruders* (*Outpourings of an Art-Loving Monk*), published anonymously by Ludwig Tieck (1773–1853) and Wilhelm Heinrich Wackenroder (1773–1798), though mostly written by the latter, in 1796. The volume consists of a series of lives of painters of the Italian Renaissance; a life of Albrecht Dürer; fantasies about the nature of art, attributed to the eponymous monk; and finally a fictional, but nonetheless evidently autobiographical, narrative, 'Das merkwürdige musikalische Leben des Tonkünstlers Joseph Berglinger' ('The Curious Musical Life of the Composer Joseph Berglinger').

Why was the public primed to receive it? Four factors combine to explain this. First, there was the continuing popular taste for sentimental-moral writing. Second, there was the increased status of art as the focus for problems of personal and national identification. Third, the Renaissance setting and the inclusion of Dürer conflated not only the neoclassicism of Weimar and German art but also the Middle Ages and the early modern period as periods from which Germans have the right to draw inspiration. Fourth, there was a rapidly widening market for print culture, in which readers' tastes had a voice alongside the dictates of opinion formers. To these four, one might speculatively add a fifth: Wackenroder's text displayed in full colour not just the scene of mental pleasure, animated by displaced eros, that *Werther* had revealed but, if one may put it this way, it revealed this form of mental pleasure now conscious of itself. Now the drama of the mind, its despair and exaltation, is confirmed, in the metaphor of 'the artist', as a stage for contemporary, widespread and complex reading pleasure.

With this speculation, we move from what was familiar about the work to new territory. Four key aspects of *Herzensergießungen* provide a working definition of the Romantic attitude. First, and most obviously, there was the preference for the Catholic iconography and 'medieval' atmosphere of southern Germany which inspired Wackenroder to write. In this style preference, he expresses revulsion at the Prussian ethos of his father. It is not important that Wackenroder's Middle Ages are peopled by Renaissance painters and are thus no more historically correct than Goethe's reaction to Strasbourg; what matters, as it had with Goethe, is the radical reckoning with excessive rationalism in the field of art by means of identification with artistic achievements of the past other than those of classical antiquity.

Second, there was the notion of ineffable truth touched by feeling but not accessible to reason or even words in any direct sense. In effect, 'art' was celebrated as the new religion. The Renaissance mixture of superb mimetic skill and Christianity provided the basis for the secular 'saints' lives' of Raphael, Leonardo da Vinci, Dürer, Michelangelo, etc. The book culminated in a fictionalized autobiography of a musician: music enjoys access to the lived reality of feelings too inchoate or complex for precise verbal definition, but it was becoming homeless in the contemporary world, as its liturgical and courtly incarnations diminished in importance before popular consumption which obscured its intrinsic spirituality. Music was destined to become the Romantic art *par excellence*, and Romanticism had from the beginning a corresponding tendency to dramatize itself (illogically) as extra-social and thus misunderstood.

Third, there was the revaluation of problematic subjectivity to mean not that you are of a melancholic disposition or a 'Schwärmer' ('enthusiast'), nor indeed that you are 'sentimentally' equipped to be a member of modern society, nor even that you are a tragic casualty of historical change, but that you (and by implication, all human subjects, properly understood, and who properly understand what they are reading) are suspended between this world and another. Wackenroder's problematic artist initiates a German and European topos that lasts for at least a hundred and fifty years (in 1948, Thomas Mann's Adrian Leverkühn in *Doktor Faustus* is still a 'Tonkünstler', literally 'sound artist', like Berglinger). The topos of the problematic artist can be interpreted as a dispersal of the Fall into an endless plurality of texts and objects which are always at once connected to, but separate from, the truth.

Fourth, there was the effacement, as a result of these ideas, of wit and skill as the criteria by which the products of culture are received, and of the distinctions between genres and media that provide the indispensable social guide in judging wit and skill in its concrete manifestations. Judgement itself is unfeeling regimentation of that which can only be felt. Literature, painting, music: they are now all refractions of the same transcendent truth that cannot be expressed without mediation (and thus inevitable loss) through the lives and things of the sublunary world.

In short, the *Herzensergießungen* offer infinity for all in the form of a book. It is not only what the book is about but the way it is read and the collectivity of readership it implies. This collectivity is very intimate, yet entirely abstract ('imagined'). The pose of being 'outside society' (the essays and the commentary that accompanies them 'are not set down in the idiom of modern society', as the narrator says on the first page) is in fact the coming to self-consciousness of the *new* society defined by print culture and mental pleasure. The account of the tragic failure of Berglinger the musician to live his music as purely as he hears and composes it is not evidence of a society in which such things happen but evidence of one in which an increasing number of people enjoy reading about such things happening.

The consolation of philosophy

The specific university culture in the German lands fostered the formulation of a theory for the kind of reading practice of which the *Herzensergießungen* are an early example. This culture began with the foundation in 1737 of Göttingen University, where J. M. Gesner introduced reforms of the study of classics so as to dispense with rote learning and imitation of Latin texts in favour of the study of classical writing as a means to train the mind. It culminated in the foundation in 1810 by Wilhelm von Humboldt (1767–1835) of Berlin University, the very administrative structure of which reflected the belief in a family of interconnected scientific knowledge ('a symphony of professors', in Friedrich Schlegel's phrase). Under the benevolent guidance of the discipline of philosophy, Germany developed a unique form of higher education devoted to disinterestedness of learning in tandem with the development of the individual personality.

The University of Jena in the 1790s played a central role in this development in at least three major ways. First, it was a stage in the relay between the progressive court culture, which was the context of Goethe and Schiller's neoclassical bid to define a contemporary social function for works of art, and a university-driven modern redefinition of what art was. Goethe was directly involved in the modernization of the university, which fell partly under the jurisdiction of the Duchy of Saxe-Weimar, and he was instrumental in securing Schiller's brief tenure there as a professor of history. The reforms were designed to overcome the notoriously asocial behaviour of the student population, which in the 1790s began to shade into Jacobinism. The result of these reforms, as well as of the simple proximity of the two most charismatic German authors of the previous generation, was to attract a succession of brilliant young teachers in many areas of higher education, including medicine and law but crucially involving the secular theologians J. G. Fichte (1762–1814), Schelling and Hegel. They deflected inchoate rebellion into the discipline of abstract thought.

Second, Jena became the conduit through which the philosophical legacy of Immanuel Kant reached the outside world. It was a scene galvanized not only by socio-political upheaval but by Kant's epistemological revolution also. It was here that the philosophy professor K. L. Reinhold popularized Kant's critical philosophy. Fichte, Schelling and Hegel went on from Jena to spectacular careers at other new or modernized German universities, where they developed the implications of Kant's rigorous delimitation of the competence of pure reason and his further and consequent expositions of practical reason (ethics) and judgement into their own vast abstract philosophical models of how consciousness exists in nature and history.

Third, Fichte linked his high post-Kantian theory with the question of the German national mission in the post-revolutionary world. The effect of this linkage was to transform the cultural cosmopolitanism with which Goethe and Schiller responded to the political upheavals into an – at least theoretically political – nationalism (from which, it must be stressed, benefit for the whole world was nevertheless predicted).

What does this mean for the theoretical formulation of Romanticism? It was in this atmosphere favourable to abstraction and explosively modern in its intellectual identity, especially in the intoxicating form of Fichte's ideas, that two brothers, both Göttingen-trained scholars centrally interested in questions concerning art and literature, invented it in the last years of the eighteenth century. By 1803, August Wilhelm Schlegel (1767–1845), the elder brother and more meticulous and gifted scholar of the two, was preaching 'Romanticism' in public as the new discourse for the modern age. Through his later lectures in Berlin and Vienna, and his association with Mme de Staël, the Romantic attitude was broadcast throughout Europe and beyond (for instance to America). The younger brother Friedrich (1772–1829), also briefly a teacher at Jena, was the more mercurial and brilliant of the two and is the most quoted theorist of German Romanticism.

Originally a classical scholar with the ambition to do for literature what Winckelmann had done for the plastic arts, Friedrich Schlegel supported the neoclassical aesthetic in the early 1790s. In *Über das Studium der griechischen Poesie* (*On the Study of Greek Poetry*), written by 1795 and published two years later, he contrasted the timeless merits of classical art with aspects of an attitude he arranged under the heading of *das Interessante* ('the interesting'; Lovejoy 1948). These qualities are effectively a list of the properties of the enthusiasms of the 1770s: resistance to boundaries and demarcations, especially those of genre; an attitude of longing (*Sehnsucht*) preferred to one of fulfilment; expressiveness and uniqueness preferred to formal beauty; an interest in exceptional individuals; a penchant for the unfamiliar, 'piquant', ugly or grotesque; and the expression of personal interest or attitude preferred to artistic detachment.

In the mid-1790s, Schlegel reversed the order of this hierarchy. The properties listed above return, now affirmed at a higher point in a spiral of sophistication, and conscious of themselves, as 'Romanticism'. By this is primarily meant 'characteristic modern European literature', quintessentially Shakespeare, but also a whole panoply of other literary forms (for instance, popular 'romances') and characters, defined as modern in opposition to the classical models of antiquity.

It was the modern affirmation of self-consciousness flourishing at Jena (Fichte in particular) that provides the explanatory context for this decisive, startling, and rather brilliant volte-face. While academic German philosophy from Kant onwards pursued the implications of the inaccessible status of things in themselves and the condition of the subject in relation to nature, the Schlegels and others in the Romantic circle at Jena and beyond pursued the issue in the context of the history of literature and art criticism.

Irony

The *collective* aspect of the genesis of Romanticism is part of its cultivation of self-consciousness as the motor of cultural renewal. It was in conversation and collaboration between the Schlegel brothers, Dorothea Schlegel (1764–1839), Caroline Schlegel-Schelling (1763–1809), Schelling, Fichte to an extent, Novalis (Friedrich von Hardenberg, 1772–1801), Tieck, Clemens Brentano (1778–1842), Sophie Mereau-Brentano (1770–1806) and others that the mood of a new type of cultural practice was formed. The Berlin literary salons of two assimilated Jewish women, Henriette Herz and Rahel Varnhagen von Ense, also contributed to the affirmation of new cultural diversity. Herz from 1780 and Varnhagen from 1790 entertained most of the individuals, from various intellectual disciplines and social ranks, who contributed to the definition of the Romantic attitude.

For the early Romantics, as post-Kantians, 'nature' and its enabling metaphors were no longer naively accessible as they had still been for Goethe, Lenz and the other writers of the 1770s. They saw that nature was inaccessible to civilized modern human beings, no matter how much they talk about it or lay out their gardens in an asymmetrical manner. Friedrich Schlegel therefore took the brilliant step of declaring that for man, the artificial is natural.

This way round, Winckelmann's Greece approaches something like a (strictly impossible) art-historical version of the Kantian thing-in-itself, inaccessible to the (modern) human subject, while the art of imperfection, the 'interesting', varied, subjective, unfinished, fragmentary, arabesque, provides an aesthetic for post-Kantian man, who knows his subjectivity to be non-transcendable and takes the consequences: epistemological, ethical, and now, at last, aesthetic.

Yet the kind of cultural authenticity (as opposed to imitation culture) preferred by the young Goethe and Lenz and preached by Winckelmann and Herder is safe because subjectivity, while always separate from nature, is also always oriented towards it by the very condition of its existence, by the light of the very reason that is simultaneously the separating agent. In this way the inner '*Gestalt*'-driven model common to Herder and Winckelmann (and central too to the ideal of education which Humboldt, directly advised by Schelling, Friedrich Schleiermacher [1768–1834] and Fichte, embodied in the Berlin University) is accommodated within a post-Kantian model of the mind.

Schiller had opposed naive to sentimental poetry, ranging Shakespeare on the side of the naive poets, and his own post-Kantian generation on that of the sentimental (self-conscious) ones, for whom spontaneous representation of nature was not possible. The change of emphasis in Schlegel's otherwise cognate (and exactly contemporary) version of the difference between classical and modern models is clear from the fact that Shakespeare swaps sides. For Schlegel, Shakespeare did not belong to the 'naive' (pre-critical) party but to the post-Kantian, Romantic one.

Since the Romantic theorists were no more willing to give up the sanction of nature than Kant, for all his epistemological rigour, was willing to be an atheist, they used the unbridgeable divide between subject and object as a prolepsis, or rhetorical anticipation, of its overcoming. The brilliance of this shift, its timely modernity and public astuteness is clear from the circumstance that, at a stroke, you could be at once modern, in the sense of self-conscious, and still keep on your team the great creative minds, Shakespeare, Dante, Cervantes and indeed (without his consent) Goethe. Through all the proliferation of 'characteristic' literatures, it was argued, there was a *negative* connection between a representation of the things of the world and their secret connection to an invisible centre. The authenticity of this connection was identical with the creative genius of the individual who gave voice and shape to it in the form of a 'work'. The work becomes the trace of subject and object's division, a division which always points to, but can never finally embody, its overcoming. This is what Schlegel meant by his famous gnomic definition of the Romantic as 'progressive Universalpoesie' ('progressive universal poetry').

The inevitable separation of subject from object was given an urbane twist by the gift of the name of irony. Romantic irony means a perpetual awareness of the 'artificiality' which is a 'natural' property of the mind. No Romantic work of art is complete in the sense hitherto required by a conventional view of art and assumed in the philosophical aesthetics of A. G. Baumgarten (who had pioneered the discipline in the mid-eighteenth century), Kant himself and Schiller. The self-consciousness that prevents 'naive' closure is also the guarantee of authenticity.

The cooperation between the natural and the artificial, the naive and the self-conscious had its most enduring concrete impact in the work done by Achim von Arnim (1781–1831), Clemens Brentano, and the brothers Jakob and Wilhelm Grimm (1785–1863 and 1786–1859 respectively) in bringing traditional national literature into modern consciousness. Arnim and Brentano's collection of folk poetry, *Des Knaben Wunderhorn* (*The Boy's Magic Horn*, 1805 and 1808), and the brothers Grimm's *Kinder- und Hausmärchen* (*Fairy Tales*, 1812 and 1815) became two of the most influential books in the history of German – indeed in the case of the latter, world – literature. Both emanating from the academic Romantic environment we have described (which had spread by the early nineteenth century to the University of Heidelberg), they blurred the boundary between philological exactitude and modern Romantic creativity. Not only did they edit and prepare the 'found' materials they collected for publication, but these materials themselves were by definition examples of spontaneous artifice: inscrutable blends of individual and collective expression.

The cultural acknowledgement of folk poetry had begun with Herder, as had its conflation with the contemporary lyric when Goethe's 'Heidenröslein' had been cited as an example of it. Arnim, Brentano and the brothers Grimm now brought this to a high point. Against the background of the Napoleonic war and Romantic nationalism, these songs and fairy tales were not only at once personal and collective but also specifically but timelessly German. The gesture of imitating folk poetry became an important way in which subsequent lyric poets such as Ludwig Uhland (1787–1862) and many others who we shall encounter in the next chapter produced poems at once recognizably literary, profound and national. This accessible spirituality recommended them not only to Romantic academics and authors but also to those German composers who saw in them the opportunity for music to convey profundity in an increasingly secular age.

The Schlegels and the urbane progressive network around them achieved the aim of uniting the classical and the modern. What is more, by seeing Goethe and the national inheritance of folk poetry as embodiments of this new synthesis, modern German letters seemed naturally to settle into the vanguard of European culture.

Spilt religion

Whether on the level of writing practice, as with Wackenroder, or the high theoretical one, as with the Berlin theologian Friedrich Schleiermacher who was closely associated with the Jena Romantics, Romanticism was not just manifestly modern, in the sense of self-conscious and proud of it, but at the same time *religious*. An agnostic definition of the psychological yield of established organized religious belief might be that it facilitates humility before one's own mortality, an attitude that, in the right circumstances, also promotes the ties of human society. This humility is inaccessible to the ordinary life of the individual mind, which by itself is unable to frame such an attitude (being always *life* of the mind). If we can accept T. E. Hulme's famous description of Romanticism as 'spilt religion', it might be the case that, where the established forms of religious belief and observance had regulated the impossible congruence between mental activity and death, now, under the Romantic disposition, we have a potentially infinite plurality of significant individual failures of the life of the mind to grasp its own boundary.

The poet/artist can distil the substantial message through the inevitably self-conscious artificiality of cultural activity but is at the same time the centre of an awareness of a personal fall from grace. The glory of the Renaissance 'holy men of art' ('Kunstheilige') and the agonized sense of unfulfilment of the modern Berglinger are equally indispensable components of the Romantic model.

Novalis was the writer in the Jena network in whom the religious tendency of Romantic literature was clearest. When it came to producing a kind of literature that conformed to the theoretical requirements of the circle, Novalis was really the only one with both the philosophical enthusiasm and the poetic gifts to make a serious contribution.

He had in common with Wackenroder that, as a pious Protestant by upbringing, he experienced Catholicism as seductive. In the essay 'Die Christenheit oder Europa' ('Christendom, or Europe', written in 1799), Novalis, inspired by Schleiermacher's theology, argued for the pre-national, pre-Reformation medieval religious community (as he saw it) as a model for a post-conflict Europe. The attraction of Catholicism in the context of the intellectual framework sketched out above is precisely that its spirituality was written symbolically on 'artificial' things in the world, untainted by materialism or rationalism.

The erotic language used by Novalis to evoke the conception of the new church is indicative of the reintegration of the Dionysiac element at large in the 1770s, and civilized in the Apolline pleasure of classical form and self-cultivation, into the mystical nexus from which it had initially re-entered modern discourse through Hamann (who in his own mind had been protecting it from this very discourse). Novalis conflates the powerful sublimation of mystical longing with Fichte's affirmation of the principle of subjectivity as the formative principle of the universe. The result is an extraordinary vision of an unfolding of general redemption through the creative transfiguration of individual suffering.

The loss of his fiancée, Sophie von Kühn, when she was only 15 became for Novalis that Romantic oxymoron, a personal myth. The *Hymnen an die Nacht* (*Hymns to Night*, 1800) construct a vision of creation, fall and redemption based upon this traumatic loss and a vision experienced at the graveside of the beloved. Somewhat like the virtual theatre of the 1770s, only on a more exalted (post-revolutionary, Fichtean) plane, they are virtual hymns, hymns written in default of a congregation but in the hope and intention of creating the community that in turn will summon a utopian future.

In the subjective area of the lyric, then, the transfiguration of experience that found a glorious secular language in Goethe's early love and nature poetry takes on the function of transforming this expression of subjective experience into the communication of an eschatological message. Yet the division of literature into genres (epic, lyric, dramatic) was alien to the Romantic attitude. The reason that Schlegel praised the novel above all genres was because it was, by virtue of its historical constitution, a mixture of different kinds of discourse. It was poetic as well as philosophical and scientific and, above all, able to sustain self-consciousness – that is, make ironic play with awareness of its own significant artificiality.

With *Heinrich von Ofterdingen* (1802), Novalis undertook the ultimate 'novel' as understood by the Romantic theorists. Friedrich Schlegel had cited Goethe's *Wilhelm Meisters Lehrjahre* (*Wilhelm Meister's Apprenticeship*) as the model of modern (Romantic) literature because it is a novel (*Roman*) in which there is a mixture of styles; subjectivity mixed with the material things of the world; a dissolution of realism into symbolism; and, governing all this, a sovereign irony which holds the knowledge of the artificiality of the text as its proud and significant substance. Novalis initially agreed, appreciating especially the way in which everyday reality progressively dissolved into a symbolic configuration, within which it was only a part and from which it gained its universal significance.

Novalis then turned against it, calling it a *Candide* aimed against poetry. This is an interesting moment since it suggests how intimately linked Goethe's neoclassical organic view of art is with the apparently very different, self-consciously artificial, but as such hyper-real, writing promoted by the Romantics. It is, in other words, fairly evident here, and in other instances of Novalis's choice of genre, that there is, to use Harold Bloom's concept, an 'anxiety of influence' operating. Goethe's choices as an artist (the aesthetic and moral closure he allows, albeit deeply ironically, to play over his novel) must be repudiated and replaced by other choices, at once more poetic and (thus) more moral. But this rivalry is the mark of close dependence.

What Novalis attempts is a writing that actively dissolves our ordinary sublunary sense of reality to reveal the infinite vistas its light obscures: the human subject is the strange point of refraction in which the infinite and the finite touch, and poetry is the trace of this contact. What sustains the narrative is the erotic-mystical mythology of the lost mother-bride, such that, characteristically for the aesthetic theology of the Romantics, the very unspeakable nature of the loss itself guarantees its future overcoming.

This gives rise to some breathtaking effects, especially when the Fichtean context is explained, as it is by Géza von Molnár in his analysis of Novalis's Fichte studies (von Molnár 1987). Abstraction is movingly transformed into a poetry of yearning, intuition and recognition. But poetry should not depend upon explanation. This – rare – *example* of 'progressive universal poetry' loses its way between the alternatives of pointless fantasy and dry allegory.

What Germans really read

Novels had been read in Germany throughout the eighteenth century. The high-altitude theorists simply co-opted the novel for their own programme, because they grasped that they couldn't change the development of literature *de haut en bas*, even with the best humanistic intentions, as their great predecessors and rivals from Lessing onwards had tried to do.

The popularity of translations of great works like *Robinson Crusoe* (1719), *Pamela* (1740) or *Julie ou la nouvelle Heloïse* (1761), as well as hundreds of forgotten novels, gave rise to calls for native equivalents. The modern novel from Richardson onwards was a compromise formation between providing pleasure and moral instruction. In this combination of aims, and in the further one of appealing to as wide a readership as possible, the novel became an important resource for the representation, working through, and the effecting of social changes. At issue (as in the more utopian theatrical dimension of the new German drama) was the relationship between morality and feeling. The epistolary novel – the novel in letters – as in Richardson or Rousseau was the preferred form. In these curious productions, the opportunity to represent the subjectivity of individuals and their relationship to others and to themselves proved of greater interest to a general readership than adventure narratives. Christian Fürchtegott Gellert (1715–1769), a professor at Leipzig, conferred some respectability upon the

Richardson model with the first modern novel in German: *Das Leben der schwedischen Gräfin von G ... (Life of the Swedish Countess of G ... , 1747–8).* Gellert mixed the familiar narrative novel of entertainment with the new novel of sensibility and he was also the author of a work on the correct way to write letters (1742), but it was left to Sophie von La Roche (1731–1807) to write the first Richardsonian epistolary novel in German.

Geschichte des Fräuleins von Sternheim (The History of Miss von Sternheim, 1771) was a significant literary success. Wieland wrote an introduction, and the younger generation such as Goethe and Lenz were enthusiastic about it. La Roche spanned the tastes. What for Wieland was a way of excusing the informality of his cousin and former fiancée's novel for the purposes of the male-dominated market was for the younger men its greatest merit, namely unaffected naturalness. La Roche's novel refracted through the subjectivity of the protagonist and that of other actors in the plot, which also features unreformed licentious and power-abusing aristocrats, components of contemporary social circumstances. The educated class of German state officials blends into the reforming nobility in the circumstance that Sophie's paternal grandfather was a professor and her maternal grandmother an enlightened English noblewoman. It reflects, in Sophie's sorely tested aspiration to be true to the benevolent authority of her father who is an ennobled bourgeois with a social conscience, the importance of the family as the matrix of public as well as private values in contemporary German self-consciousness. In constructing a heroine less perfect but with more congenial parents than Richardson's Clarissa, it encouraged complex identification for readers, especially the women who had established themselves as the prime market for novel fiction. La Roche's novel belongs in the landscape marked out by Richardson, Rousseau and Wieland, but it was also an original feature in that landscape because it proceeded from the woman's point of view and defied enlightened aesthetic expectations by being at once intelligent and popular.

Women in the German lands had no immediate access to the artificial realm of high literature because they were barred from state service and the universities. But many of them connected with the networks linking civil servants, professors, publishers and members of the enlightened nobility did publish novels, and Sophie von La Roche was only the most successful. Whereas Gellert had explicitly wished to reach, as he put it, clever women and low-born men of sound understanding, Moritz, Goethe and Schiller had been keen to distinguish 'art' from what was happening on the ground. In 1790 Schiller coined the term 'dilettantism' as a phenomenon of the age, to refer to the English style in gardening (Vaget 1970:

22–3), but it came to stand for the escape of culture from responsible control. The many women who found their way into print (examples – all persons with substantial literary or academic connections – are Caroline von Wolzogen, Therese Huber, Friederike Unger or Sophie Mereau, a woman who was able to support herself through her writing and whose accomplishments Schiller grudgingly described to Goethe in 1797 as 'dilettantisch') were by definition outside the control of the dominant theoretical masculine culture, yet bore witness to the anarchic liveliness of the book market and the publishing industry in German in the last decades of the eighteenth century.

It is probably true that Jean Paul Richter was the most widely read author in Germany in the mid-1790s, when the ideas for high Romanticism were germinating (Berend 1974). It is also probably true that his writing was more influential on the following generations of writers (for instance Börne, Herwegh, Hauff, Hebbel, Stifter and Keller) and readers in the nineteenth century than that of the Jena thinkers and critics. Jean Paul's writing straddles conventional literary-historical divisions. From the publication of *Hesperus* in 1795 on, it is clear that he holds a very potent attraction for a broad-based readership, the educated and urbane, as well as the learned, and especially for women readers. While Jean Paul was topical enough to reflect and consider elements of other contemporary literary attitudes, including Classical and Romantic, his popularity was probably due to the extent to which he did not break with eighteenth-century sensibility, either in relation to religious feeling or to the place of morality and sentiment in serious literature.

His writing and the European style it adapted for German readers (Sterne, Diderot) flouted all rules of form and exuberantly transgressed against ancient decorum. Here, the age speaks informally and directly to the age in a language it can understand, mindful of both mortality and the absurdities of modern life, disturbing as well as engaging. It seems that Jean Paul was available to people who, unlike the implied neo-Greek readers of Goethe and Schiller or the imagined community of inspired dilettantes of the Romantics, needed to feel they were not alone with the feeling of what the next generation would call *Zerrissenheit* – modern alienation.

Jean Paul was an actual social and moral presence to a greater extent than his contemporary rivals – an author whose wisdom was anthologized widely (two dozen anthologies at his death), as Richardson's had been – and it is legitimate to speculate that it was this immediacy that attracted the Romantics and led them to define their cultural programme in such a way as to include his form of discourse within it. In retrospect, both Clemens Brentano and Joseph Görres identified Jean Paul's affinity with early Romanticism as residing in the way literary idiosyncrasy mingled nostalgia, for the lost simplicity of eighteenth-century life, with hope for a future in which the secular and the spiritual would be co-present in indefinite proportions. The model of how he was read and appreciated, largely by serious women readers, defined a form of sensibility and literary community that the early Romantics wished to appropriate, albeit in a purified, 'virtual' and more exclusive form.

But then, Jean Paul's world was itself already a 'virtual' one since it was by writing in line with village values that he was able to speak to the new solitary readers, people whose sensibilities were nevertheless still formed upon the basis of immediate commerce and contact. This is why he did not become one of the literary aristocracy during his life like Goethe and the Schlegels (preferring the warm domesticity of the Herder household in Weimar). Jean Paul was the old sensibility for the modern market.

Ludwig Tieck, on the other hand, was a Berliner through and through and a born networker. If Novalis wrote high-Romantic texts with little hope of wide readership, and Jean Paul provided a sort of pre-existing popular writing that could be co-opted as a guarantee of the timeliness of what the programmatic Romantics were proposing, Ludwig Tieck was the author who was able actually to produce modern Romantic books which people read. He was a man of the modern book world. His wide range of involvement is clear from his presence in all those areas of the 'Romantic' with which we have dealt up to now. He cooperated with his boyhood friend Wackenroder on the historically important volume of *Herzensergießungen*. He was loosely attached to the Jena network, moving there in 1799 and becoming a close associate of Friedrich Schlegel, while later it was he who edited the posthumous works of his friend Novalis, having to be dissuaded from finishing *Heinrich von Ofterdingen* himself.

As an author, he was a kind of sponge for the voracious literary reading pleasures of the time, from the Gothic novel to Shakespeare. Jean Paul was the living novelist he most admired. He started his career as a jobbing writer for the highly influential Berlin publisher Friedrich Nicolai, and he developed, through parody of this sort of higher pulp production, into an innovator across a broad range of early modern German and European types and styles, including popular ones, making them *salonfähig* in modern German literature.

What the Schlegels affirmed in theory was really *diversity* in literature. At one end, this diversity is connected to all the post-Kantian elaborations of the stake of subjectivity in nature but, at the other, it is exactly what the expanding market for books and reading matter demanded. Tieck was a tireless provider of literary product for this market. What his example also underscores is that in Germany from Gellert onwards, through Wieland, La Roche, Jean Paul and Tieck, and on to E. T. A. Hoffmann, Keller, Storm, Raabe, Ebner-Eschenbach and Fontane, a tradition of good popular writing coexists with those moments of high culture, rightly treasured by the western world.

Spirit in the age of modern literature

To sum up: on one hand, the Romantic elaboration of post-Kantian theories about the potency of subjectivity in nature provides the impetus for a view of culture that opposes the steady advance of what later came to be called instrumental rationality. It seemed like a reaction against the rise of capitalism or, as Raymond Williams argues, like the very founding of what we nowadays think of as 'culture'. But on the other hand, it provides exactly the diversity required for the ongoing capitalization of the literary marketplace which is inseparable from the expansion and diversification of literary tastes. The popular success of folk songs and tales illustrate this, as does the 'cult' of the ballad, in which lyric, epic and dramatic dissolve and which the publisher Cotta (see chapter 2) enthusiastically promoted.

In order to save the one distinction that really mattered – that between the part of life blessed with spirit and the clockwork of causality that had freed the mind only to shackle it again – the Romantics sacrificed all familiar cultural distinctions (affirming the protean forms of all literature), save that between the human and the merely mechanical. As a result, impulses from above and below flow together into a potentially infinite reservoir of literary material. On the other hand, the whole field of literature becomes distinct from the utilitarian reality of industrial modernity. While this in some sense constitutes it as a critique of that reality, criteria of discrimination for placing poetic productions in a system of assessment, while not abandoned, become invisible, since they take their terms from Idealist philosophy. Literature therefore becomes difficult to defend against the depredations of industry and trade. One contemporary commentator criticized the 'factory-like manufacture' of the ballad (Beutin et al. 1993: 360).

The representation of life in the era of quickening and technically improving modes of reproduction rapidly becomes simply more insidiously artificial. 'Romantic' scientific illustration, for instance, which reflected the new holistic philosophy of a unification of all disciplines of thought, now represented images of living things, rather than autopsies of dead ones. But of course, these 'animated' illustrations could only come about because of the technical advances which facilitated travel and improved reproduction (Knight 1990: 22).

In literature, the inner life, once an area to be revealed in confession or opened to the hope of divine intervention is established as the sphere of mental pleasure, the virtual scene of the mind; the world for which the angry young men of the 1770s wrote plays and Novalis hymns. And this new continent was immediately and inevitably colonized by the publishing industry. The life of the mind, refracted in the plethora of fantastic genres and kinds of world literature, supplied the raw material for an industrial literary culture. The two attitudes of mind that Isaiah Berlin picked out as characteristic of Romanticism, namely nostalgia and paranoia (Berlin 1999: 104), correspond to the two great quarries mined by mass culture: Kitsch and horror.

Yet the genuinely great period of German literature coincided with the establishment of the modern book market. Modernization and literary quality were by no means mutually exclusive. The writers whose works are still with us today were often supported by state incomes or pensions, at the same time as playing important roles in the new literary world of publishing and distribution. Schiller, who battled manfully to be both a professional writer and an uncompromising aesthetic and moral authority, but in the end could not survive without noble sponsorship, was probably the best-selling (not the most widely read) German author of the day (Berend 1974: 164). 'Literature' therefore came to self-consciousness in Germany with the sort of aesthetic authority we have talked about in relation to the ideas of Moritz, Schiller, Goethe and the Romantic theorists. This 'autonomy' was both an expression of special cultural value and something the book trade could promote and sell. Amplified by the publishers, literature as autonomous art became a proud German product description. In the century to come, the miraculous disembodied 'soul' of modern German literature was to continue a long struggle with the 'body' of modern political and industrial interests, keen to co-opt this 'autonomy' for its own ends.

2

Poetry and Politics

After the defeat of Napoleon and the Congress of Vienna, literature in the German lands was in a new and unfamiliar situation. Occupation and war have the advantage of shelving problems of national, and thus to a significant extent, personal identity. After 1815 this apparent simplicity gave way to a more complex picture.

The period before 1848 was characterized by a fascinating stand-off between opponents who were not playing by the same rules. The restoration governments, those taking the tone from Catholic Austria and the regime of Metternich, as well as the more dynamic Prussia, at once understood the need for progress in education, trade and industry, but did not know how to control its effects. Eighteenth-century moral and religious attitudes are used to condemn the new ways of thinking of the post-revolutionary period, and these attitudes are partly transparently politicized, the ancestors of modern propaganda, and yet partly still the expression of seriously held beliefs, capable of giving rise to genuine poetry. On the other hand, the perception of a change that seemed to have arrived but was then painfully deferred is also now so deeply felt as to generate serious literature.

We thus have a scene in which absolutism and the development of the modern industrial world shadow-box in a grey area between brute force and legality. Georg Büchner's Danton (we will return to Büchner below) finds himself in exactly that disconcerting area when he tells himself that the Jacobins 'will not dare' to send him and his faction to the guillotine, while he suspects, half hopes, that they will, and the drama is driven by the audience's knowledge that he is right. Büchner's letters are full of anguished requests for information about exactly how far the authorities have gone in their reprisals against his fellow conspirators.

The classical inheritance in the modern world

Goethe, Schiller and Romanticism were pervasively influential in the literary practices that developed after the defeat of Napoleon. Yet the double impact upon this remarkable inheritance of the heavily politicized atmosphere and the rapid expansion of the modern market for culture inevitably changed it.

For instance, nobody did more than the Stuttgart publisher J. F. Cotta to establish the classical inheritance of German literature (Wieland, Herder, Goethe, Schiller, Hölderlin). Cotta was opposed to the mixture of literature with politics, and the prestige of his house contributed, for the first time to a sociologically significant extent, to the establishment of a 'Church of Culture' (Sengle 1971: 104). From the 1820s onwards, Cotta's new classical authors were published for the first time in cheap editions, and when his heirs published Schiller's complete works in a twelve-volume pocket edition of 100,000 in 1837–8, only 3,000 remained unsold in 1844 – a unique event in the publishing world of the time.

This conservative promotion of a classical non-political or, in Schiller's case, a kind of trans-political, literature, reaching out to broad areas of what Metternich called the 'große Lesewelt' ('broader reading public'), cannot have been unwelcome to the restoration governments, seeming as it did to seal off the sphere of *belles-lettres* from the hurly-burly of contemporary political controversy. Yet Cotta's position was not defined by politics but by business (as well as a good publisher's respect for the quality of the work he published). Thus, exploiting the relatively lax regulation in matters of censorship in Württemberg, his influential cultural periodical, the *Morgenblatt für gebildete Stände* (*Morning Paper for the Educated Reader*), launched as explicitly non-political in 1807, became in the restoration period an organ of liberal, even dissident, writing because there was a vibrant market for it (Cotta did not tend to allow political writers, not even Heine, to feature in the prestigious catalogue itself).

Of the older writers, the early Romantics tended to throw in their lot with the *ancien régime*. Friedrich Schlegel, now a Catholic convert and working for Metternich in Vienna, inaugurated the tradition of 'un-political' German cultural politics with his *Geschichte der alten und neuen Literatur* (*History of Ancient and Modern Literature*, 1815). Goethe, living on into the new era, was notoriously anti-political.

The writers who came to maturity in this new situation tended to absorb or assimilate aspects of the inheritance to express their own deeply felt attitudes. The Silesian Catholic Joseph Freiherr von Eichendorff (1788–1857) reconceived the Romantic moment in entirely religious terms. Where Novalis, in *Die Christenheit oder Europa* (known in manuscript before its posthumous publication in 1826), had proposed a revolutionary renewal of Christianity for the modern world, Eichendorff sees no option but to withdraw to the traditional Catholic position. In his novel *Ahnung und Gegenwart* (*Intuition and the Present*, 1815), his mouthpiece-hero Friedrich defends the arch-Romantic novel Achim von Arnim's *Gräfin Dolores* (*Countess Dolores*, 1810), which was notorious for its extravagantly 'arabesque' style. Friedrich insists upon its spiritual authenticity. His impassioned defence meets with great success among his lady listeners, but Friedrich feels that this very success signals failure ('in euch wird doch alles Wort wieder nur Wort' ['in you all words are reduced to mere words']). The modern world is too 'frivolous' to hear the real spiritual message to which the great literary art of the previous generation had borne witness in all its manifestations. For Eichendorff, the attempt to link *Ahnung* ('intuition') with *Gegenwart* ('present'; the splendidly apposite title was the suggestion of Dorothea Schlegel) can only be represented as a failure, and a neo-Catholic literature as the only remedy.

Another case of the conservative reception of the first wave of modern German literature is that of Franz Grillparzer (1791–1872). By the first decade of the new century the impact of Romanticism was felt in Vienna. Grillparzer assimilated the traditions of Viennese popular and baroque drama, as well as impulses from Spain, to the new attitude. Grillparzer also wished to emulate Shakespeare and Schiller as a writer of national tragedy, and in *König Ottokars Glück und Ende* (*King Ottokar's Rise and Fall*, 1823) hits the appropriate political notes (celebrating the founding of the house of Habsburg and exploiting an historical parallel between the Czech King Ottokar and Napoleon), at the same time constructing a timeless tragic representation of the dangers of political ambition. However, so sensitive were the censorship authorities to political content of any sort that, fearing offence to the Czechs, they wished to prevent the play from being performed. The Emperor himself tried to have another play touching upon Habsburg issues, *Ein treuer Diener seines Herrn* (*His Master's Loyal Servant*, 1826), banned. Grillparzer turned instead to non-political subjects. His career is marked by a profound meditation upon the place of classical drama in the modern world, and he clearly doubts that it has one. In an autobiographical fragment, he wrote that he felt like the last poet in an age of prose.

In lyric poetry, the inheritance of Klopstock, Goethe, Hölderlin and the folk song was taken up and developed by religious poets such as the Swabian pastor Eduard Mörike (1804–1875), and the Westphalian noblewoman Annette von Droste-Hülsoff (1797–1848). Lyric poetry in this tradition invites a reading practice that recalls the intensive reading required by the Bible and other devotional texts and resists the extensive reading that fed the rapidly growing market. At the same time, it aspires to the popular accessibility and timeless simplicity of folk poetry. Mörike, Droste-Hülsoff and other writers, who sometimes come under the heading of *Biedermeier*, aim to be redemptive amid a culture of consolation and distraction. This is an attitude that entails pathos, an undercurrent of melancholic foreboding, given that the times are against it. Yet this pathos enriches the poetic attention brought to representations of personal experience, the aim of which is often to convey a sense of how it is more than just personal (examples, among many, are Mörike's 'Besuch in Urach' ['Visit to Urach', 1827] or Droste-Hülsoff's 'Im Grase' ['In the Grass', 1844]).

Finely wrought poems offer themselves as artefacts at once unpretentious and authentic. They are testimony to a spirituality threatened with homelessness in the new age and they specifically oppose what Marx defined as the fetish of commodities, which means an attitude to the objects of ordinary life (in this case, beautifully made poems) that forgets they have a provenance and a history (in other words that they are the fruits of human labour; see Cooper 2008: 92–5). Eichendorff and Droste-Hülsoff were Catholics, and Mörike, a troubled Lutheran minister married to a Catholic, was attracted to Catholicism. This counter-reformationary tendency bore witness to dismay at the usurpation of material existence by – to use Marxian terms once more – exchange value, in place of the sense of indwelling meaning that 'autonomy' had preserved in art, and which Mörike expresses poignantly in the final line of 'Auf eine Lampe' ('On a Lamp', 1846): 'Was aber schön ist, selig scheint es in ihm selbst' ('Yet blithely beauty seems to shine in self-content', trans. Middleton 1972: 205).

In December 1835 Metternich wrote to his official representative in Frankfurt about a group of writers whose works he wished to see banned everywhere in the German-speaking lands. His point was that drama, novels and poems were being used by these authors to undermine the religious and moral fibre of the reading public, and that this would inevitably have effects in the political sphere. On 20 December, the parliament of the German Confederation issued a decree banning the works of a group of writers it referred to as *Junges Deutschland*, mentioning the names of Heinrich Laube (1806–1884), Karl Gutzkow (1811–1878), Ludolf Wienbarg (1802–1872) and Theodor Mundt (1808–1861). On the following day the name of Heine was added to the list, and not only all his existing writings, but all his future ones too, forbidden. The terms of the decree suggest that the authorities felt that the danger posed by literature that was accessible to all classes of reader was great enough to warrant such draconian measures.

The immediate occasion of this climactic example of the endemic state repression of literature was precipitated by the scandalous publication, earlier in the same year, of the novel *Wally, die Zweiflerin* (*Wally the Sceptic*) by Gutzkow. Although very much a product of the 1830s, Gutzkow's novel was an intertextual mobilization of the old Classical-Romantic culture. It had clear links to *Werther* and to Schlegel's programmatically Romantic erotic novel *Lucinde*. Its discursive style, a mixture of narrative and essayism, is unthinkable without the Romantic theory of the novel as a kind of meta-discourse in which representation, narrative and critical reflection combine.

It was the liberal publisher Campe who thought up the perfectly pitched title *Ästhetische Feldzüge* (*Aesthetic Campaigns*, 1834) for Wienbarg's collected inflammatory lectures in the dedication of which the term 'Young Germany' had first been used. What was at issue in the writing of the Young Germans was the appropriation of aesthetic activity for effectiveness in the modern political-commercial environment. The nature of the aesthetic provocation in *Wally* is encapsulated in the one scene that caused the most outrage (and some embarrassment to Gutzkow, who removed it from the 1852 edition). In this scene the heroine Wally, in a Romanticizing *tableau vivant* based on an episode from the medieval poem *Titurel*, reveals herself naked on the night of her marriage (to somebody else) to her lover Cäsar as an earnest of her feeling for him. It is an erotic act but also a sublimation of the erotic, since this is not the prelude to a sexual encounter but a substitute for it, a climax in itself. Like so much of Goethe and indeed Classical-Romantic literature as a whole, it is an act of sublimation, but in the 1830s this takes the form of a moment of intensified but desexualized transgression pesented as significant resistance. It is in this rather convoluted sense political (but it was a sense Metternich understood well enough). This glimpse of something on the threshold between beauty and desire, of something involving Wally and Cäsar in a bond more authentic than Wally's arranged marriage, embodies the 'message' that contests the reactionary moral and religious discourses against which Gutzkow and his friends were conducting their aesthetic campaigns.

The 1835 ban was enough to silence and scatter the Young Germans (some of whom went on to considerable careers in the theatre, literature and publishing in the later part of the century). Their curious application of literature to politics (in a way it was also an evasion of politics by recourse to literature and literary criticism) did not lead to great writing. But this in itself may have been symptomatic of the period. If you wished to make a voice and a name for yourself, there was no time to write for eternity.

On the other hand, the experience of aesthetically conservative writers was that writing professionally was not compatible with what it meant to be a poet. As Adalbert Stifter (1805–1868) wrote in an essay programmatically called 'Über Stand und Würde des Schriftstellers' ('On the Status and Dignity of the Writer') of 1848, those caught in the maelstrom of the urban print culture could not hope to achieve 'the higher, moral purification and tranquillity ... necessary to confer solemnity, human fullness, edification and reconciliation upon the work as a whole' (quoted in Goetzinger 1998: 54). Droste took a more detached view of the same problem. While by no means immune to the temptation of fame, the reflection (in fact wrong) that the notorious Heine was already forgotten lead her to the conclusion that it is better 'to stretch your legs out on the sofa and with half-closed eyes to dream of eternity' (quoted in Goetzinger 1998: 45).

What kind of writing will be adequate to 'times out of joint'? The choice seems to be between giving in to the demands of the day and forsaking the deep eternal truths, or pursuing these at leisure and risking irrelevance. To put it another way: while the achievements in artistic literature of the previous generation had built a poetry in which authentic human feeling could be formed and expressed in a way at once historically and philosophically valid, now any attempt to possess this legacy and put it to use in the modern world will only leave you with half the synthesis, either the world or eternity, plus, in each case, the aching sense of the lack of the other. It is no wonder that *Zerrissenheit* (literally: 'torn-ness') became the fashionable word to describe the state of the sensitive individual, and that madness, to a remarkable extent, became a theme (in works by Hoffmann, Gutzkow, Immermann and Büchner, for instance).

German realism

The kind of writing that flourished in 'times out of joint' is novel realism. Modern European realism from Stendhal onwards deals with individual subjects who are out of sync with the objective circumstances in which they find themselves. It is often argued that German literature did not reflect this until the second half of the nineteenth century because the objective circumstances in the German lands lagged behind France or Great Britain. But it is not that the Germans were too backward but that their literature was too advanced. The symbiosis of German and European writing of the earlier generation had brought literature to the threshold

of general cultural modernity in the form of Romanticism. German literature, in other words, had taken a huge leap forward, only then, in the
period 1815–1848, to stumble.

It is true that Immermann's novel *Die Epigonen* (*The Epigones*, 1836) – the
very title of which (as well as its main themes) addresses the sense of a
temporal dislocation – comes quite close to being a recognizably realist
novel. The most obvious indications of this are that the author includes an
account of the building of a factory installation in the countryside and that
he gives a psychologically authentic account of the Napoleonic equivalent
of shell shock. On a stylistic level, he struggles with the excess of different
ways of seeing the world. However, Immermann, for all his real merits,
was not a great novelist, and the ending of *Die Epigonen* lapses into a rather
embarrassing idealism, a kind of literary restoration.

The mid-nineteenth century was to see a growth in the popularity
of regional writing which was political in the sense that the liberal lobby
co-opted it in the national cause, and realist in the sense that it reported
on actual social conditions and prided itself on its closeness to reality.
Immermann, and especially the section of his *Münchhausen* (1839)
that became popular under the title *Oberhof*, was an important reference
point for Rhineland authors, with Uhland fulfilling a similar function for
Swabia, Jeremias Gotthelf (1797–1854) for Switzerland and Theodor Storm
(1817–1888) for Schleswig-Holstein. The most popular regional writer of
this sort, though less remembered now, was Berthold Auerbach (1812–1882)
whose *Dorfgeschichten* began to appear in 1843. He came from a Jewish
background in Württemberg, and as a radical liberal had been in his youth,
from the point of view of the authorities, a political extremist. Auerbach's
writing and fame were important reference points for German national
identification, since with his most successful story 'Barfüßele' (1856), for
instance, and his narratives of contemporary peasant life, such as 'Die Frau
Professorin' ('The Professor's Wife', 1846) and 'Diethelm von Buchenberg'
(1852), which were often about the psychological repercussions of social
mobility, he raised consciousness about historical change. The international resonance of realistic stories about regions of the German-speaking
world is reflected in Auerbach's fame abroad as well as in German-speaking
places, which also paved the way for that of Gottfried Keller (1819–1890).

The forces of reaction lacked the social popularity which would have
made it possible for them to colonize effectively the area of *belles-lettres* for
their purposes, as they realized they needed to do. Instead, they had to rely
on varying degrees of effectiveness in the realm of old-fashioned mind
control, largely based (apart from the censorship itself) on guilt and the

promise of redemption. Meanwhile, the moment of Romanticism itself, a moment of explosive cultural diversification, arranged the cultural resources for the new market. This market was governed by the laws of enterprise and oriented towards the establishment of a gratification-driven consumer sphere. *Zerrissenheit* was grist to its mill. The deformations of mental life – nostalgia and paranoia as Isaiah Berlin said – provided a huge new resource to be quarried for the modern mind to recognize itself in and be entertained by.

Not only as a writer, but as a musician and as a drinker too, E. T. A. Hoffmann (1776–1822) is an important transitional figure in this respect. The first thing to say about him is that, although he certainly did not fit into the official definitions of what a writer should be, neither among such as Eichendorff and other conservative German cultural pundits nor among moralists from further afield such as Carlyle or Sir Walter Scott, he was nevertheless a significantly successful and representative modern author. It is a simple paradox. His example showed that the unaccommodated post-Romantic individual, whose pleasures, though intense and genuine, are not welcome in salon or church, is at home in the modern book. Solitary pleasures can be shared; the lack of metaphysical certainty is compensated for by a modern imagined community of partial souls.

The second thing to say is that Hoffmann is a serious popular writer (in the tradition of Jean Paul). He brings paranoia to the market (in *Die Romantische Schule*, Heine described his work as a 'frightful cry of terror in twenty volumes') and makes it humorous and enjoyable, but that does not devalue at all the subjective reality of the fear, nor its objective basis. The Romantic project was to dissolve all distinctions in culture, save that between humans and machines. It is exactly the leering possibility of the disappearance of this last distinction that animated Hoffmann's fantasies. Nathanael in 'Der Sandman' ('The Sandman', 1816) finds out that the living subject who has attracted and excited his passion is in fact nothing but an automaton – machinery has invaded the very apparatus of vision, while the economy of the body occupies the territory of the spirit. Consciousness, once made conscious of itself as inhabited by error, excess and irregularity, is haunted by the spectre of its own merely material constitution. How are we to know if our transports of yearning, the glimpses of surpassing order experienced in the pleasure of musical composition, are oriented upon the truth of the spirit, or simply the effects of too much punch? In face of imponderable questions like this, Hoffmann's advice is to carry on drinking.

The movement towards the culture of the modern consumer takes a further step with Heinrich Heine (1797–1856). Heine is the one great author who seems thoroughly at home in this period, playing off nostalgia for the lost innocence of Romantic folk song against the political clamour in which it got lost and paranoia about what might emerge from it, and creating an effective public image for himself as a modern author – lyric poet, travel writer, journalist, popular cultural historian – in the process. Heine occupies a place in modern German literature left empty by the absence of an indigenous realist novel.

On one hand, Heine's opposition to the reactionary political implications of Romanticism could not be clearer. In one of his two great essays on Germany, written from the point of view of an exile writing about Germany for the French, *Die Romantische Schule* (*The Romantic School*, 1836; the other is *Zur Geschichte der Religion und Philosophie in Deutschland*; [*On the History of Religion and Philosophy in Germany*, 1834]), he represented the Schlegels as vain and uncreative cultural pundits whose claim to be taken seriously had ceased with Goethe's dismissal of them, and who had set the seal on their own historical irrelevance by going over to the reactionary Austrian Catholic camp.

On the other hand, Heine's ambivalence about the imagination is the constitutive component of all his writing. In him, the question of the place of aesthetic pleasure in the force field of modern political life is posed perhaps for the first time, but at any rate very clearly. Heine was for a significant period, and at the height of his powers, a friend of the Parisian Saint-Simonian doctrine of sensualism. But the importance he attached to beauty within this broad religious-moral-political affirmation of sensualism was a preoccupation of his own, and evidently a legacy of the great period just passed. Heine coined the term 'Kunstperiode' (literally 'era of art') to define its anachronistic status in what Hegel called the 'age of prose'. Nobody wanted literature (broadly defined, across a Romantic range of genres and modes of discourse) to contribute substantially and materially to general emancipation more than Heine. Yet, in order to be genuinely emancipatory (and in order for there to be a point to emancipation), there must be a pleasure associated with literature which is sharply distinguished from the redemptive earnestness of religious observance. It must not be conceived as contradicting the pleasures of the appetites, because this would be politically reactionary. No wonder Eichendorff saw in Heine the epitome of that frivolity that devalued the more recent manifestations of Romanticism in Eichendorff's view, and not only Droste, but Mörike too was repelled by how comfortable Heine was in the modern age. But the pleasure in question would be equally threatened if poetry were to be subordinated to political purpose. In a sense, the pleasure of the poetry, a pleasure for those modern city-dwellers who are familiar with the consolations of material gratification, is its very political force, since it opposes the torture-obsessed, gratification-postponing culture of Christianity. Its political meaning is that in a period when reason and technology make it possible for everyone to share in the pleasures of the world, there is no reason either to put them off until the afterlife, or to deny them to as many people as possible.

Heine's choice not to put his feet up and dream about eternity meant nonetheless that he suffered the identity split of those who tried the impossible trick of being a German *Dichter* and a modern journalist at the same time. Perhaps his modernity resides in his ability to embrace and affirm that split (since it connected him with his audience). The dual allegiance to poetry and politics informs his two great narrative poems, *Atta Troll* (1843), which described itself ironically as 'das letzte Freie Waldlied der Romantik' ('Romanticism's last free sylvan song') and *Deutschland. Ein Wintermärchen* (*Germany. A Winter's Tale*, 1844).

Heine made a virtue of the excessive self-consciousness of the epoch that his friend Immermann had made a theme of *Die Epigonen*. Heine's response to the need to write in, about and for a time out of joint was to cultivate a subjective ironic style which permitted the poetic subject to affirm itself while still responding to, satirizing, mocking but also attacking contemporary circumstances, including the stupidity of the censors.

Heine spent the last eight years of his life bedridden in Paris. Yet in his last poetry the ironic intelligence and the verbal facility of the earlier writing play against this nightmarish physical condition, refusing to be silenced by it. Although gratification will inevitably fail in the end, Heine's example goes to show that a culture which affirms gratification and, failing that, consolation, rather than the promise of redemption, is by no means a hollow or easy thing. The 'Afterword' to the collection *Romanzero* (1851) is a masterpiece of modern secular spirituality, whistling in the dark, for the benefit not only of the whistler but also for those in the light. Heine's poetry from the beginning bore a trace of the horror of a world without redemption, and at the end of Book Two of *Zur Geschichte der Religion und Philosophie in Deutschland* he announced the death of God fifty years before Nietzsche's Madman did the same to a complacent crowd, thinking themselves secure in the rational light of the midday sun.

In 1834, Georg Büchner (1813–1837), then just twenty-one, co-wrote a propaganda pamphlet, *Der hessische Landbote* [*The Hessian Messenger*], inciting the peasantry of Upper Hesse to open revolt. This politically direct act went beyond the territory upon which the new liberal print culture shadow-boxed with the authorities. In this, Büchner cannot be included in the range of writers from 'left' to 'right' who found ways of relating the poetic legacy to the new reality. He was not a dissident but a revolutionary, albeit an unsuccessful one.

Yet in Büchner's literary writing – three plays and a short prose piece – there is a powerful, if anguished, connection to the older literature. He was certainly trying to co-opt its best aspects for his cause. He had no interest in sacrificing literature to politics. When the issue was one of drafting propaganda, that is, after all, what he did. He was a great realist in a literary culture as yet innocent of the modern realist novel.

There is first of all a passionate commitment to the importance of literature as a discourse of human sympathy. In the prose fragment 'Lenz' (written 1835–6), Büchner backdates 'the Idealist period' to the late 1770s so that his fictional Lenz can articulate an aesthetic credo of authentic humanity against it. It is an indication of the politicization of aesthetics in this period that Büchner should identify Schiller with the forces of reaction because of his support of classical form in drama. Büchner's Lenz insists upon what one might in retrospect certainly recognize as realism but which is defined not by style but by the ability to give rise to 'feeling'. The feeling that Lenz / Büchner argues for is not simply gratification, however deferred, of the sort Heine proposed as an instrument of emancipation. It is, despite Büchner's hatred of Schiller's idealism, itself profoundly idealistic. The aspiration is that of the Enlightenment ideal of the family of Man. This belief is not put forward theoretically but realized through the medium of poetic prose or drama into an affirmative experience of shared humanity.

Lenz's programme has something of Romanticism in its resistance to genre and conventional form in literature. His vision of nature as an organic continuum also owes something to Goethe. The dream is to serve an aesthetic perception in which the individual human subject, as object and subject of the representation, is able to grasp in reality and its extension, history, the enduring values to which this intensity of feeling and unbroken authenticity of perception and sympathy bear witness.

This redemptive trajectory of Büchner's writing is also clear from his declared ambition as a creative writer to breathe life back into the documents of history, a history which threatens nihilism. This was his revolutionary method in *Dantons Tod* (*Danton's Death*, 1835), where he used historians' accounts and other contemporary documents (speeches, for instance) in the construction of the drama, in 'Lenz', where he used Pastor Oberlin's diaries, and in *Woyzeck* which he based upon actual cases of domestic homicide.

This was his radical form of literary opposition to the petrifying inhumanity of the restoration and the redoubled repression after 1830. The radical nature of his vision also reveals, however, that vision might not be enough. If Hoffmann was haunted by the loss of the founding distinction between man and machine, and Heine, somewhat comparably, is dismayed at the prospect of the instrumental brutality of what a revolution would actually be like (see the figure of the lictor in *Deutschland. Ein Wintermärchen*), the spectre haunting Büchner is that of materialist determinism. Like Hoffmann, Büchner suspects in his worst moments that human self-consciousness is machine-like, even suggesting to his fiancée (7 March 1834) that he could have been a model for one of Hoffmann's bizarre mirror characters (and earned some money doing it!). The underlying fear is that words (we are reminded of Eichendorff's Romantic apologist Friedrich here) will always only be words, severed from substance by the material social conditions in which they are uttered. The underlying theme of *Dantons Tod*, a play concerning the private lives of public figures, is the relation between rhetoric and meaning. This is a paralyzing fear for literature, threatening a nihilism in regard of the very practice (that is to say, literature) passionately pursued in order to resist it.

Where Heine's ironic affirmation of a sensualist industrial modernity pointed forward to a culture of gratification and consolation, Büchner's concern with the social determination of language itself and all its resources, including literary ones, anticipates theories of alienation. His resistance to Schiller cannot be to Schiller's hopes for drama, since nobody more than he grasped the threat of alienation resulting from the modern division of labour and tried to deploy dramatic art to resist it. Büchner's resistance to Schiller must be to the alienation of Schiller's dramatic practice from the reality it was developed to correct. Büchner senses the limits of affirmative literature, limits set precisely by the alienation of the discourse of a whole class by virtue of its being at odds with the true interests of the oppressed of history. His rejection of restoration authority, but also of wordy, worthy liberal opposition, and his analysis of social malaise in terms not of birth but of money identify him as a proto-Marxist.

Despite the absence of a German novel realism, then, this epoch out of joint saw the stirrings of much of the future of modern literature. Hoffmann continued the tradition of serious popular literature, following Jean Paul, while Heine and Immermann were on the right wavelength to find some sort of literary solution to the multi-temporality, that is to say the simultaneous existence of several different historical conditions, that characterized the *Zerrisenheit* of the epoch and to indicate some directions the popular tradition represented by Jean Paul and Hoffmann might take in the modern literary marketplace. Büchner was both a realist (carrying forward the realism of the German drama of the 1770s) and the manifestation of a time warp in which the forms of serious literature of the future appear before their time. *Danton's Tod* and 'Lenz', and, especially, *Woyzeck*, have long been recognized as precursors of Modernism. For the next fifty years or so, however, the time warp was to operate in the other direction, and the dimension in which the sensibilities of an Eichendorff, a Grillparzer or a Stifter were at home was to determine the scene of German literature.

An affirmative literature

In the second half of the nineteenth century, German literature took a back seat to politics. This was the period during which Germany really did enter the modern world, but German literature did not begin to behave much like other European literatures again until nearly the end of the century.

Historians have argued a great deal about the German *Sonderweg* in the nineteenth century, by which they mean the claim that the social development of the countries / country did not match the economic one (the point being to try and trace a German democratic deficit in the pre-history of Nazism). One reason why there might be grounds for talking about a *Sonderweg* in relation to German literature, as opposed to German history in general terms, has already been mentioned: the highly advanced nature of the first literary effloresence, which then finds itself out of joint with a time of political pragmatism.

Another aspect was revealed once Metternich departed in 1848, following the year of liberal revolutions throughout Europe, and the modernization of the German lands started to accelerate, despite the reversals suffered by the liberal cause. What historians see is a convergence of two kinds of middle class, the educated and the economic. This did not occur in the same way in the other advanced European countries because the German development was staggered. The intelligentsia and the mercantile capitalists had little in common under Metternich; indeed in some senses they were rivals. After 1848, their interests did begin to coincide, since both groups, though for different reasons, were now able to conceive of themselves as united within the same progress towards modernization. While what we nowadays call the business community welcomed further advances towards a strong modern economic state, the liberals, sobered by the reality of civil violence in 1848, were defensive in relation to the incipient proletariat and thus willing to compromise in pursuit of political stability and material progress.

The mercantile capitalists made the new reality; the intelligentsia dressed it up with poetry. The intelligentsia were able to keep their Classical-Romantic habits of reception (art is art and not politics or popular entertainment), while the new pragmatic spirit was nevertheless affirmed. On the one hand, the terrific impact of industrial technology (factories, railways, usable roads, photography, electricity) could be softened by a conservative sense of transfiguring mediation while on the other, literature itself became part of industrial modernity, since this new coalescence of the practical and the imaginative confirmed its transformation into a complex commodity.

These developments led to *Kitsch* (a word apparently coined by Munich art dealers in the 1860s and 1870s) but also to the creation of a literature with broad appeal across social boundaries. If they set the stage for the kind of 'alienation' Büchner anticipated, they also provided the modern literary conditions in or against which certain authors – one might call them problematic – produced great writing.

Before the actual unification of Germany, the main manifestation of a literary *Sonderweg* was the attribution of a curious meaning to the term 'realism'. In the way it was used by Julian Schmidt in his influential journal *Die Grenzboten* (*The Border Courier*, 1841–1923) during the 1850s, it really meant: 'Don't rock the (national-liberal) boat.' The idea is something like what we mean in everyday language when we say: 'Be realistic!' *Die Grenzboten*, and those in its cultural penumbra during the 1850s, accordingly opposed the 'extravagances' of the earlier literature. They questioned the excessive imaginative freedom of the Classical-Romantic heritage. Goethe and Schiller were too 'Greek', and this idealizing distance from the real world had grown 'monstrous' with the Romantics. Furthermore, they revised the earlier revision of the great authors by the oppositional authors of the pre-1848 period, or the *Vormärz* as it is called in German (seen by Schmidt as a second Romantic generation), who objected to the apolitical or reactionary aspects of the heritage. In the political situation after 1848, this earlier politics seemed utopian and needed to be replaced by a more pragmatic attitude. Yet the programme for literature proposed by Julian Schmidt was not really thinkable without Classical-Romantic German literature and its refractions in the preceding decades. The idea was to produce an idealized or poetic representation of 'the world' which is understood as a manifestation of nature in historical circumstances.

Goethe's pantheism and the Romantic conviction that infinity plays among the products of the human mind are subliminally co-opted to posit a literature that can represent 'the world'. Because the emphasis was now on reality (that is, on the progress of Germany towards a practical solution of the difficulties lying in the path of its economic and political potential), these aesthetic-cultural properties were surreptitiously projected onto this 'reality', making it into an aesthetic entity. The function of literature is that of a litmus paper that tinges the pragmatism of prose with the colour of poetry when timeless regularities are discerned within historical circumstances.

The thought that representation can somehow capture 'the world' attributes an irrational completeness to the notion of representation. It is only here, and paradoxically, that the question of the 'autonomy' of literature becomes philosophically problematic. Before, from Lessing to Herwegh, literature had always been a specific form of discourse, or perhaps a variety of specific forms of discourse, but either way always part of a complex social world in its very specificity. Now, the 'autonomy' of art is smuggled out into 'the world', thence to be revealed in literature.

This is the quintessential model of 'affirmative' literature. The forms of affirmation in the period between the defeat of Napoleon and the revolutionary year of 1848 had necessarily been factional and therefore *zerrissen* in nostalgia for the no-longer-possible oneness implicit in the aesthetics of Goethe, Schiller and the Romantics (albeit in different ways). Now an affirmation was proposed predicated upon the coherence of a historical reality that had sense and direction.

Whereas elsewhere (England, France, Russia), 'realism' meant the concession on the part of literature to the dynamic informality of urban modernity – the imaginative exploitation of historically complex, multi-temporal conditions, inevitably involving socially critical moments, just as 'society' in 'reality' is charged through with critical moments – in Germany the word was used to describe a literary style that expressed the common enterprise of pragmatic realism in the matter of bringing about a new political Germany.

Even more paradoxically, Schmidt argued that realism, far from being the literary genre of modern informality, should be a bastion against the kind of anarchy in the order of genre which had been one of the hallmarks of Romanticism. He set his face against what was most substantively modern in the Romantic revolution: the dissolution of literary genre.

This affirmative circumscription of literature had the subsidiary effect of shaping it as a commodity and thus affirming too its niche in industrial modernity. Paradoxically once more, the movement towards cultural commodification – encouraged by the Romantic loosening of culture into a scattered and diverse series of entities and events – was continued in this attempt to oppose and reverse Romanticism.

The affirmation of a certain realism by Julian Schmidt and many others who, like him, had modified a radical liberal stance to a more pragmatic national one in the post-1848 period, amounted to a sense of the German nation 'growing up'. It is as if the censorship that had crudely borne down upon the writers of all stamps during the restoration period has now been internalized successfully. Before, the necessity of internalizing censorship of one sort or another had led to *Zerrissenheit*. Now, in the manner of a boy negotiating the Oedipus complex correctly, German 'realism' identified with rules prohibiting excessive exercise of the imagination that had formerly threatened mutilation. They become stiffeners for the politically mature personality instead.

This is intimately linked with the question of commodities in general, as it is represented in the novel *Soll und Haben* (*Debit and Credit*, 1855). Its author, Gustav Freytag, was a co-editor of Schmidt's on *Die Grenzboten*. While one can legitimately wonder how representative the ideas of a journal with a circulation of no more than circa 4,000 actually were, there can be less doubt about the importance of this book which became (possibly) the best-selling novel of the century. It was promoted as the paradigm for the 'programmatic realism' propagated by Schmidt and Freytag and remained acknowledged as a classic of German realistic fiction until well into the twentieth century. For better or for worse, it reveals something about the mind of the new Germany.

Soll und Haben tells a very particular story about pleasures in the capitalist age. The hero is a mercantile capitalist *Bildungsroman* hero by the name of Anton Wohlfart. Less a Wilhelm Meister than a Werner figure (Wilhelm's cousin, whose major intellectual passion is double-entry bookkeeping), he represents the proper attitude to the emancipation enjoyed by the modern commercial individual. Anton is the boy who correctly internalizes, and identifies with, the censorship rules relating to the dangers of too much fun. Freytag (in eerie anticipation of the famous italicized punch line from the 'Snow' chapter of Thomas Mann's twentieth-century *Bildungsroman, Der Zauberberg* [*The Magic Mountain*]) summed up the morality of his book thus: 'Der Mensch soll sich hüten, daß Gedanken und Wünsche, welche durch die Phantasie aufgeregt werden, nicht allzu große Herrschaft über sein Leben erhalten' ('A man must be on his guard lest thoughts and wishes whipped up by his imagination obtain too great a sway over his life'). The novel (as a novel) recognizes that 'an aesthetic libidinal desire for commodities' (Berman 1986: 89) is indispensable for the modern individual, since it is the motor of commerce. But, so the message goes, this appetite must also be countered by an asceticism that regulates it. It is this pattern of regulation that Schmidt and Freytag advocate through realism of the 'don't-get-carried-away' sort.

This realistically regulated pleasure is carefully differentiated from other, less socially acceptable, sorts. It is not so much the aristocracy, the old enemies of the middle class on the plane of pleasure, who represent unacceptable licentiousness. In another reversal of *Wilhelm Meister*, it is they who have to learn to live with the new mobility, while bringing their old virtues (such as bravery in battle) into the equation. This was the alliance upon which the new Germany had to be built.

The new models of licentiousness are the Jews and the Poles. They are propagandistic 'others' to the correct new German character. The Jewish character Veitel Itzig (whose surname became the German equivalent of such English anti-Semitic terms as 'yid' and 'Jewboy') is too given over to the lure of capital accumulation. His pleasure is unbounded, tied up with the bad infinity of speculation. The traditional association of the Jews with licentiousness is also allowed to swing along with Freytag's distasteful characterization of them. Stifter associated insurrectionary behaviour with sexual depravity, referring to Hungarian separatists in a letter of 1849 as driven by 'appetites and cravings' (quoted in Naumann 1979: 13) and was no doubt not alone in this. In this novel, the people addicted to the vice of civil disorder are the Poles. They are characterized also by another manifestation of an addiction to undeferred gratification: they are almost always drunk. In this way the vicious aspects of modernity, revolution and speculation are projected on to others, while the affirmative ones, the commitment to work, trade and self-control, are attributed to the Germans.

This differentiation of permitted from unpermitted pleasures frames a realism that offers a reading experience perfectly suited to providing a bridge between the intelligentsia, whose area of competence is handling the aesthetic inheritance of the incipient German nation, and the men charged with the creation of a modern commercial German state. *Soll und Haben* was the first novel in German with which men specifically could – indeed were expected to – admit to being familiar and this cross-over in appeal accounts to a significant extent for its unique success in sales.

An essay of 1852 in *Die Grenzboten* ('How to Create a Home Library'; quoted in Berman 1986: 292) exemplifies the kind of lifestyle advice being dispensed to the modern population by that journal as well as others.

(Gutzkow's *Unterhaltungen am häuslichen Herd* [*Conversations by the Fireside*, 1853–64], its ideological rival, had a permanent column on the 'Art of Living', including such features as 'The Aesthetic of Food'.) The advice about setting up one's own library is really advice about how to put a brake on the pleasures to be found inside books. What the reader has to do is to regulate, order and generally clean up his own book collection. He is advised to buy his own copies (rather than put up with library copies soiled by the attentions of others), have them bound tastefully and keep them ordered and catalogued in an appropriately appointed domestic area. On the other hand, conduct books of the nineteenth century repeatedly stressed that *Prachtausgaben*, luxury editions, should not be just for show but also read.

Soll und Haben, unusually for the time, was first published as a book and not in serial form in *Die Grenzboten* or any other journal. This chimed with the campaign for the book as a complex commodity, a possession not just for passive consumption but defining and affording socially sanctioned pleasure.

The German literature myth and what Germans really read

In 1859, one hundred years after Schiller's birth, the propaganda potential of the German literary inheritance in the years leading up to German unification was demonstrated when the liberals used the occasion as a huge party-political event. Schiller's patriotism, his vaunted closeness to the common people and his idealism were the focus for popular celebrations all over the German Confederation (not to mention Switzerland where Schiller's *Wilhelm Tell* had made the playwright a national hero). Not only did this high-profile occasion distract attention from the 'de-idealizing' tendencies of the pragmatic realists to the classical inheritance itself, but it transformed a celebration of the cultural inheritance into an unambiguously political act, involving broad swathes of the population.

With the Prussian military victory over Austria in 1866, and the creation of a unified modern German state under Prussian conservatives in 1870–1, the logic of modern propaganda led to the identification of the great achievements of the Romantic generations – which had been the result of a symbiosis between German creativity and wider European influences – not just with Europe, nor yet with the diffuse cultural identity within the Confederation which made regional patriotism a rallying point for German literary self-consciousness in the mid-century, but with the history of

Prussia. It was contended by Wilhelm Dilthey (1833–1911) in 1866, for example, that the German literary tradition was founded upon the specifically German marriage of absolutism and enlightenment.

Dilthey is the originator of the myth of the German *Bildungsroman*. It is not true that there is a 'tradition' of the novel of personal development in German literature (athough there are some examples of it, as there are in other literatures). Dilthey claimed that there was. He made this claim in relation – surprisingly enough, since few have since referred to it as a *Bildungsroman* – to Hölderlin's tragic novel *Hyperion*. But at the moment at which modern political Germany came of age, it is not surprising that one might assert that the German version of the European novel in fact dealt with the maturation of subjective inwardness into political and social responsibility. *Soll und Haben* literally told the same story.

Dilthey is an important figure, less for the cultural history of literature than for the cultural history of the image of literature. On one hand, in his work he completed the definition of the German literary heritage as a Classical-Romantic symbiosis, finally fully integrating Romanticism into the mix and completing the trend towards a philosophizing homogenization of the varied components of the first effloresence into an overarching notion of the specifically German.

On the other hand, his contribution to the establishment of a history of German literature was no longer itself literary. He produced an intellectually dazzling account of the *Geistesgeschichte* ('intellectual history') informing the German nation, but he did this for a professional scholarly audience. The history of histories of German literature from Schlegel to Schmidt had involved an address to at least a notional, and notionally gradually expanding, public. Dilthey is for the professionals. He represents what sociologists call the 'systematic' differentation within modernity, by which they mean that what had been a unified though changing 'public sphere', from the Enlightenment onward, separates out in modernity into different systems which no longer map on to one another. *Realpolitik* is, for example, the system of politics severed from that of morality.

If with Dilthey we see the establishment of a severed theoretical literary consciousness, the enormous success of the family literary periodicals in the period after 1850, especially Ernst Keil's *Gartenlaube* (*The Arbour*), represents the body from which it has been severed. Keil, like Gutzkow, his predecessor in this branch of publishing, was a liberal whose commitment was channelled into the modern market for culture after 1848. Keil, as well as Gutzkow and Auerbach whose earlier 'village stories' were held to be exemplary by the *Grenzboten* realists, provides and exploits literary pleasure for the actual readers of the time. In this they are the real heirs of Wieland, Jean Paul, Tieck and Hoffmann (not to mention the early Schiller and Goethe) in the actual tradition in German literature of serious popular authorship.

If we recall that the circulation of *Die Grenzboten* was about 4,000, and Gutkow's *Unterhaltungen am häuslichen Herd* about 6,000 at its height, the statistic that *Die Gartenlaube* had reached a circulation figure of 382,000 by 1875 has more expressive power than most. The magazine itself claimed to have the largest circulation in the world which, whether true or not, again says something about the arrival of Germany in modernity and vice versa.

While with Dilthey German literature was reconstituted as *Geistesgeschichte*, with Keil it was popularized (*Die Gartenlaube*, unlike its predecessors, eschewed literary criticism). Goethe and Schiller dominated the literary programme, Schiller featuring 90 times in print and 15 times in illustrations between 1853 and 1880, Goethe 75 and 14 times. The journal highlighted lyric poetry as a sort of metonym for literature itself. The function of 'poetry' in the *Gartenlaube* ethos is effectively expressed in the poetic motto provided by Friedrich Bodenstedt for a popular anthology of verse edited by Elise Polko entitled *Dichtergrüße (Poets' Greetings)*: 'O spirit of poetry, thou divine gift: thou coverest with flowers the abyss' (quoted in Becker 1996: 123). It is clear that this recourse to poetry, in part a conscious defence against the shock of the new, was a less theoretically elaborate version of Schmidt's programme for realism or Ludwig's 'poetic realism'. Otto Ludwig (1813–1865) coined the phrase that came to represent the brake applied to German literature in the name of timeless literary values in the second half of the nineteenth century, during the same period as that which witnessed the beginnings of Modernism in Paris.

There is a certain schizophrenia involved in the mass distribution of material, the explicit aim of which is to mask the industrial reality upon which mass distribution depends. Yet the Marxist view of one economic class deploying a culture of its own (as if it were universally valid) as a defence against the interests of another ignores the historical fact of the reading pleasure to which the success of *Die Gartenlaube* attests. Keil's line was decidedly (though not explicitly) liberal, at least in the first decades after 1848, and, by the logic of free enterprise, other journals like it spanning the spectrum of political opinion were successfully launched. They had broad appeal for millions of readers (taking multiple readerships into account) who as far as one knows were minor officials, office workers, artisans, village schoolteachers and domestic servants. One estimate is that the family magazines reached 60–70 per cent of the population

(Helmstetter 1998: 59). This was literature (among other things) as popular mass entertainment, and it gives an insight into the actual literary taste of the time: the taste that was refined, but not dismissed, in the writers whose work is still read with pleasure. As Theodor Fontane (1819–1898) said in a letter to the editorial board of the *Die Gartenlaube*: 'I shall gladly eat from a bowl from which three hundred thousand Germans also eat' (quoted in Helmstetter 1998: 34).

A popular prose culture came about in modern industrializing Germany. *Soll und Haben*, Otto Ludwig's *Zwischen Himmel und Erde* (*Between Heaven and Earth*, 1856, originally intended as a *Novelle* for the *Gartenlaube*, but growing too long), and *Goldelse* (1866) by E. Marlitt (1825–1887), the serial novel that made a significant impact upon the already impressive circulation of the *Gartenlaube*, inaugurating the practice of novel serialization in that journal, are all examples of this. The 1870s saw an increase as sudden and great as that in the circulation of the family magazine in what is known as the *Kolportageroman*. Enterprising publishers saw the opportunity afforded by the exponential growth of the urban proletariat (by a factor of approximately six in the years after unification). Travelling salesmen (*Kolporteurs*) had sold tracts and pictures to peasant families since the Middle Ages. Now this traditional method was allied with the latest marketing ploys, notably huge printings of the first episodes of novels distributed free of charge in order to produce and maintain a readership for the dozens of ensuing ones. The result was that serial reading spread deep into the populace. The function of these novels in stimulating and meeting a sustained need for reading material was taken over by the popular press towards the end of the century.

The *Novelle*

Against this background of the commercialization of literature – which, as across Europe, favours the novel – one literary form stands out as historically characteristic for this phase of time-resisting German literature: the *Novelle*.

The *Novelle* is the prose form par excellence for journal publication and was explicitly envisaged from the start as part of Ernst Keil's programme (before novel serialization proved economically irresistible), as well as that of Julius Rodenberg's *Deutsche Rundschau* (*German Review*), of which more below. Like lyric poetry, it is more obviously literary, in the sense of poetically formed, than the novel. It comes into German literature as part of the first great symbiosis. Goethe, Kleist and Tieck adapted the old tradition of Boccaccio, Cervantes and the French *nouvelle* for contemporary use. It is a good example of the kind of cultural material made available (largely through the literary enterprise and versatility of Tieck) for the modern market for culture. The Young Germans recommended its use as a means of spreading the liberal doctrine precisely because it was an established and popular genre (if it can be called a genre, so diverse were its manifestations).

Before 1848, although the *Novelle* was ubiquitous, it was simply part of the rush to diversification taking place in the wake of Romanticism in the almanacs and *Taschenbücher* (pocket-sized books) of the developing literary market in Germany. It was only after 1848 that it became a focus for a specifically German literature.

One can advance several possible reasons for this. The *Novelle* was particularly suited to what the Germans called realism in the two decades or so after 1848. Pre-1848, discussion elaborated a defining contrast between the novel and the *Novelle*, along the lines that the novel was linked with the feminine, the fantastic and idealism, while the *Novelle* was intellectual, masculine and realist. Its best recommendation was that it was not Romantic *Universalpoesie* (although in Tieck's hands, it had seemed the very vessel of such diversity). This provided credentials for a serious prose literature, suitable for a grown-up national culture. It has even been suggested that the self-control evinced in preferring the tight short form to the sprawl of the novel was a parallel to the preference for a lean 'little German' solution (excluding Austria) to the question of unification over that for a heterogeneous 'greater German' one (Sengle 1971: 841).

Another reason why the *Novelle* rose to such dignity in this period is the link between it and the drama. Theodor Storm, one of the most successful writers of *Novellen* of the period, as well as one of the best, famously called it 'the sister of the drama'. Otto Ludwig and Paul Heyse (1830–1914), the two most important proponents of the *Novelle* as a strictly defined, nationally characteristic genre were both also dramatists. Gottfried Keller would dearly have liked to be one. While dramatic literature had played the key role in the middle-class revolution in literary culture in the 1770s, the institution of the theatre itself, whether in Vienna or in the hands of the company of the Duke of Saxe-Meiningen remained associated with the *ancien régime*. Attempts to reinvent it for the present were not really successful (the time never did really come, as the dramatist Friedrich Hebbel [1813–1863] had hoped it would, when his dramas *about* history would find their own place in history). With the spectacular exception of Wagner's music drama, of which more presently, it languished until it became the site of a cultural revolution in German literature in the 1890s (see chapter 3). The *Novelle*, therefore, like the *Lesedrama* of the 1770s, made a bid for the prestige of dramatic literature in the realm of modern reading practices.

Finally, the *Novelle's* tight organization and propensity to symbolize made it especially suitable, to recall Bodenstedt's motto quoted above, as a literary 'flower' to cover the hard-edged technological 'abyss' opening up beneath the comforting landscape of liberal humanist pieties. Storm's *Immensee* (1848) takes up the challenge from the recently invented practice of photography to redeem by poetic description the inevitable discrepancy between the life of the mind and the narrative of a life. His last and most famous *Novelle*, *Der Schimmelreiter* (*Rider of the White Horse*, 1888), simultaneously addresses and begs the question of how technological progress and the collective values of human society are meant to relate to one another, making of this historical ambivalence an aesthetic ambiguity. Throughout Storm's prolific *Novelle* output, there is the threat of immersion, engulfment and oblivion contained within tightly organized and framed narratives. This should not be taken as a negative critique of the genre: on the contrary, this historical tension informs and intensifies the art of the *Novelle* not just in Storm, but in others such as Annette von Droste-Hülsoff, Conrad Ferdinand Meyer (1825–1898) and Adalbert Stifter.

Problematic affirmative literature

The best German novel realism of the second half of the nineteenth century is the work of those authors who, while of course shaped by their period, can be described as 'problematic' rather than 'programmatic'. Writers like Adalbert Stifter, Theodor Fontane, Gottfried Keller, Marie von Ebner-Eschenbach (1830–1916), and Wilhelm Raabe (1831–1910) are poetic or programmatic realists (affirmative writers) to some extent, and quite possibly in their deepest convictions about literature and art. Yet they all knew that there was a chink of light – or perhaps more appropriately darkness – between the social identity and goals the age has to offer and what human subjects really want.

Something of the complexity of the cultural moment can be clarified by looking comparatively at the three writers with the most established international reputation, Stifter, Keller and Fontane. Stifter was Austrian, Keller Swiss and Fontane Prussian. In each case their national identity is of determining importance in their development as writers. Stifter, as an Austrian, does not have access to the kind of reality commended by the

Grenzboten, predicated as it was upon a new Germany without Austria. It is not unexpected that poetic realism for Stifter (at one time a tutor to Metternich's son) should be essentially backward looking. Keller began his literary career as a Swiss Herwegh, writing radical patriotic verse, and he never lost his positive relation to his homeland, although it became seasoned with scepticism after the novelty of the new democratic Switzerland began to wear off. Fontane made his name as a literary journalist writing for the Prussian conservative press, but in later years he became more politically liberal. Keller and Fontane experienced what Stifter missed by dying too soon: the foundation of the German Reich, the associated triumphalism and vulgarity, the economic crash of 1873, and a lengthening perspective upon the difficulties of modernization, for instance, the dramatic expansion of an urban proletariat and the alarming materialism and moral indifference of speculative capitalism.

To writers of this generation, for whom the profession of writing was an established objective possibility, there was a choice to be made between identity as a poet or as an author or man of letters (*Dichter* or *Literat*). Stifter, slightly older than the other two, chose the former. As we have already seen, he regarded the need to write for money as incompatible with the task of the poet. His remarkable novel, *Der Nachsommer* (*Indian Summer*, 1857) was, as he said in a letter to his publisher of 11 January 1858, 'poetry [*Dichtung*], not a book intended simply to entertain'. Keller and Fontane were both ambitious as poets (and in Keller's case as an artist and dramatist also) but, given their positive commitment to their respective moral and socio-political 'realities', they had more incentive to write for the actual reading public, and this made their engagement with the market inevitable, quite apart from the question of earning an income.

All three were decisively influenced by the culture of the family magazine which reflected and shaped the popular reading taste. Stifter wrote for the *Gartenlaube für Österreich* and other similar journals. But these journals were themselves sites of cultural transition. While on one hand they embodied the cultural values of Classical-Romantic inheritance, they were also governed, with the best of intentions, by considerations of broad appeal and thus tended towards *Kitsch*. Stifter's many obsessive revisions of his stories between their magazine publication and their inclusion in books can be read as a sort of semi-conscious cleansing of the results of this effect. And there is nothing semi-conscious about his composition of *Der Nachsommer*, emphatically not for serial publication, and written in order to 'set against this miserable depravity a great, simple moral force' (quoted in Naumann 1979: 42).

Keller and Fontane were also ambivalent about the family magazine. We quoted above Fontane's splendidly double-edged comment about *Die Gartenlaube*, in which disdain and dependence compete. Keller satirized the market for fiction in *Kleider machen Leute* and *Die mißbrauchten Liebesbriefe* (*Clothes Maketh the Man* and *The Misused Love Letters*, both first published in the second volume of *Die Leute von Seldwyla* [*The People of Seldwyla*], 1874), while himself unquestionably supporting respect for the aesthetic inheritance, the morality of decent pragmatism and the civic responsibility to which the family magazines were dedicated, and recognizing quite openly that he was writing for broadly the same market.

Perhaps one should differentiate and say that Fontane and Keller did write for a market, but not quite the same one as the family magazines, or at least for the top end of it. They were part of a critical metropolitan literary culture, the establishment of which is confirmed by Julius Rodenberg's founding of the *Deutsche Rundschau* in Berlin in 1874. The intention of this literary magazine was to fill a gap in the market for a sophisticated modern journal offering entertainment but of a refined sort. It was a symptom of Germany catching up with the industrial cultures of France and Great Britain, the models for this enterprise being the *Quarterly Review* (from 1809) in Britain, and the Parisian *Revue des deux mondes* (1830 onwards). Rodenberg's journal did indeed provide an outlet for serious contemporary writing, with a clear sense of aesthetic product differentiation over the other entertainment magazines which had hitherto defined the parameters of taste and attitude. Eschewing the illustrations that were a crucial part of the appeal of the family magazine, it featured philosophy and science on a higher level than the others hitherto, and it soon had emulators – featuring contributions by Dilthey, for instance. Publication in the *Deutsche Rundschau* was a guarantee of literary quality and much valued by such as Storm, Meyer, Keller and Ebner-Eschenbach.

These writers, therefore, attest to the establishment of serious prose literature in the zone between the aesthetic cultural inheritance and the new popular and socially broad reading culture. The fault line between Stifter and the other two writers, however, lies in their respective attitudes to literary pleasure, that is, to the practical aesthetic implied by their work.

As we saw, Stifter, at least in his novel written against the novel, *Der Nachsommer*, wished to write poetry rather than provide entertainment. Yet the commitment to poetry and the opposition to entertainment interfere with each other. In the revision from the journal to the book version of his *Novelle*-like story 'Granit' (1849), for instance, Stifter finds himself sacrificing a symbolic yield in order to disambiguate a moral point. A marvellous framework narrative recounts a child innocently bringing pitch into his mother's freshly scrubbed home and being ferociously punished for it. The inner story – about the ravages of the plague upon a rural community, which evokes the aftershocks of 1848 – is told to him by his grandfather in order to help him overcome this catastrophic disturbance in his moral world. The earlier journal version allowed the ambiguity of harm coming through innocence to shape story and frame, both of which point to the inscrutable working of Providence. The workaday distinctions between good and evil can be suspended to allow a glimpse of a surpassing order (a version of the aesthetic device of sublimity). In the revision, this parallel is removed. It seems that allowing the mind to dwell on imponderables is now an unacceptable luxury, a suspect cultural pleasure.

Seen without the benefit of an anticipated Prussian utopia, poetic realism emerges as a problematic, but also genuinely profound, aesthetic attitude. The problem facing Stifter was how to distinguish between the redemptive significance of aesthetic experience (for whom the classical Goethe and Schiller provided the cultural models) and the pleasures of a 'Romantic' sensibility, which now, unless checked, seemed to lead straight to terrifying anarchy.

Stifter backtracks from excessive 'subjectivity', which seems to him to be responsible for the loss of objectively sanctioned distinctions in morality, society, politics and art. His fervent belief is that the regularities, including scientific ones, which govern the world should not only be clearly discerned and reinforced, but that they are all ultimately compatible with one another. The moral part of this correlation distorts the aesthetic one because it leaves little room for any sort of pleasure. In the preface to the collection of stories *Bunte Steine* (*Coloured Stones*,1853), Stifter defines the good life as one which is lived to the end under the regulation of stern self-control ('Bezwingung seiner selbst'). There can be no clearer instance of the post-1848 internalization of censorship. The result is a strangled didacticism which is great literature because it is the pure representation of the agony of the inner censorship. Stifter is the Shakespeare of repression.

The distinction between Stifter on the one hand and Keller and Fontane on the other is therefore that Stifter believes in a unified human subject, registering its division as tragic, while for Keller and Fontane the human subject is already split into social and imaginative selves that can never be fully reconciled.

Stifter is a precursor of Modernism because he defends an aesthetic at odds with the moral world in which he finds himself. Keller and Fontane (like their slightly younger colleagues, Raabe and Ebner-Eschenbach) are modern (not Modernist) writers because they find ways of writing commercially without sacrificing complexity.

As with Freytag, in the hands of Keller and Fontane fiction is a complex commodity, but with them, unlike Freytag, the complexity of identification is not projected on to a preferred self and an array of disparaged others but acknowledged as internal to everyone. This is because they both work within the moral horizon of their times and fellows, yet exploit the capacity of 'poetic' realism to register what might lie beyond that horizon and the permission that poetry gives to enjoy it. They are sceptical because they survive the honeymoon of modernization in their respective lands, and thus write satirically and critically, as well as transfiguratively, in a way Schmidt did see the need for in the 1850s. Yet they also express their complicity with their readers who are as split as they themselves are, and this shared partialness is expressed by means of humour, a device of which the *Grenzboten* theorists approved.

Both can transfigure ordinariness in their fiction and are skilled at the precarious judgement needed to distinguish this from sentimentality or *Kitsch*. Keller's *Novelle Romeo und Julia auf dem Dorfe* (*The Village Romeo and Juliet*, 1856, in the first volume of *Die Leute von Seldwyla*) is a programmatic piece of poetic realism, announcing at the outset that age-old archetypes, like that of Shakespeare's lovers from feuding families, can recur in different social and historical embodiments. Its crowning success is the account of the last day in the lives of the doomed lovers. Rather as in Goethe's ironic-heroic *Hermann und Dorothea* (1798), art captures the sensual and moral potential of human beings in the moment of as yet unacted-upon desire between a boy / man and girl / woman. Yet the poetic potentiation in Keller's case comes from the knowledge – shared or at least suspected, in an unusual variant of tragic irony, by readers and protagonists, but not the world around – that this visit to a fair, this exchange of gifts, this satisfaction in being seen as ordinarily happy, are all touched by the imminence of death.

Part of Keller's achievement is to have motivated his story morally as well as poetically. His lovers prefer to consummate their love and then commit suicide than to live together in a way which would compromise their embodied sense of ordinary decency. The story as a whole is a poetic realization of ordinary people. It affirms unremarkable conventional morality aesthetically.

One of the options that Keller's protagonists in that story, Sali and Vrenchen, reject is to leave the countryside and go to the city, where they would go into service, presumably mutate socially, and become, in a word, novel rather than *Novelle* characters. Keller's aesthetic vote for the country-side in *Leute von Seldwyla* is partly a function of the poetic realist difficulty with the novelistic urban culture but partly also a function of the specifi-cally Swiss political situation, in which the rural cantons were liberal and democratic, while the urban patriciates were more conservative. Fontane, as is often asserted, became a novelist only once Berlin became a modern metropolis (which happened very quickly in the last decades of the century). He incorporates poetic realist motifs into socially minutely observed and motivated narratives.

Like Keller's *Novelle*, *Effi Briest* (1894) is based on a contemporary, which is to say journalistic, anecdote. After decades of journalism, travel writing, the composition of a long historical novel (published serially in the *Garten-laube*'s Christian conservative rival *Daheim* [*At Home*]) and many *Novellen* tailored to the popular taste of this or that magazine, Fontane began to write realist novels. The story of a young married woman who is ruined because she fails to throw away letters which reveal an affair years in the past, thus forcing her husband and her former lover into a fatal duel, has the shape of a *Novelle* plot. Yet Fontane narrates this story in perfect com-plicity with his urban readers. We understand, without being told, that sentimentality and passionate irresponsibility are continuous across the social distinction that allows one and condemns the other. We are put among the characters so convincingly (Fontane's ambition was that in memory one should really not be able to distinguish between his charac-ters and real acquaintances) that we see Effi Briest with affection, while knowing at the same time that she is unremarkable, except in the sense that any attractive person is remarkable.

The tragic complexion of this story entails the danger of sentimentality. There is debate as to whether Fontane actually avoids it. Of all the ghosts that haunt the narrative – descendants of Fontane's balladic past – it is the ghost of *Kitsch* that is the most threatening. Yet at the same time, the poetic early death of the heroine, which can seem like an inauthentic redemption on the author's part of a social casualty, can also be experienced as a poetic realist treatment of a universal but ordinary tragedy, namely the loss of childhood. It is as if the real poetic aspiration of German programmatic realism (we feel this also often with Storm), that was theorized by Schmidt and others as the 'adult' correction to immature Romantic and *Vormärz* excesses, was to mourn this very loss.

Keller's success in combining commercial with aesthetic criteria was manifest in his *Novellen*, but he wrote an autobiographical novel, not well matched to commercial requirements, *Der grüne Heinrich* (*Green Henry*), which is a socially and morally carefully motivated account of the betrayal of childhood – and, by extension, artistic – potential by social realities. His difficulties with this novel, which contains a characterization of childhood experience to compete with Proust, help to clarify exactly the aesthetic issues. Keller's modern grasp of the split nature of identity, which informs his practice as a writer, was in tension with the Goethean ambition to feel and write as if human personality were somehow enigmatically unified. Keller wrote the novel twice, with different endings. The first ending from the mid-1850s, in which he killed 'himself' off poetically, was rejected, presumably because it was too poetic – which, in the 1870s, meant open on one side to the charge of extravagant idealism and, on the other, to the kind of danger of *Kitsch* skirted by Fontane in the ending of *Effi Briest*. The second ending, in which Keller gives himself a responsible job in the civil administration of Zurich, threatens to dilute poetry so completely into prose as to leave no literary residue whatsoever.

Keller's great double novel, in its very uncommercial unwieldiness, is caught between the rock and the hard place that his *Novellen* and Fontane's novels negotiate so carefully. They pay their readers the compliment of honouring their responsible adult lives, the moral horizons against which they really move, but at the same time tell them stories the very irresponsible artificiality of which gives them pleasure.

Overture to the future

Ernest Newman, the author of the definitive biography of Richard Wagner (1813–1883), judges that the composer had a 'more remarkable artistic mind' than Goethe because – despite the diversity of other activities in which both men's extraordinary energy engaged them – Wagner's mature works achieve 'organic unity', while Goethe's large-scale works never do (Newman 1933: 502–3). Components of this judgement are beyond debate but it is disconcertingly lacking in a sense of historical context.

Goethe and Wagner had very different attitudes to the waning court and rising democratic cultures of their times. Clearly, this was in part due to the different generations to which they belonged and to some extent also to their respective social backgrounds. But the point that concerns us here is that, while Goethe identified with his situation at the enlightened court of Weimar where he lived and worked from 1775 until his death in 1832, Wagner identified himself by means of a – nearly literally – violent opposition to the court culture of which he had experience as an official musician (second *Kapellmeister*) at Dresden. For Goethe, the peculiar polity into which his spontaneous public success catapulted him provided the real framework within which the problematic subjectivity of the Romantic era could be contained and represented in literary art. Like the Young Germans, who were his contemporaries and in some cases colleagues and friends, Wagner associated his artistic aspirations with opposition to the semi-feudal remnants of *Vormärz* Germany. His labours in the service of the new Romantic spirit became indistinguishable from thoughts of political change. Once the revolution came and went in 1848, he had no objectively existing social framework to check or form his productions.

Hence their completeness. Wagner miraculously delivered what the aesthetician Friedrich Theodor Vischer, in an essay of 1844 entitled *Vorschlag zu einer Oper*, had identified as necessary for German music. Thinking in the then-fashionable Hegelian categories of subjective and objective, and pursuing an interesting parallel between music and literature, Vischer argued that although music had found equivalents for the subjective triumphs of the new German literature – its Goethe in Mozart, its Klopstock in Haydn, its Jean Paul in Beethoven – it had yet to achieve its equivalent to Schiller or Shakespeare, that is to say, its objective realization. Wagner may have known the essay, which in fact went on to commend the *Nibelungen* saga as a fit topic.

The problem with Newman's judgement (of the mid-1930s) is that it is based on the assumption that it is possible for the production of an artist to be objective all on its own, that is to say without an existing social framework to hold it. Goethe did not believe this. Wagner, driven by the utopian illusions of his class and generation, did. Or rather, he and Vischer both erroneously thought the new social framework was just around the corner. Goethe progressively either produced works which bore in their very structure his awareness of the fragmented circumstances of modernity (for instance the second part of *Faust* and the later part of Wilhelm Meister, the *Wanderjahre*, *The Journeyman Years*), or else, as in the case of the highly 'composed', anti-Romantic, novel *Wahlverwandtschaften* (*Elective Affinities*, 1809), were constructed to resist the sort of easy appropriation which could lead to the misunderstandings and commercialization that *Werther* had occasioned forty years before.

It is fair to claim that Wagner completed the Romantic project. By the circumstance of his genius, he was able to work with supreme confidence and extraordinary originality in the medium to which the writers of Romanticism had aspired, ever since Wackenroder's fictional anthology of artists had culminated with the life of the problematic composer Berglinger. Friedrich Schlegel and Hoffmann are among the leading figures who claimed music as the ultimate Romantic form. Schopenhauer's views about the primacy of music not only among the arts but in the pursuit of a good life *tout court* gave Wagner himself permission to see music as the supreme art where before he had, in good Romantic style, included it as first among equals within the kinds and genres of the arts.

The second way in which Wagner completed the project of Romanticism was actually to produce the 'new mythology' for Germany, for which Friedrich Schlegel in the *Gespräch über die Poesie* (*Conversation on Poetry*, 1800) had called. During the early years of the life of the newly unified Germany, long historical verse epics, such as Scheffel's *Der Trompeter von Säckingen* (originally 1854), and there were several others, sold more copies than all but the most successful novels. Wagner's music dramas were overwhelmingly new, they were unprecedented in style and theme, but they also offered the same sort of German national-historical identification as these curiously anachronistic popular literary productions. They seemed, like some force of fate, to combine the brilliance of modern German music after Beethoven with the historical destiny of Germany as a new major European power. Nietzsche's enthusiasm in *Die Geburt der Tragödie* (*The Birth of Tragedy*, 1872) about Wagner's music drama as the rebirth of a national culture strong enough to replace the enfeebling regime of reason is testimony to this.

This provision of myths for the modern age also identifies Wagner's music drama as the completion of the Romantic project in another way. In his great compositions, as well as in his radical theory and practice for the reform of the theatre as a public institution, he took on the responsibility of managing the areas of human experience that lie outside social convention. The theme of madness accompanies the practical working out of Romanticism, from Tieck's sense that *Werther* was a stage on the way to insanity, to its insistent occurrence in Wackenroder, August Klingemann's anonymously published *Nachtwachen des Bonaventura* (*Bonaventura's Vigils*, 1804), Hoffmann, Heine, Immermann, Gutzkow, Büchner and others. Madness (*Wahnsinn*) for the Romantics is the name for those areas outside convention which both beckon and terrify. After the failure of 1848 and his reading of the atheist philosopher Ludwig Feuerbach, Wagner stabilized the concept by talking in 1851 of his concern with the purely human, beyond conventions. Thomas Mann called this 'Wagner's healthy way of being sick' (Mann 1990: 403). In seeking to provide through the stage illusions and musical effects of his dramas the kind of 'Wahn' (in the sense of 'illusion') that can speak about and satisfy an entirely convention-free sense of self- and collective identity, Wagner attempts to do what Hans Sachs, in the first scene of the third act of *Die Meistersinger von Nürnberg* (*The Mastersingers of Nuremberg*, 1868) says it is the job of the artist to do, namely to turn 'Wahn' to noble ends.

The problem with all this is the completeness which Newman praises. The task of objectification defined by Vischer and apparently achieved by Wagner is in fact an extreme form of the affirmative view of art. This was, as we saw, the post-1848 generation's way of conceiving the relevance of Classical-Romantic literature to the political circumstances leading up to German unification. What is affirmed is a 'vitalism' which once seemed to correspond to the inner truth of German destiny and seemed also, at the time and ever since, at least to some Wagnerites, to be the worthy successor to established religion.

Another way of looking at this wonderfully conceived and realized completion of the Romantic project, however, is to see it as a false totality. Art conceived as affirmative, to such an extent that its formations seem 'objective', becomes indistinguishable from a perfect totality defined not by its reference to the objective world, but by its absolute separation from it. Complete, but not objective in the Hegelian sense of partaking in the objective life of the spirit at a particular time in history. The Romantic project to define, encourage and produce artefacts touched by the spirit becomes, in its Wagnerian completion, a totality exposed to the twin predators of the actual, rather than the fantasized, objectivity that surrounds it, namely nationalism and capitalism. In other words, the completeness achieved by Wagner has nothing to do with truth. Which is not the same as saying that moments in his works do not – for some listeners and perhaps many – enable authentic subjective experiences of genuine intensity or profundity.

This is why Newman's claim about the organic unity of Wagner's large-scale works as a sign of their artistic superiority in relation to Goethe needs to be questioned. Goethe understood the dangers of a completeness that bore no relation to the objective world and hence avoided it in his later years. The 'organic unity' of which Newman speaks is a Romantic metaphor. Of course, one knows what he means. But as a metaphor, it will no longer really do. What this totality is is not organic but artificial. The Romantic project that began by sweeping away all artificial distinctions and affirming the spiritual significance of the sort of artificiality understood by the term art, in order to safeguard the one distinction – between the spiritual and the machine-manufactured – that really mattered, ends by leaving this whole huge spiritual enterprise in a state in which it threatens to mutate into propaganda, or assume properties of the modern industrial commodity.

Wagner wanted to bring the institution of the theatre into the modern age. He felt that the theatre was the most powerful instrument in the shaping of a nation's culture. We know how his version of the theatre looked and sounded. If we imagine not the theatre but the technological power of the twentieth century's equivalent media of public communication, allied to the sort of aesthetic control and manipulation of the senses Wagner brilliantly pioneered, we see that his claims for the theatre were not only a heavily amplified echo of Schiller's enlightened and human hopes for it but an accurate prediction of the awesome power of both the culture industry and modern propaganda techniques.

The musicologist and aesthetic philosopher T. W. Adorno (1903–1969) analysed the ways in which Wagner's music drama is at once high musical art and incipiently commodified. Like the later Nietzsche, he sees in Wagner a great miniaturist, the totality of whose works is in fact composed of a myriad of anthologizable moments. (It is particularly telling that Wagner was compelled to take highlights from his only recently triumphantly premiered *Der Ring des Nibelungen* [*The Ring of the Nibelung*, 1853–76] to the Albert Hall in an heroic, but sadly unsuccessful, attempt to raise funds for Bayreuth – an institution conceived to facilitate the complete performance of the Cycle.) Moreover, Adorno sees Wagner's music as 'already predicated on that ego weakness that later became the operational basis of the culture industry' (Huyssen 1986: 37). The way it treats its listeners, by binding music to characters in 'musical pictures', 'flattered the regressive listener, amounting to the double insult of the claim to mythic totality at the level of the disposable commodity' (Steinberg 2004: 16).

Unlike Modernists such as Baudelaire or Mallarmé, neither Keller nor Fontane were enthusiastic supporters of Wagner. Fontane felt that one is confronted with nothing but base appetites in his works and associated the emotionally deficient Innstetten (in *Effi Briest*) with him, implying that a love of Wagner is a kind of compensation gratification for those too busy in the Weberian 'iron cage' of modern bureaucracy to live a rounded life. Keller, in fact a friend of Wagner's from his Zurich days, musing on the Swiss *Schillerfeier* of 1859, wanted a more genuinely popular and participatory form of folk festival than Wagner's for his own – as he admitted self-indulgently utopian – vision of what the theatre could be in a modern republic. Both these writers, in their acceptance of the market of their time, point forward to a certain important strain in capitalist democratic literary culture. Wagner, in whom the Romantic project culminates and mutates, points forward to the deeply problematic and contested future awaiting literature and the arts amid the technologically enhanced and predatory public media of the next century.

3

Imperial Modernity

During the first two decades after the unification of Germany, a vigorous renewal of German literature seemed inevitable. At the time it seemed as if a 'revolution in literature' was on the horizon (this was the name of polemic published by Karl Bleibtreu in 1886). The new writing was to be recognizably German but also modern both in its aesthetic resources and in its commitment to what since the 1830s had been known as 'the social question'. Yet this renewal of literature never happened. Instead, it began to become apparent that it was no longer possible to separate the practice of literature from the market, media and machinery of modern society.

The revolution that never was

The young writers and publicists of this generation evoked the honourable tradition of social realism in German, emphasizing the seminal contribution of the young writers of the 1770s (the *Sturm und Drang*) and especially Lenz. The progressive patriotic arts journal *Kritische Waffengänge* (*Critical Skirmishes*), edited and written by the brothers Heinrich and Julius Hart in the early 1880s, recalled in its title the *Ästhetische Feldzüge* (*Aesthetic Campaigns*) of the *Vormärz* period. The realist novelist and scholar Karl Emil Franzos published his edition of the half-forgotten 'Revolutionsdichter' ('poet of the revolution'), Georg Büchner, in 1879. The watchword of this literary revolution was 'realism', and it prided itself on its national pedigree. The name 'Naturalism' came from France, Germany's defeated rival, where it had been coined and promoted by Émile Zola. Zola's brand of social realism, based on a preference for determinist physiology over metaphysics, provided the scientist ideology that identified the new writing as modern.

The outlook for a new literature, progressive and integrated in the life of modern Germany, seemed particularly bright when Kaiser Wilhelm II came to the throne in 1888, committed to technological modernity and, for a brief moment, promising to be a democratic 'people's Kaiser'.

A Naturalist revolution was staged (in both senses) in 1889, when a programmatically Naturalist play by Gerhart Hauptmann (1862–1946), *Vor Sonnenaufgang (Before Sunrise)*, caused a sensation at its premiere. The theatrical template for the promotion of modern international drama had been provided by the *Théâtre-Libre* in Paris in 1887, which staged Naturalist plays performed realistically by carefully rehearsed ensembles. The theatrical approach adopted in Paris, and shortly thereafter in Berlin under the name *Freie Bühne (Free Theatre)*, had in fact been pioneered in Germany in the 1870s by the famous court theatre troupe of Meiningen. They were the first to reject the declamatory individual style of classical acting, to choreograph crowd scenes dynamically and to cultivate meticulous realism in their productions of historical drama.

There was excitement about a fusion between German literature and European Modernism. Hauptmann's was the only German contribution to the first programme of the *Freie Bühne*, which included plays by Strindberg, Bjørnson, the brothers Goncourt and Tolstoy, and had opened with a production of Ibsen's *Ghosts*. *Vor Sonnenaufgang* provoked an identity shock by revealing in the work of the young Silesian playwright the modern sensibility and willingness to innovate that had hitherto been associated exclusively with foreign authors. Arno Holz and Johannes Schlaf, for instance, had previously published their programmatically un-Shakespearean *Papa Hamlet* under Scandinavian pseudonyms.

Hauptmann's play deals with the social impact of industrialization upon Silesian farmers, made rich by the sale of rights to the coal beneath their infertile land. Sudden wealth has led to moral collapse in the form of conspicuous consumption, adultery and alcoholism, which are conveyed with aggressive, taboo-challenging realism, for example the sounds of a woman in labour. The plot depends upon the determinist notion that alcoholism is hereditary (an infant shockingly – and improbably – turns out to have been born with it). The hero, Alfred Loth, who represents the scientistic and socially reformist sympathies of the Naturalist persuasion, turns away from the woman with whom he has fallen in love because of the corruption of her family, which, according to his conviction, will taint her and any children they might have together via the laws of heredity. Did such scenes represent a scandal for traditional German culture, or the breakthrough for modern German art? Hauptmann, to some, was a dangerous subversive anarchist, to others the long-awaited modernizer of German letters.

The subtitle of the leading Naturalist journal *Gesellschaft (Society)* was 'Realistic Weekly for Literature, Art, and Public Life'. The aspiration of the Naturalist publicists in Berlin and Munich to integrate, involve, and educate was clear. But in fact the expansive discourse about realism or Naturalism was theoretically not very different from the programme proposed by Julian Schmidt in the 1850s (and indeed, *Soll und Haben* continued to be an important model). Bleibtreu, like his literary hero Lenz a hundred years before, made an assumption that artistic realism, if properly executed, could only reinforce moral and political values. In other words, he (and the others) assumed that the political, moral and aesthetic spheres were clearly defined and integrated with one another. An unexamined belief in the redemptive power of art remained that was foreign to Zola. The same dubious (but characteristically German) assumption that art retained its old privileged mission even in capitalist modernity is reflected in the fact that, cosmopolitan and realist as the founders of the *Freie Bühne* were, they distinguished their version of theatrical modernity by agreeing from the outset that, unlike the Parisian model, it should not be run for profit but for the cultivation of art alone.

The genre description of Hauptmann's play, 'Social drama in five acts', reveals the divergent tendencies within Naturalism. On one side, there was the pull towards the depiction of milieu, in which art bore undimmed witness to the reality of social determinism. This sort of documentarism was attempted by the theoretically most radical of the Naturalist circle, Arno Holz (1863–1929), to whom Hauptmann had dedicated his play. On the other side, there were the requirements of conventional five-act dramatic form, in which the presence of a Naturalist hero has at once to introduce certain ideas into the discourse of the play, and at the same time function as the catalyst for a plot that will produce dramatic closure. Hence the suicide of Helene, the heroine, and the tragic guilt of Loth in relation to it, though technically caused by a set of social circumstances, have no significant expressive meaning in relation to these circumstances. The particular anecdote does not represent the general truth.

The clamorous division over *Vor Sonnenaufgang* was one manifestion of the objective truth that the sphere of culture had become problematic in its relation to society. The moment of Naturalism – and it was just a moment; by the mid-1890s it was already old fashioned – was the last historical point in German literature at which it was possible to imagine that the cultural sphere could embrace in its productions pride in German national identity, social awareness and critique, modern science, and aesthetic Modernism, all at the same time.

The social question

The incipient fracturing of the cultural sphere becomes clear if we look briefly at the issue of the 'social question'. What had been part of the cultural life and philosophical-political agenda of educated Germans since the 1830s had, by 1890, long since also taken the form of real socialist opposition, with a powerful, developed publicity universe of its own, and political expression in a Socialist Democratic party which became the most numerous such party in Europe by the beginning of the First World War. This changed political reality drove a wedge between the social and the aesthetic components of the Naturalist programme.

The difficulty posed by the cultural question for socialism, while not its first priority, was a real one, and it is not surprising that those on the left did not manage to solve it straight away (if indeed they ever did). What kind of culture is appropriate for the new working public? There was a strong logic in favour of finding effective means of engaging that public with the German literary and dramatic heritage since at least the 1770s. This was attractive for several reasons. First, the tradition had moments of revolutionary pathos and political engagement within it (notably in the drama of Schiller and the explicitly political writing of the *Vormärz* period). Second, there was a familiarity about the traditional construction of art, the very familiarity that made it unattractive to avant-garde publicists in the 1890s but which meant that it was comprehensible to newcomers to the table of culture. Third, it offered the most available and obvious bulwark against the manifest lures of mass popular entertainment.

But on the other hand, the Marxist analysis of class conflict suggests persuasively that the culture of one class is likely to be a means of oppressing another. Moreover, the Naturalist concentration upon social misery hardly appealed to those for whom this misery was reality and whose organizations were devoted to eliminating it, not imitating it in the form of artistic representation.

In essence this was a question of identification: should the new social class identify itself with existing culture or strive to create a new one of its own? The problems encountered by members of the *Freie Bühne*, notably the Marxist literary intellectual Bruno Wille, to take this cultural institution devoted to theatrical Modernism to the people (*Volk*) in the form of a *Freie Volksbühne*, founded in 1890, reflect the practical, institutional difficulty generated by these debates. Wille, coming from the side of the arts, was soon ousted by political party interests and replaced by Franz Mehring who, while initially expressing admiration for Holz and Hauptmann, later took the view that the sphere of culture was, at least at this stage of the political struggle, simply irrelevant to the proletariat. Wille himself went on to found a further splinter association in the form of the *Neue freie Volksbühne*.

The exception that proves the rule was Hauptmann's, and Germany's, finest Naturalist play, *Die Weber* (*The Weavers*). This was staged with spectacular success by the *Freie Bühne* in February 1893, then by Wille's *Neue freie Volksbühne* in October and by Mehring himself in December of the same year, where it assumed the character of a political event. Hauptmann's play solved the problem that had bedevilled *Vor Sonnenaufgang* of how to devise a drama without falling victim to an individualizing anecdote that has no inner relevance to the social problem with which the work is really concerned. In this play, the oppressed and exploited weavers themselves are the protagonists of the action, and the play is not only aggressively realist in style, diction and so on (the original version was written in Silesian dialect) but both clear and effectively emotive in its class analysis and allegiance.

The German claim to art

The curiously precarious moment of Naturalism in 1889 is highlighted by the extraordinary popularity (dozens of impressions in a couple of years) of a book published anonymously in the following year, *Rembrandt als Erzieher* (*Rembrandt as Educator*). If the reality of the socialist movement drove a wedge between the social and aesthetic parts of the Naturalist programme, Julius Langbehn's polemic revealed a gulf between the aesthetic and the nationalist elements. Langbehn's text amplified all the pro-German components of the literary revolution and condemned all the others. This was the bible of anti-modernity, a voice raised against the influential popularizers of modern science such as Ludwig Büchner and Ernst Haeckel, against capitalism and materialism (Langbehn insisted the book should be sold for no more than two marks, and renounced royalties), against foreign influence upon German culture (following Zola was 'poetic treason'), against cosmopolitan sophisticated Berlin. Instead, in a vulgar modern echo of Herder, he demanded that the German spirit (*Geist*) must bring forth its own specific culture once more, the expression of its true soul, throwing off the nihilistic eclecticism of the present. Rembrandt, for whom, according to Langbehn, the practice of art was integrated into everyday life, functioned as the exemplary German, and Langbehn insisted upon the merits of closeness to one's own background, praising the peasants of Schleswig-Holstein, where he came from, as the genuine model of integrated personal and communal identity. This was nostalgia for the mutual reinforcement of individual and national identity of the late eighteenth century, expressed in, to use Fritz Stern's phrase, the radical language of 'cultural despair'.

Langbehn's opposition to Naturalism (as the name of un-German Modernism) is easy to understand, and might be seen as a straightforward aesthetic disagreement. The success of his book, however, also signals a deeper disjuncture: that between the spheres of culture and political pragmatism. The *Gartenlaube*, which might have been expected to approve of a text passionately in favour of German art, recoiled in its review from the radical nature of Langbehn's polemic. There could be no doubt that this was a work of opposition, opposing 'Art' not only to the science and socialism of the Naturalist position, but to the very acquiescence in modernity, in capitalism, industrialization, and urbanization displayed abroad by what in German is referred to as the *Bildungsbürgertum* (educated classes). Whether or not this term is tendentious, one thing is clear: its widespread use is evidence for the historical split between culture and official national identity.

Surprise best-sellers provide one of the few clues to what a modern public, so various and mobile in its constitution, is actually thinking or feeling. The resonance enjoyed by Langbehn's book is testimony to the traumatic impact of accelerated modernization upon Germans at the end of the nineteenth century. There was a tension between the demands of everyday life on the one hand and abstract values on the other. The majority of reading Germans clearly distrusted the promises of modern society as they experienced them, preferring nostalgia for stable, integrated individual and national identity.

Langbehn's evident contemporary 'legibility' reminds us that, while literary history records Naturalism and the other symbiotic moments to which we shall come presently, a substantial part of the literature of the time was committed to a Germanic ideology which glorified peasants (common folk but not the urban proletariat) as exemplary Germans, close to their native soil, loyal, brave and united against foreign threats. The villains were materialist incomers, often Jews. Although this theme was frequently expressed in historical settings, as for instance in the ballads of such as Börries von Münchhausen and Lulu von Strauß und Torney or the still-anthologized Agnes Miegel, its propagandistic relevance to the present was transparent.

In an aggressive version of the mid-century regionalism, the term *Heimatkunst* (literally: art of the homeland) came into usage in the 1890s to identify this defensive, anti-symbiotic aesthetic position. In *Der Kunstwart* (*Guardian of Art*), it had a journal that, taking its cue from Langbehn, propagated it. Although *Heimatkunst* was not necessarily proto-fascist or even regressive (significant earlier writers like Storm and Stifter were co-opted, and the main theme in the contemporary *Heimatkunst* novel was the impact of social change), the repertoire of views and prejudices promoted in its name for instance by the anti-Semitic literary historian Adolf Bartels in *Der Kunstwart* provided a cultural template for the Nazis.

Literature on the ground

While significant public debates about the meaning of literature in relation to society raged, the novel was unquestionably the dominant form of literature actually read. The three best-selling authors of the period were Karl May (1842–1912), Hedwig Courths-Mahler (1867–1950) and Ludwig Ganghofer (1855–1920, a writer of sentimental fiction set in the Bavarian Alps, whose work had the enthusiastic approval of Kaiser Wilhelm II). Karl May is unique to the German literary universe and his popularity reveals something specific and genuine about readers' needs in the Wilhelmine period. His beginnings as a writer were at the bottom end of the literary market, the serialized *Kolportageroman*, described in the previous chapter. His narrative *Der verlorene Sohn oder Der Fürst des Elends* (*The Prodigal Son or the Prince of Despair*, 1883–5, delivered in 101 episodes at 10 pfennig each, totalling over 2,000 pages in all), a story whose hero has been described as a mixture of the Count of Monte Cristo, Father Christmas and Jesus (Waldmann 1982: 127), contains a graphic and emotive representation of the exploitation of weavers in the *Erzgebirge*. Although the plot enfolds these circumstances within a simple revenge story with no social analysis and a simplistic moral horizon, the novel nevertheless provides evidence of a sense of public resentment at industrial alienation of labour in the Bismarck era (one of the sections of the book is entitled *Slaves of Labour*) and of a will to social criticism in both author and hundreds of thousands of readers, even at this most transparently commodified end of the sphere of public representations.

May is renowned everywhere in German-speaking countries for his adventure stories set in the American Wild West (for instance, the *Winnetou* novels) and other exotic places, such as the near east, especially those featuring the heroes Old Shatterhand and Kara ben Nemsi (Karl the German), both paradigmatially German adventurers. These books were aimed at a slightly higher economic level of consumer than the tenpenny serial novels. Their extraordinary success (and May's celebrity status) in the 1890s and onwards reflects another kind of symbiosis, namely a sort of imaginary national self-confidence with regard to the rest of the globe. On one hand, the ravages of rapid industrialization, urban development and the kind of economic, social and psychological dynamism-cum-instability inseparable from developed capitalism left their imprint upon literature, also of the best-selling variety, as we shall see. On the other, the kind of easy identi-fication offered by Karl May, who transparently projected himself into his Superman-like heroes, thereby inviting his readership to do likewise, suggests how hundreds of thousands of Germans were able to find com-pensation in dreams of a Germany able to *transfigure* the modern world by combining traditional merits of idealism with new-found industrial-military muscle, in a sort of poetic realist foreign policy. Emmanuel Geibel, whose *Poems* reached their one-hundredth printing in 1884, famously summed up this public fantasy in the lines: 'Und es soll am deutschen Wesen / Einmal noch die Welt genesen' ('By the German soul the world will one day be made whole'). This attitude had lost its innocence by about 1916 and had become pathological by 1933 when Goebbels quoted it to representatives of the German book trade.

May's readers were offered a predominantly masculine identification. The struggle-cum-opportunity for commercial success in fiction publishing inevitably acknowledged the needs of women, spectacularly evident in the effect of Eugénie Marlitt's fiction upon the circulation figures of *Die Gar-tenlaube*, mentioned in the previous chapter. Courths-Mahler, who wrote over 200 novels in the course of her life that sold in their millions, supplied this market with stories for women to identify with, in which the heroines are rewarded for moral integrity and self-denial with social advancement and personal satisfaction. While this sentimental and stereotype-confirm-ing culture was exactly what all the progressive (and not so progressive) elements opposed, it was popular and durable.

A certain type of novel, going back to Freytag's 'social novel' *Soll und Haben*, was differentiated from this sort of thing by the claim that it was suitable for men (or not suitable for old women of either sex, as Michael Georg Conrad had quipped, borrowing Huxley's renowned joke made in defence of Darwin). The sexist idiom of the day notwithstand-ing, this meant 'serious'. These were novels that engaged with real intrac-table social issues, even if, being novels, they could not claim or aspire to solve them.

In fact, it was in relation to women that the real social significance of this stratum of literature, as opposed to the public debates about literature as a theoretical or ideological proposition, emerges most clearly. Conrad and Langbehn were agreed on one thing: what passed for literature in the family magazines like *Am häuslichen Herd* or *Daheim*, and in the hundreds of anthologies of lyric poetry (for example, *Im Heiligtum der Familie* [*In the Sacred Heart of the Family*], 1879; or *Für Haus und Herz* [*For Home and Heart*], 1881) published each year, would no longer do. The deleterious separation of literature from the serious business of the day, its trivialization as commodity for the continued infantilization of women, stimulated both Naturalist and *Heimatkunst* tendencies to make their proposals for the reintegration of art with the pragmatic demands of modern life. To them, this paradoxically entailed re-establishing its masculine credentials. But in the real world, many women authors neither accepted these overheated male fantasies, nor the anachronistic identification offered to them by industrialized cultural *Kitsch*.

Like 'the social question', 'the woman question' had gained objective organized form by the 1890s, and, although thematically central to the 'revolutionary' new literature (as in Ibsen's *Doll's House*, to name a prominent example), it could no longer be subsumed within a cultural agenda, the imagined unity of which was in fact simply nostalgia. Realistic analytical depictions of the condition of women by women themselves, inspired by the Naturalist manner, could hardly reinforce moral and political values, as Bleibtreu had complacently assumed, because here a new and genuinely subversive consciousness was finding a voice, in literature as well as elsewhere.

As Raymond Williams has observed, Naturalism as an avant-garde banner is one thing and naturalism as a literary attitude quite another (Williams 1988). The first was short-lived and publicistic; the second remained the default style of twentieth-century literature, not to mention drama, film and television. Gabriele Reuter's *Aus guter Familie* [*Of Good Family*, 1895], another spontaneous best-seller, had reached 14 editions by 1908. Inspired by the prevailing Naturalist taste for authenticity, it provided a point of identification for women readers by narrating the failure of its female protagonist to identify with the social possibilities conventionally available to her. If Reuter's plot shares with other Naturalist productions a sense of helplessness in the face of existing conditions, other women writers, for instance the prominent feminist Hedwig Dohm, found in the medium of the novel the opportunity to offer more positive critiques of the conventional subject construction of women.

The point about these popular Naturalist novels was that, although they were embedded in the real reading culture and were not the effects of publicity, they did not conform either to the pattern of 'easy' identification for readers offered by those writers at the bottom end of the commercial and aesthetic spectrum. Authors like Gabriele Reuter, Gustav Frenssen, Wilhelm von Polenz, Hermann Sudermann and Clara Viebig who cut across the Naturalist/*Heimatkunst* divide achieved significant commercial success by offering a kind of fiction that engaged directly with the impact of change.

Three best-selling examples of now forgotten German popular fiction are Max Kretzer's *Meister Timpe* (1888), Gustave Frenssen's *Jörn Uhl* (1901), and Bernhard Kellermann's *Der Tunnel* (1913). These three texts, evenly distributed across the period as they are, give an indication of how the mediation of social change itself changed in the course of these years.

Meister Timpe, which went through nine printings before 1928 and whose million-selling author was celebrated as the German Zola, deals with the triumph of mass production over traditional handicraft. The setting is Berlin east, and the plot concerns the physical and commercial displacement of a family wood-turning workshop by a factory. Kretzer was from an impoverished background, knew the Berlin proletariat at first hand and saw the task of what he called his 'social literature' as the representation of character in circumstances of poverty. Kretzer evidently did take the cue for his Berlin social novel from Zola, whose *Au bonheur des dames* its central topic echoes. But while Zola affirms the inevitable replacement of small retail outlets by the modern department store, Kretzer's treatment is rooted in character and deals with its topic tragically. Contemporary opinion read Kretzer's text as the Berlin novel everyone had been waiting for: at once naturalistic, German and artistically defensible. In terms of the specific sort of complex symbiotic process going on in German letters at the time, it is interesting that the aesthetic judgement is pre-modern: the author of a contemporary literary survey described it as 'a genuinely classical work'.

Frenssen's *Jörn Uhl* was the first literary best-seller of the new century. Unlike Kretzer's Berlin novel, *Jörn Uhl* is set in the north German countryside, thus by its very setting distinguishing itself from the aesthetic front lines in Berlin and Munich. Frenssen was a pastor in the town of Hemme in Schleswig-Holstein before becoming a full-time professional writer. But this does not mean that *Jörn Uhl* is not a novel about contemporary life or that it was irrelevant to the needs of the inhabitants of the big city. On the contrary, here too (and in many other serious popular novels) the impact of industrial modernization and the effects of degeneration upon contemporary Germans is the stuff of the plot.

The great lyric poet Rainer Maria Rilke (1875–1926) wrote an enthusiastic review of Frenssen's novel in 1902, in which he insisted that although it was unmistakably *Heimatkunst*, it was not what is usually sold under this name (for Rilke, this tended to consist in the literary exploitation of rural nostalgia by authors in and for the modern city). Rather, it is a realist novel in the defining sense that it shows how human beings are imprinted with their background. In this sense, the novel has the same commitment to the entwinement of social and psychological elements that defines the aesthetic behind Kretzer's work. Frenssen, however, and this reflects not only his own background but also the later historical moment, produces a melodramatic narrative of loss – the eponymous hero loses the family property – which gives way to a muted affirmation of technological modernization when the hero studies modern methods of land management.

This novel, and other best-sellers like it, such as the almost as successful *Der Büttnerbauer* (*The Smallholder*) by Wilhelm von Polenz (1895), of which Fontane, Tolstoy and Lenin all approved, was regarded at the time as Naturalist. Although there is no doubt that they were not objective analyses of contemporary history and were tainted by stereotypes (such as anti-Semitism), there can equally be no doubt that they engaged with uncertainties and concerns experienced by readers at the time and therefore contributed in reality to the difficult process of adaptation to the shock of the new. They offered more complex identifications and more hybrid aesthetics than the simpler forms of fiction. They provide examples of how good popular fiction can mediate between the need of readers for simple identification and the requirement placed upon them by social change for more complex perspectival mobility.

If Kretzer regarded technology as fatality, and Frenssen as an instrument of national renewal, in Germany's first global best-seller, Bernhard Kellermann's *Der Tunnel* (1913), it becomes the protagonist. In this text, modernity has entered into the very language and value system of the writing. The perspective is now not from a defined locality or *Heimat* within Germany but from the United States, as imagined by a European. Indeed, the central, post-Titanic, motif is the construction of a tunnel connecting the two continents. The horizon of reality is now not, as it was with Kretzer, the social question, the plight of human subjects in the face of modernization, nor, as with Frenssen, the creative and adaptive response of a rooted local Germanness to the depredations of the new. Reality is now the acceleration and efficiency of modern life, its pervasive technologization (Kellermann is indebted to H. G. Wells and Jules Verne). To be sure, human suffering is indivisible from this fatality, and the industrial catastrophes that play an important stylistic and thematic part in later productions such as the *Gas* dramas (1918 and 1920) of Georg Kaiser (1878–1945) and Fritz Lang's film *Metropolis* (1927) would not be thinkable without the disastrous collapse of the Tunnel which threatens to destroy the entire global project in Kellermann's novel. But the penetration of technological reality is reflected less in the content, at which level it is ambivalent, than on the level of style. Kellermann's novel is clearly written for a readership for which the experience of going to the movies, if not yet of enjoying sustained cinematic narrative, can be taken for granted (this was so by 1913; not yet for the readership of 1900). Kellermann affects a disjointed idiom, with montage-like juxtaposition and flashback, as if to say this is how the world now comes to us: via measurements, statistics, records. One must conclude from the enormous success of this novel that the sort of perspectives, or identifications, it offered were helpful to those whose private and working lives were being redefined from every angle by impenetrable forces expressing themselves in the language of industrial technology.

Many other aspects of contemporary attitudes were fictionalized with great public resonance, from satirical novels such as Heinrich Mann's *Professor Unrat* (1905), which deals with the emergence of metropolitan nihilism from within the sclerotic structures of provincial social morality, to exteme localist and xenophobic works, such as Hermann Burte's *Wiltfeber der ewige Deutsche. Die Geschichte eines Heimatsuchers* (*Wiltfeber the Wandering German. The History of a Seeker of the Homeland*, 1912), a sub-Zarathustrian-Wagnerian fantasy, or Hermann Löns's *Der Wehrwolf* (1910, over 800,000 copies), in which a kind of German Robin Hood defeats the enemies encircling his people during the time of the Thirty Years' War.

This flourishing and varied market absorbed influences from England, France, Russia and Scandinavia, and moulded them to German needs. But the Geman novel gave as well as received. Two of the most successful popular authors in the world literature of the twentieth century, Thomas Mann and Hermann Hesse (Nobel Prize winners for Literature in 1929 and 1946 respectively), have their roots firmly in this literary environment. This is where they met with their first – substantial – public success. Both writers came from within Prussian-dominated modern Germany, Mann from the free port of Lübeck in the north, and Hesse from Württemberg in the south. Together, they represent a specifically German contribution to world literature because they both found means of formulating nineteenth-century metaphysical concerns in the arena of the twentieth-century popular novel, without collapsing into *Kitsch* (just – both came extremely close in this period, Hesse with *Gertrud*, 1910, and Mann with *Königliche Hoheit* [*Royal Highness*], 1909; Hesse has rarely been free from accusations of writing *Kitsch*, especially in regard to his lyric poetry which is closer to the *Gartenlaube* than, say, to the aesthetically elitist George Circle [see below]).

It took Thomas Mann's *Buddenbrooks* (1901) as long to sell 1,000 copies as it took *Jörn Uhl* to sell 130,000. But *Buddenbrooks* won out in the end, selling over a million copies in the course of the century on the threshold of which it was published. Rilke reviewed Mann's novel shortly before his review of Frenssen's, and there is nothing in the poet's tone to suggest that he thought they belonged to different categories of literature. (Frenssen himself had no doubts about where he belonged in the pantheon: his view was that he had been denied the Nobel Prize in 1913 only by a French–Jewish plot.) We are left with the question: what is the categorical difference between these two basically realist-Naturalist novels? As so many of the serious literary novels of this period, they are both about change. Change is the constant of all history: cultural consciousness of change is much more variable. Mann's novel is a superbly crafted representation of consciousness of change. While the change he describes in the *Verfall einer Familie* ('Decline of a Family' – the novel's subtitle) belongs to the nineteenth century, the consciousness of it belongs to the twentieth.

In *Buddenbrooks*, what happens in the story impacts upon the way the story is told. Mann contrives to tell the story of the separation of the cultural from the pragmatic sphere, without himself leaving either. This can perhaps be most concisely illustrated by comparing two extended accounts of short periods of time, one the first chapter, the other a chapter from near the end of the novel, both covering about fifty pages. The day of the dinner party at the *Buddenbrooks* home, with which the novel opens, displays the strengths of nineteenth-century novel realism. These are rooted mainly in the ability to hold psychological, social, commercial and moral perspectives within a single narrative style and against a unified horizon that author, narrator, characters and reader agree to see as reality. Physical details are coextensive with the pattern of complex meaning that informs and inhabits them. This is a perfect private–public occasion (guests and family are carefully seated alternately at the dinner table), in which the success of the family firm, manifest both physically and symbolically (there is no difference!) in their recent occupation of a fine house, is acknowledged in speeches and toasts by dignitaries of the town in recognition of the family's contribution to its prosperity. Interwoven with this display of confident representation is a sub-story concerning the disinheritance of a family member from whom a letter has just arrived, the contents and import of which neither the reader, nor the head of the family, get to hear about until a private interview between father and son at the end of the day. This injects into the social description an engaging psychological-social content that goes some way to conveying the inside, as it were, of the outside being celebrated.

The sequence at the end describes, again at considerable length, one day in the life of the youngest generation of Buddenbrooks, Hanno. The point of this sequence is to show how the various determinants of 'reality' in the old literary convention, psychological, social and moral, have fallen apart in the course of the historical developments described in the plot. Hanno is all too aware of his lack of identification with the world of his school. The worst aspects of Wilhelmine shallowness are represented in it (the excessive authoritarianism, insensitivity and superficiality of the school system and its dire effects on pupils was a literary topos of the time, treated by, among others, Frank Wedekind [1864–1918] and Hesse). This day is not a special day, one with a legible significance in which private and public converge, but just any day, a slice of life, a Naturalist day. The artistic contradiction at the heart of Naturalism is encapsulated: the kind of poetic, creative, artistic, dissenting mind (in Hanno's case, musical) that could enter and engage with this moral reality to produce literary fiction is far too demoralized to have the inclination to do so (or to summon a public to do it for). The social novel contrives to tell the story of the end of social novels. Immediately after the final line of the chapter ('this was one day in the life of little Johann'), there follows an entirely impersonal ('scientific') description of typhoid fever, from which Hanno has died in the unnarrated space between two chapters.

One thing Rilke did get right about *Buddenbrooks* in his review of April 1902 was that Hanno, had he lived, would have embarked upon 'the infinitely endangered life of the artist'. The novel knowingly points to a space beyond the representations of the social novel, but does not, itself, go there. We return to the question of where the novel genre did go in chapter 6.

The world of publicity

The promotion of Naturalism as well as the vogue for Langbehn (like that for other ideological best-sellers of the time like Nordau's *Entartung*

[*Degeneration*, 1892], or Weininger's *Geschlecht und Charakter* [*Sex and Character*, 1903]), are effects of the phenomenon of publicity, which I define as the dialectic of supply and demand in the market for ideas and opinions. As Fritz Stern says, trying to explain the impact of Langbehn's eccentric rant: 'above all, it sold' (Stern 1961: 153). Heinrich Mann, in the final chapter of his bitter satirical novel on the Wilhelmine era, *Der Untertan* (set in 1900, finished by 1914, but only published in 1918 when, in the aftermath of the era, it had a major political impact) characterized the period as 'absolutism tempered by the craving for publicity'. The regime did occasionally attempt to regulate literary production through the courts but was not always successful in making its charges stick. Indeed, court cases were themselves, then as now, an extremely effective form of publicity.

The point is that, while culture became oppositional rather than an adjunct to a national project or a zone of eternal verities, publicity tended to neutralize opposition. This was because the machinery of publicity was at once essentially the enemy (as Heinrich Mann's formulation captures so neatly) but also the medium through which opposition was inevitably conducted.

The instructive example here is that of Nietzsche, whose oppositional position could hardly have been more radical and whose opinions could not have had greater impact than they did. Yet they were consumed, rather than comprehended. Zarathustra's main concern is less with what he has to say than with how to say it so that it is not misunderstood or misappropriated. In *Also sprach Zarathustra* (*Thus Spake Zarathustra*, 1892), Nietzsche remembers how the Wagner who had once seemed to him to embody the glorious potential of the new Germany and the rest of Europe had been debased by the vulgar industrial reality of the *Gründerzeit*. Georg Simmel, in his famous essay of 1903 on the new mentality of modern urban individuals, 'Die Großstädte und das Geistesleben' ('The Metropolis and Mental Life'; Simmel 1950), identified the characteristic paradox that Nietzsche's alpine anti-metropolitan moral radicalism spoke directly to the contemporary city-dweller whose threatening subordination to the urban environment creates the need for ever greater individualism. In the ten years from 1890 until his death in 1900, Nietzsche had been applied across the political and cultural spectrum from feminism to *Heimatkunst*.

From the early part of the period, culture becomes a function of competing publicistic claims for its ownership. Once the powerful claim of Naturalism had broken like a wave, there was a divergence, perhaps most easily read off from the journals that arose thenceforth. If *Die Gesellschaft*, with its integrative programme, enjoyed intellectual leadership for a while, after 1890 the various components that it had sought to combine developed in separate directions. *Der Kunstwart* (from 1887) became the focus for conservative national values in matters of art; *Die Freie Bühne* (from 1889) represented forms of cultural cosmopolitan Modernism; *Jugend* (*Youth*, from 1896), inspired by the British arts and crafts movement, went with the market, radically updating the broad popular appeal of the family journal and emulating its success by tracking and developing the interests of consumers. The editors of these journals in their separate ways all proposed versions of what art was, recognizing Simmel's point that what modern city subjects wanted was ways in which to express their own difference.

Jugend gave its name to *Jugendstil*. Culture here becomes explicitly separate, a matter of 'style' (the symbiosis here is with the wider European movement of art for art's sake, sometimes called 'aestheticism'), but at the same time eroticized and linked to personal desire and its gratification. In this, it at once distinguishes itself from modernity – the arts and crafts movement is specifically resistant to the fetish of commodities (the anonymity of industrial manufacture) – and at the same time, by its attention to the market and its pronounced use of a kind of soft-core eroticism, itself comfortably a commodity. This strand of literature, in Germany as much as in Paris or London, was precariously balanced between the delivery of sophisticated aesthetic effects and a subversive oppositional stance, threatening public morals.

The marketing of exclusivity

The case of Stefan George (1868–1933) and his circle at first sight looks like an historical curiosity, sealed off from literary and other sorts of history. In fact, it offers a quintessence of the public situation of literature in the Germany of the period between about 1890 and 1914. Although George was not an unconditional Nietzschean, like Nietzsche he was motivated by profound distaste for *Gründerzeit* philistinism, materialism and vulgarity. The fashion for Naturalism was anathema to him, and the George Circle's famous journal, *Blätter für die Kunst* (*Pages / Leaves for Art*), was founded as an aesthetic rebuttal of Conrad's socially conscious *Gesellschaft*. In other words, George's critical opposition was not within political reality, but to political reality. He announced that his practice and promotion of art, and that of his followers, wished to have nothing to do with state or society, since these were not the domain of poetry.

George's opposition was inspired from abroad and, as such, a moment of symbiosis. It absorbed and redefined wider European Modernism for German literature (George was active as a translator, for instance of Baudelaire). In fact, George was a Rhinelander and thus inclined to be anti-Prussian. His decisive influence was Stéphane Mallarmé, the influential and significant French Symbolist poet, at whose feet the young George sat in Paris in 1889. This was the source of his sense of the sacramental importance of poetry for the present day.

George would have preferred to write in French but his facility in that language, though near-native, was not up to the demands of a messianic vocation. Hence, and here too he is typical in a way, the foreign impulse is transplanted into the German situation and becomes the vocation to transform specifically German literature. Indeed, George and his circle saw themselves, and came to be seen, as stewards of a 'Secret Germany' which provided an alternative spiritual reality to the fallen modern one.

The phenomenon of the George Circle does, at first glance, seem to be atypical because its oppositional stance is not neutralized by publicity. This would not be true of other representatives of a broadly similar kind of aesthetic Modernism: for example *Jugend*, which was commercially successful (and thus made compromises with public taste, particularly in relation to eroticism), or the journal *Pan*, which, though high-minded and aesthetically ambitious, was unable to compromise sufficiently with the demands of a large enough niche to maintain its high production standards and still remain viable. George saw to it that his poetic mission was carried out with complete control of the means of production, from his relationship with the publisher Georg Bondi, through the arts and crafts-inspired care and attention given to the physical appearance of the books and the journal associated with the Circle, to the de-fetishization of print culture implied by the commissioning of designer Melchior Lechter to create a typeface that resembled George's own handwriting.

Neither did George countenance surrendering control of the distribution of his poetry and that of his acolytes to market forces. *Blätter für die Kunst* announced that it was available to an invited readership only, and in fact was partially supported by money provided discreetly by a wealthy member of the Circle.

Yet this seeming independence from the hurly-burly of industrial modernity is illusory. For one thing, George's circle opposed what the sphere of publicity does and means and therefore helped to define it. Despite its considerable achievements, in literature as well as in literary criticism, the Circle with all its high-profile mannerisms was reactive, not creative.

Secondly, the notion of publishing a journal or books which announce themselves as intended for an invited readership only is already self-contradictory: it is the marketing of exclusivity and fits exactly the explanation Simmel (who in fact contributed to the *Blätter*) put forward to explain the dispersal of the alpine purity of Nietzsche in the pressing need for self-differentiation in the mentality of the modern city-dweller. In this, the example of the George–*Kreis* demonstrates what Nietzsche knew, that the market was too strong to be opposed by thoughts and words alone, however beautifully packaged they came. Looking at it another way (as Brecht did, when asked by *Die literarische Welt* in 1928 to make a tribute to the poet on the occasion of his sixtieth birthday), George was a highly skilled publicist; less of a lonely prophet than a media event.

But there is a more sinister aspect of the story of George that is also representative, not of the hothouse of publicity of the beginnings of modern democratic-capitalist Germany but of Germany's subsequent embrace of political irrationalism. George criticized Nietzsche for never having found disciples to carry his thought over into the practical world, and himself amply made good the deficiency. What began as a mission within literature, and defined itself as categorically severed from state and society, became for George the cultivation of a lifestyle that he and his friends believed would eventually transform state and society. In an even more aggravated case of the anxiety of influence than the one that defined his relation with Nietzsche's work, George despised Wagner as a charlatan. Yet George intended the same sort of translation of the aesthetic into the social as Wagner had dreamed of. In the case of George, then, one can discern a genealogical link between the isolation of the sphere of culture, the establishment of this charismatic fiction in the minds of a public, and the catastrophic, irrational reapplication of it in the political sphere.

German art meets advertising

In one crucial aspect it is Expressionism that marks the culmination of the effect of modern publicity on culture in pre-First World War Germany. This effect is to excite and stimulate it but at the same time to marginalize it.

Around 1910, a generation of artists and intellectuals came of age that was completely identified with Wilhelmine modernity. Its identification, its sense of itself, was therefore informed by the aggressive urban self-differentiation described by Simmel and by a sense of radical opposition to the hegemony of industrial interests, to vulgar imperial pretension and to cultural philistinism. On the other hand, its sense of the need for community in the modern world could not have been stronger, yet this sense was severed from a feeling of common purpose with the actual institutions and attitudes surrounding it.

As Nietzsche, a figure admiringly contested by many writers in this generation, had known, the market is strong enough to accommodate cries from the edge, even welcome them. While the imperial institutions of official art, from which culture as we have come to understand it had seceded, disapproved, impotently and indeed counter-productively, of the new practices of distortion and abstraction, the logic of the market penetrated, neutralized and canonized them. From 1910 to the real end of the 'long' nineteenth century in 1914, 'Expressionism' was at the same time, and inextricably, both a vibrant Modernist moment and high cultural fashion. The more ecstatic the address, the more sincere and intense the anguish at the lack of a political constituency, and the more strident the insistence upon what art actually is, the more 'Expressionism' provided the irresistible spectacle of art roaring in a cage.

Hermann Hesse, asked in 1918 to pronounce in *Die neue Rundschau* on the word 'Expressionism', made the point that the difference between it and Impressionism was not really that one fashion followed another, but that whereas the Impressionists were called Impressionists by others, the Expressionists were called Expressionists by themselves. This brings out, first, the paradigm shift of these last phases of the German long nineteenth century: we are not dealing with a continuous development, within which one form of artistic sensibility and set of practices follows another, but with a sociological change. And, secondly, it points to the self-consciousness with which this moment for culture was situated in the sphere of publicity.

What Hesse's shrewd *aperçu* fails to bring out is the dialectical reverse of this high-profile self-consciousness, namely that this generation in this milieu has *no choice* but to market itself. There is, in the moment of pre-war Expressionism, a defining tension between a sense of the threatened integrity of the cultural sphere and that sphere's need to name and explain itself clamorously, to make itself public. As the Austrian poet and film-maker Ernst Angel said in 1920, making the exact opposite point to Hesse's, any poet calling himself an Expressionist is unlikely to be one.

The name Expressionism was originally a synonym for 'modern', just as realism and Naturalism had been in the decades immediately preceding. It was the art dealer and publicist Herwarth Walden, who invented Expressionism as a movement, or, as we would say now, as a brand. The word came about in order to organize a public for innovative work in modern painting. The impresario of Modernism in Germany, Walden found many ways of promoting the new art, for instance in the familiar device of founding a journal (the influential *Der Sturm* [*The Storm*]) or by producing inexpensive art cards for sale in his own book store. Importantly, he also mounted exhibitions (he opened a *Sturm* gallery in Berlin in 1912), and it was he who brought the Italian Futurist painters – the most immediate models for the new generation of Wilhelmine German artists and writers – and other cutting-edge modern painters to Berlin for an epoch-making exhibition in 1913.

Although the marketing of the new art by Walden and others, such as Franz Pfemfert, was not primarily for commercial profit (at least before the war), the phenomenon nevertheless came unintentionally close to the forms of life of the world it so vehemently wished to countermand. In its very bid for Dionysian authenticity, it had the quality of a fashion, of a distraction among the distractions of the new metropolis, even something of the essence of advertising as a medium and genre: a public culture of attention-getting. Advertising is indistinguishable from the world of publicity; it has no objective reference and enjoys a constitutive and pragmatic contempt for truth. Expressionist manifestos were, in the words of Brecht, who was not an unbiased commentator, full of the excitement of ideas but without the ideas.

Attempts to generalize about the German literary Expressionists run the risk of parroting some of the frankly nonsensical slogans produced by the pressure to position culture in the sphere of publicity. The Futurists promoted themselves consciously, shrewdly and radically by advocating the abandonment of inwardness in favour of a fusion of machines and instinct. The young German aesthetic radicals who frequented Berlin cafés from 1908 or so onwards and adopted the identification of Expressionists, wanted to keep that radical pitch but retain the cultural aura of art the very demolition of which made the Futurists (and would make Dada) categorically distinct from the aesthetic of the preceding century. The Futurists wanted a new technology of the word; the Expressionists (as announced by Walden) wanted a new art of the word (*Wortkunst*). In lyric poetry (August Stramm [1874–1915]) and especially the staging of drama (for instance, the producers Karlheinz Martin and Leopold Jessner), there is a case to be made in favour of the genuine cultural innovativeness of the Expressionist generation. Yet if one tries to form a judgement upon the phenomenon as a whole, it is hard to escape the conclusion that Brecht had a point: it was sound and fury. It is notable that, if one seeks a 'typical' example of

Expressionism, one has to go to distinctly second-rate writers, or simply publicists and manifesto-writers to find it (a Johannes Becher, a Walter Hasenclever, a Kurt Hiller or a Kasimir Edschmid), while no genuinely great literary artist of this period (not Gottfried Benn [1886–1956], Alfred Döblin [1878–1957], Georg Trakl [1887–1914] or even Georg Kaiser) is unambiguously identified with the word or significantly 'typical' of the moment as Marinetti is of Futurism. Georg Heym (born 1887) who died in 1912 might be the exception.

Although the selling point of Expressionism is to this day that it was 'the first German Modernism', a more accurate assessment (at least as far as literature is concerned) might be that it was the way the German Idealist tradition looked in the glare of modernity: outwardly hugely ambitious; inwardly bewildered; tantalized by the almost infinite possibilities of the urban, industrial and technological modern world and clueless as to what to do about it. As we shall argue in the next chapter, the advent of the First World War changed that. It was the war that added content to the forms developed by the Expressionist writers (where it didn't kill them).

Publicity as a creative force

The realm of publicity has a liberating as well as a constraining aspect. Frank Wedekind (1864–1918), once the advertising director for Maggi, the soup stock manufacturer, sworn enemy of the artistically inert earnestness of Naturalism and entirely at home with the erotic subversiveness implicit in *Jugendstil*, was perhaps the first major German dramatist to respond creatively to urban modernity (which is why he was a hero to the Expressionist generation and Brecht). Wedekind became a kind of avant-garde rival of the unofficial laureate Hauptmann. There was a bohemian anarchism about his theatricality, touched not only by the traditional bourgeois stage but also by other forms of spectacle like the cabaret and the circus, implying aesthetics of effect and performance, and an eye to public reception rather than private insight. At the end of *Frühlings Erwachen* (*Spring Awakening*, 1891), a masked man leads the adolescent antagonist away from the claustrophobic provincial setting of the play towards what is understood to be the greater freedom of the modern metropolis – the greater freedom to define yourself in relation to your own sexuality, the greater freedom to invent yourself and play roles. The complications and limitations of the loosening of the constraints of sexuality are then dynamically dramatized in the famous *Lulu* plays (*Erdgeist* [*Earth Spirit*] and *Die Büchse der Pandora* [*Pandora's Box*], 1892–4), especially in relation to the role of women. We encounter the kind of ambivalence we noted in the context of *Jugend*: what is sexually liberating is also immediately made available for commercial exploitation, and thus constrained again, just in a more modern way. More disturbingly: at the end of *Die Büchse der Pandora* it is not a masked roué but Jack the Ripper who represents metropolitan modernity, anticipating the lesson of the First World War about what happens when the patriarchal culture loses its grip on responsible political and social governance.

If one literary figure provided testimony to the pervasive presence of publicity in this period, it was Karl Kraus, who did so by contesting it. Kraus (1874–1936), an admirer of Wedekind, whom he knew, and whose *Die Büchse der Pandora* he produced in Vienna in 1905, made himself the champion of language precisely in view of its abuse at the hands of the proliferation of publicists. He combated the 'ideological saturation' (Timms 1986: 28) of language in contemporary Austrian political discourse in the journal he controlled from 1899 until 1936, *Die Fackel* (*The Torch*). Grasping how words used without responsibility were a powerful means of oppression in modern print society, he attacked the irresponsible use of language by developing an art of satirical quotation that unmasked it. In so doing he remained, as he himself said, distinct from (what was then seen as) the literary avant-garde because, unlike them, he remained 'within the old house of language' to wage his war against its abasement. By contrast, many attempts can be discerned, particularly in Austria-Hungary, to quit this old house. To this revolution in literature at the level of language itself we now turn.

Language becomes self-conscious

Arno Holz (1863–1929), whose extreme Naturalism destroyed the traditional structure of drama by doing away with plot, preached and practised a radical formal revolution in lyric poetry (*Revolution der Lyrik* [*Revolution in Lyric Poetry*], 1899; *Phantasus*, 1898), advocating inner rhthyms, rather than formal metres, and syntactic abbreviation, anticipating practices of interior monologue and Expressionist 'telegram style'. Wedekind and Hauptmann thematized poor communication in their plays, thus clouding the traditional transparency of language as deployed in literary and dramatic art. Wedekind transgressed intentionally against uniformity of linguistic register in his drama, thereby, again, making language use itself visible rather than transparent. Thomas Mann's Hanno swooned away from the rigours of social identity towards the non-linguistic sweetness of music. Even the unashamedly popular best-selling novel, *Der Tunnel*, acknowledged the impact of technological modernity on the level of style.

This pervasive tendency reflects a Europe-wide development, for instance in the plays of the Belgian playwright Maurice Maeterlinck, the poetry of Mallarmé and Rimbaud in France, or later the Futurists in Italy. It is the most significant manifestation of a fresh symbiosis of German and European literature. Within the German-speaking world, it is at its most intense and creative outside the new Prussian-led Germany, where even the extreme aestheticist edge of lyric poetry, the George-*Kreis*, was preoccupied with its public image and touched by overheated nationalism. It was in Vienna, Prague and stations of exile that the paradigm shift towards Modernist literature begins to emerge most clearly.

Austria-Hungary, while not immune to the corrosive effects of the sphere of publicity (as the work of Karl Kraus reflected), was nevertheless less affected by the technologically amplified clamour of national self-confidence on the other side of the border. The publicist Hermann Bahr's *Die Überwindung des Naturalismus* (*The Overcoming of Naturalism*) of 1891 was a move against the cultural holism of Berlin Naturalism, which, as we saw, complacently united aesthetic Modernism, national ambition, social critique, and scientific rationalism under one banner. That the disintegration of programmatic Naturalism should be registered prominently in Vienna is not an accident. Not only did Austria-Hungary, as the losers in the war of 1866, have less stake in the national pride and hope driving even the oppositional discourses in Imperial Germany, it was also a polity lacking a compelling political rationale, constitutionally decentred, multinational, and past its days of imperial glory. As a citizen of Austria-Hungary, it was easier to attune to the inner hollowness of the brash new European order than it was elsewhere.

One document in particular crystallizes with astonishing comprehensiveness the new challenge for literature. 'Ein Brief' ('A Letter') by Hugo von Hofmannsthal (1874–1929), published in the Berlin newspaper *Der Tag* in 1902 and commonly known as the 'Lord Chandos Brief', is a fictional letter from a young writer to Sir Francis Bacon, explaining why he has been unable to write creatively for the past two years. It is in effect the announcement of disintegration, positioned all the more tellingly by virtue of its fictional historical setting within a fully integrated culture. The addressee, Bacon, was a figure who personified this integration: politician, philosopher, writer, scientist, and jurist. The young author Chandos, master of both the English and the Latin languages, was steeped in the historical literary practice of the transmission and renewal of traditional models, and his letter is rhetorically faultlessly formulated in dizzying contradiction to what is being announced.

What is being announced is a crisis of language. Not only is the habitual recourse to rhetoric, by the self-conscious logic of the fiction, empty, but language itself, Lord Chandos explains, no longer does what it is supposed to do, namely give coherence to the world and the self. This has profound implications for the human subject. The hierarchy of metaphysical concepts henceforth leads only into emptiness. Inner experience and outer experience, feelings and behaviour, are no longer knitted together along the line of language. On the outside, there is only empty observance; on the inside, moments of overwhelming and unmediated fullness, which no words are adequate to express. These experiences are unendurably intense, ranging from a sense of supra-individual oneness with the continuity of all creation to a horrific awareness of the *bellum omnium contra omnes* when Chandos cannot defend himself against an all-too-vivid mental representation of the last moments of rats he has routinely poisoned in a sealed cellar.

The human subject falls into two modes of being, on either side of language which once united them. One relies on paternal discipline for the performance of external life, the other turns towards the possibility of a new language 'of the heart' which would facilitate an unprecedented relation between the subject and existence. The Chandos Letter ends without hope, and Hofmannsthal drew back from threatening silence to devote himself to the production of opera libretti and subtle, knowing dramas.

Perhaps the great insights of turn-of-the-century Austrian writers like Hofmannsthal, and the slightly older Arthur Schnitzler (1862–1931), into the dissociation of language and experience (Schnitzler was one of the pioneers of interior monologue in *Leutnant Gustl* [1901], and the dramatic structure of his play *Reigen* [*Round Dance*, 1900], in which characters change sexual partners in a sort of relay from scene to scene, is such as to emphasize the mutually determining but divergent relationship between discourse and sexuality), did not lead onto radical linguistic innovation in their own cases for the same reasons that led them to have the insights in the first place. If the social and cultural circumstances were propitious for this revelation, they were also the objective circumstances in and for which Schnitzler and Hofmannsthal wrote. To these they remained committed, adapting and modifying their potentially radical opposition to a cityscape less rebarbatively false than that of Imperial Germany. This was a culture of political and existential prevarication, primed to appreciate a drama or a literature which represented, and thus in a sense affirmed, this reality.

Their fellow Austrian, Robert Musil (1880–1942), by contrast, did go on to make a substantial contribution to twentieth-century literary Modernism in the form of his huge unfinished novel *Der Mann ohne Eigenschaften* (*Man without Qualities*, 1930, 1933, 1943), of which more in chapter 6. *Die Verwirrungen des jungen Törleß* (*Confusions of Young Törleß*, 1906) is a precursor. Musil's background was in mathematics and engineering, and he was the author of a critical doctorate on the Austrian scientist and philosopher Ernst Mach. Mach's 'psychotechnological' epistemology dissolved the distinction between the mental and the physical, proposing a view of the human subject as a composite of sensations. Musil's starting point was therefore different to that of Hofmannsthal's Chandos. Mach's influence is clear in the Chandos letter, but the letter is an expression of something lost (as well as an incipient literary response to the challenge posed by this loss). For Musil, less problematically, the challenge was to find the appropriate literary discourse for this reconceptualization of subjectivity.

His novel can be understood as a psychologically naturalistic account of the mental life of a sixteen-year old. It has affinities with many other quasi-autobiographical school stories of the period (for instance, Hermann Hesse's *Unterm Rad* [*Beneath the Wheel*, 1906]). However, Musil explained that the novel's realism and its psychology were pretexts for a much more radical writing than these expectations imply, a writing alert to the structure of subjectivity itself. The advantage of adolescence as a pretext is that what is 'unfinished' in the life of the mind is less hidden than it becomes in the correctly socialized adult. The starting point is therefore less the crisis of language than the recognition that, within language, the subject is only apparently unified.

Musil's language is constantly reformulating the difference between what is distinct in and for the mind, and what is hidden in and from it. The book's juxtaposition, in its style and story, of *fin-de-siècle* nuance regarding the inner life, probing ever further into the secret connections therein, and the eruptive experience of transgressive sexuality (feelings of incestuous desire and homosexual rape) suggests this. The two are categorically different but somehow also linked. They are both constitutive of subjectivity, but not unifiable.

There is something disconcertingly and fascinatingly fluid about what Musil puts on one side of the divide and what on the other. If we draw up a list of the qualities juxtaposed, on one side we appear to be able to talk about the 'character, soul, line or timbre of a person', or else one's 'self', or, better, one's 'most inner self', or 'that which stands wordlessly before the mind's eye', or 'the life that one feels, senses, sees from afar', or else 'that which gathers in the soul, the mind, a thought that one finds between the words of a book, or before silent lips of an image'. On the other 'thoughts, decisions, actions', or else 'one's own feelings', 'oneself', 'events'; 'the life that one lives', or more extensively, how or who one is 'when composing documents, designing machinery, going to the circus or engaging in one of a hundred other similar activities'.

Although a superficial glance at these complementarities might suggest a difference between 'inner' and 'outer', a closer look reveals that the dividing line slides, especially when it is a matter of the life of the mind: feelings and thoughts can appear on either side, and so can the 'self'. The definitions of both qualities often tail off into indeterminacy ('or whatever you want to call it'; 'a hundred other similar activities').

The life of desire particularly blurs the distinction, while being animated by it: 'between events and his self, indeed between his own feelings and some most inner self, which desired understanding of them, there always remained a borderline, which receded like a horizon' (trans. and quoted in Webber 1993: 37). This translation admirably captures the double possibility of the German ('[begehrte] nach ihrem Verständnis'), which contrives to convey the thought that both sides of the divide desire the understanding of the other. What the translation cannot keep is the ambiguity of the German word used for 'borderline', 'Scheidelinie', which, in using the word for vagina ('Scheide', and in another example there is said to be an 'enges Tor' between the two sides), specifies a transition which, like birth, is at once constitutive of our subjective existence and inaccessible to our consciousness.

All this is to suggest that, given Musil's enthusiasm for the theme of the division in subjectivity, his ever-repeated search for the clinching formulation of the division is in effect a performance of language's role as that which divides the two. This role is experienced here not as a disaster as with Chandos but as a challenge of writing and an opportunity for literature to inscribe itself between the forces that it cannot name without, as the novel's motto from Maeterlinck says, 'diminishing them strangely'.

What is achieved on the pretext of psychological realism is a kind of writing that becomes two-dimensional in an artistically productive way. It only apparently presupposes a reality that it represents, but in fact makes of the life of language the surface or screen upon which the constitutive disunity of mind and body, the never satisfied life of desire and the loss of a metaphysical horizon can be acknowledged but crucially also savoured as a network of what Musil called 'Inbeziehungen' (a neologism indicating something like 'relations within').

In Rilke's *Die Aufzeichnungen des Malte Laurids Brigge* (*The Notebooks of Malte Laurids Brigge*, 1910), the pretext of realism is dropped altogether and only the relations remain ('Bezug ist alles', or ' "relationality" is all', Rilke elsewhere maintained). If Hofmannsthal expressed the crisis of the word in historical costume, and Musil ironically showed the corruption endemic in a school chosen by the parents of its pupils to escape the corrupting infuence of the modern city, Rilke sets his text, and the artistic challenge, in contemporary Paris itself.

Malte is the record of the traumatic impact of the forces of modernity, as they are condensed in the form of the French capital, upon the sensitive young Danish patrician named in the title. Rilke's text has formal and artistic affinities with the *Petits poèmes en prose* of Baudelaire (one of which is quoted) and Dostoevsky's *Notes from Underground*, as the word 'Notes' or 'Jottings' in the title suggests. Rilke himself was at various times in Russia and Paris, and lived in a form of serial exile, the only incipient domesticity he experienced being in the programmatically non-bourgeois sociality of the artists' colony Worpswede near Bremen. Like Stefan George, he resolutely resisted the forms of ordinary bourgeois life and, like him, committed his life to the search for meaningful form in words. Unlike George, whose inspiration from Mallarmé gave way to the identification with – at least an imaginary version of – Germany, Rilke in his lifestyle as well as his work (as the affinity with Baudelaire and Dostoevsky suggests) personified the internationalism of artistic Modernism, and the symbiosis of German-language literature with wider modern European writing.

Like Musil's, but more radically, Rilke's language in *Malte* lives from the position it is shown to occupy between a secure sense of self and an intimidating sense of other. The antithesis could hardly be more pointedly established: on one side, the sensitive inward-looking poet, on the other, Simmel's excessively 'objective' modern metropolis. Yet the discourse does not take sides. On the contrary, what it shows is that the self is only apparently a safe interior space, and in fact the stark objectified otherness of the city is uncannily familiar to Malte because it recalls the repressed other in the self.

The most pressing concern of this language is that there might be a wholly different semantic order adequate to the new experiences of self and other that are the condition of Malte's 'Aufzeichnungen'. There is 'eine andere Auslegung' ('another interpretation') that is just around the corner. The (impossible) property of this new language will be that it will not subordinate, and thus diminish, what it names. The work closes on the words 'not yet', situating the whole text in the proleptic light of a dawn of meaning about to break.

What must change is a matter of relationality ('Bezug'). Chandos reports the strange experience of words congealing into eyes and staring back at him. In Musil's novel, too, at a crucial moment Törleß feels that the light in the school attic – scene of the transgressive acting-out of desire – is like an eye that looks back at him. Malte in a famous passage reports that he is still able to write in response to his experiential revolution, but its real import escapes his discourse because he himself is the impression that will be transformed, that he himself will no longer write but will himself be written.

In the context of a review of a novel by Gustaf af Geijerstam in 1903, Rilke had criticized the introduction of a third character in order to bring out the problems between a married couple. This third person, he argued, was a device to personify the forces at work separating two people who are held together by their circumstances, and that these difficulties would be more honestly and accurately represented in relation to the two characters alone. While Rilke was making a specific criticism here, and perhaps also thinking of the circumstances of his own marriage to Clara Westhoff, the point was important enough for him to introduce it into the fifteenth section of *Malte* as a kind of general proposition on the fallacy of representation: 'And I should have known that this third person, who runs through all life and literatures; this ghost of a third person, who never existed, who has no significance, that he should be denied. He is one of the devices of nature, which is always striving to distract the attention of mankind from her deepest secrets.'

This 'third' is language itself, the 'trennende Macht' ('separating force'), which has a triangulating effect, positioning two subjects in relation to a third point of reference which they have in common but which also masks their respective uniqueness, and thus makes it impossible for there to be a direct relation between them. Language also objectifies the self before itself, one's familiar identity revealed as the personification of something basically other or unfamiliar, a false inward exterior masking a terrifyingly unbounded subjectivity. Against this, Rilke adumbrates a notion of intransitivity which, when expressed in the terms of the socially recognized relation between two people, for which marriage can be taken as the paradigm but which is generalizable to all 'relations', is expressed as 'intransitive love'.

This intransitive love is the figure in Rilke which corresponds to the possibility of a new aesthetic. *Malte* leaves it as a possibilty, and Rilke's later poetry continues to weave itself around the possibility, rather than fulfil it (since an intransitive relation is either a mystical notion or a logical contradiction). The point is that Rilke's writing, in prose and especially in poetry, moves into an area of relations between subjectivities that is not defined or constrained by language but that is constitutive of subjectivity itself from within, as it were. He does this in such a way as to make of literature one means of deepening culture's understanding of its own inevitable discontentment.

Literature and technology

Jürgen Habermas, in *The Philosophical Discourse of Modernity*, recognizes the key position Nietzsche occupied in relation to the sort of modern practice initiated by Hofmannsthal, Musil and Rilke: 'Nietzsche is the first to conceptualize the attitude of aesthetic modernity before avant-garde consciousness assumed objective shape in the literature, painting, and music of the twentieth century' (Habermas 1987: 122). This attitude consisted in the perception that scientific rationality and the assumption of universally valid morality had ceased to exercise a life-enhancing function. The way Nietzsche analyses the predicament in *Zur Genealogie der Moral* (*On the Genealogy of Morality*, 1887), these mainstays of European civilization are expressions of what he calls 'the Will to Truth', which in turn is the expression of Christian worldview. For Nietzsche, it is not the 'Truth' part that matters, but the 'Will' part. As long as Christianity, for all its ascetic aversion to 'life', provided a framework for the activity of the will, then it also supported the health of the communities it informed. But by the strength of its own logic, the Will to Truth has examined its own presuppositions and thereby eliminated them. It has become 'problematic to itself' and thus unconducive to the health of the community. This is the meaning of the grim news that not only 'God is Dead', but that we have killed him, announced by the Madman in *Die fröhliche Wissenschaft* [*The Gay Science*] §125.

Western civilization is in the position of the hunted cartoon character that runs off the edge of a cliff, confident that he is outrunning his pursuer but about to realize that there is nothing left beneath him to support the exertions he thought were his salvation.

Those at this juncture who spoke on behalf of scientific rationality, for instance Mach, or the German Darwinian Ernst Haeckel and his Naturalist followers Wilhelm Bölsche and Bruno Wille, resemble the bystanders in the marketplace who mock Nietzsche's mad messenger and who have simply not yet understood the implications. For both groups, there is still a perfectly viable place for the human subject at the heart of a single-decker, non-metaphysical world, although each group frames this complacent assumption differently. Even those who, while accepting the anti-metaphysical position of the scientists, opposed technological modernity from the point of view of a superficially Nietzschean 'life', such as Dilthey and Ludwig Klages, did so only by ignoring the part of the Madman's message that urges the enormity of what has been done: 'How were we able to drink up the sea? Who gave us the sponge to wipe away the entire horizon? What did we do when we unchained this earth from the sun? Whither is it moving now? Away from all suns? Are we not plunging continually? Backward, sideward, forward, in all directions? Is there any up or down left? Are we not straying as through an infinite nothing? Do we not feel the breath of empty space ...?'

The poets we have mentioned, and indeed the Expressionists also, were vitally concerned with the psychologically devastating repercussions of the disappearance of the metaphysical horizon. But at the same time, they engaged with the reality of technological modernity: Lord Chandos writes his letter to Sir Francis Bacon, one of the founders of modern empirical science; Musil takes as his starting point Mach's ontological demotion of the human subject; Rilke takes his *Jugendstil* soul to modern Paris, where the trolley buses glide through it and physiological detail penetrates the surfaces of Naturalism. The Expressionists, even while they were caught in the glare of Wilhelmine publicity, took their cue from the Italian Futurists, who affirmed technology precisely because it eliminated the musty space of interiority. In other words, this writing, far from turning away from the modern world, is on the contrary perfectly attuned to the encounter between the human subject and technology.

The crucial insight determining the attitude of aesthetic modernity referred to by Habermas is its self-consciousness. And what else does this mean, in the context of that branch of art concerned with language, but that writers discover the mediality of their own medium? That, in other words, language itself is a technology. For Friedrich Kittler, the most radical theorist of what is new about literature at this historical moment, the 'Aufschreibesystem' ('discourse network') of 1900 is a network of information technologies, with no metaphysical referent. But even if we accept this extreme deconstructive view, the poetic realization of this technological invasion of the privileged interiority of the human subject has the effect of acknowledging that very bedrock of meaningless suffering that, according to Nietzsche, gave rise to the ascetic ideal in the first place. As we read in the very last section of *Zur Genealogie der Moral*, the ascetic ideal, the only meaning humans have ever devised for themselves, had had the incomparable merit of giving meaning to suffering.

By permitting the scientistic paradigm, by way of the recognition of literature as a form of information technology (as Kittler has it), into the heart of the process whereby the human subject is constructed, the medial self-consciousness of Modernism manufactures the screen, the 'surface', upon which, as Hofmannsthal said, profundity could best be hidden.

Kittler explains the 1900 discourse network of literature as the transformation of madness into information. By this, he means that the art of these writers consists in devising ways of capturing for culture otherwise unsocialized subjective experience. Chandos and Malte's nervous breakdowns, the very 'Verwirrungen', confusions, of Musil's title are examples of this, but there are many others, for instance Alfred Döblin's *Ermordung einer Butterblume* (*The Murder of a Buttercup*, 1913), Georg Heym's *Der Irre* (*The Madman*, 1913), Gottfried Benn's *Gehirne* (*Brains*) *Novellen* (1916). Yet the use of language against itself to expose dysfunction, vulnerability, disorientation, confusion, and to endow these things with the quality of cultural pleasure is by any measure a major achievement. This holds true even if it is not pleasure in the traditional aesthetic sense but, in Lionel Trilling's words, the gratification of unpleasure, the bracing touch of the 'breath of empty space' of which Nietzsche's Madman talked in the midst of the benighted sane.

In 1912, Rilke seriously considered undergoing psychoanalysis, either with a friend, Emil Gebsattel, or with Freud himself, but decided against it. The choice for him seemed to be between the analysis and his writing, and the successful completion of the First *Duineser Elegie* decided him in favour of the latter. This biographical circumstance is notable because it is symptomatic of a wider sense that literature at the rarefied level at which Rilke pursued it came into a kind of rivalry with the science of psychoanalysis. Freud's practice was a socialization of mild kinds of madness, and his concentration on the specificities of idiosyncratic language use brings his activities very close to the area of language use previously occupied by literary practice: even more specifically now in this matter of converting interference, the 'noise' of mental confusion, into culturally coded information.

From the point of view of a cultural history of literature, the rivalry between Modernist poetry and psychoanalysis needs to be seen in the context of a third rival for occupation of this space: Nietzsche's *Also sprach Zarathustra*. The three kinds of language use embody different attitudes to traditional patriarchal authority. Nietzsche writes from the perspective of a prophet, and much of the book is taken up with trying to get round the contradiction that this very position is rendered terminally unstable by his own radical demolition of western values. The subtitle suggests it: a book 'for all and none'. As Nietzsche himself observed, where solitude ceases, the market begins, and it is to be doubted that many of the German soldiers going to war with *Zarathustra* in their knapsacks were sensitive to the finer self-modifying points of Zarathustra's message from the mountain. Freud's work with language (his famous case studies though often inconclusive are often celebrated as – a sort of – literary art instead) adopts a different attitude to authority. Here the affective life of patients that has been sidelined by technologies of socialization is given a voice, and, through the interactive mediation of the analyst, which exercises a kind of softened authority, made more compatible with the regularities of objective modern culture. Modernist literature, finally, moves ever closer towards a kind of language use, as we saw, that tricks language into betraying the authority it habitually serves, and speaking, without correction, for the excluded, the outsider, the shamed subject.

4

The Literature of Negation

Man arbeitet heut zu Tag Alles im Menschenfleisch. Das ist der Fluch
unserer Zeit.

(*Dantons Tod*, III, 3)

The Great War

The Naturalists had been intent upon a realist revolution, only to find that
there was no longer a consensus about what reality was. Culture diversified
into competing versions, either claiming this or that reality (*'Heimat'* versus
cosmopolitan urban modernity; *Kultur* versus *Zivilisation*), or, as with the
art for art's sake movement and its commercial penumbra, declaring independence from reality, whatever it was. All this was grist to the mill of
publicity, which actively adumbrated a virtual universe. Public words
gained in immediate impact but lost in secure referential authority. This
was the condition heroically opposed by Karl Kraus, and the reason why
Expressionist literature (as opposed to Expressionism in the plastic and
performance arts) was excited but empty.

The advent of what was once called the Great War changed this because
reality now received a new name (i.e. 'War'), providing a single content for
the previously divergent or detached forms of culture. The Kaiser could
say that he no longer recognized political parties, only Germans; spectacular numbers of people wrote sentimental poetry to express their emotion
at the heroic turn of events; artists and intellectuals of all persuasions
believed they felt the historical earth move. Hyper-efficient mass mobilization seemed to betoken the fusion of industrial technological power and
German *Geist*. It was a perfect Hegelian synthesis. An until-quite-recently
powerless 'interior' (German culture) and a mighty modern ironclad 'exterior' (industry, technology and centralized, rationalized social organization) formed a synthesis in which the latter was to be informed by the
former, for the eventual benefit of Germany and, as Emanuel Geibel had
foretold, the whole civilized world (see chapter 3).

By 1916, it was difficult to sustain without considerable effort the sense that history was going to confirm the Schlieffen plan, let alone the Hegelian plan for the historical trajectory of *Geist*. The initial sense that the meaning of German, or any other, culture, was now manifest in history (and vice versa) became the preserve of political factions, and to this development and related ones we will turn in the next chapter.

The impact of the war on the discourse of Expressionism can be illuminated by the case of August Stramm, one of the linguistically most extreme of the Expressionist lyric poets. It is clear both from his own pronouncements and from the characteristic attitude of the *Sturm* circle in which his writing was encouraged and appreciated that, for all the provocative experimentalism of his lyrics, his aim was affirmative. He wished to develop linguistic means of bypassing consciousness, even the already-coded category of 'experience', and of expressing feelings without any mediation. His pre-war experimentalism lent itself readily to the poetic representation of the clinically traumatic conditions of the Western Front:

> *Sturmangriff*
>
> Aus allen Winkeln gellen Fürchte Wollen
> kreisch
> peitscht
> das Leben
> vor
> sich
> her
> den keuchen Tod
> die Himmel fetzen.
> blinde schlächtert wildum das Entsetzen

> *Storm Attack*
>
> From all corners shriek fears willing
> screech
> whips
> life
> before
> it
> gasp death
> the skies tatter.
> blind slaughters wildabout with terror

In a letter written in March 1915, Stramm expressed his fury at the way journalists, who seldom actually came to the front line, were representing the war for the audience at home. This was a widespread complaint among soldiers. Stylistic and narrative conventions that had worked well enough for the purposes of war reporting in 1870 no longer matched the reality of exponentially increased efficiency in the distribution of men and materials on the one hand, and a war of attrition on the other which 'lacked spatial and geographic markers to which one could attribute beginnings and conclusions' (Natter 1999: 64). Stramm was incensed about the 'pack of lies' he read in the papers, which, he felt, desecrated the magnitude and power of what he was living through at the Front: 'this desecration of everything mighty and great that we are living through here' (quoted in Jordan 1981: 124). The aesthetic and religious diction Stramm uses to convey what the modern language of publicity betrays reveals the traditional assumptions underlying his experimentalism. Significantly, however, he went on to reflect that perhaps it is not just the mendacity of journalists that is exposed by the discrepancy between event and representation, but the mendacity of language itself ('die Lügenhaftigkeit unserer Sprache' [quoted in Jordan 1981: 124]).

In other words, the shocking gap opened up by the war between the lived event and the discourse used to represent it brings the Expressionist Stramm close to the position of language crisis and critique discussed at the end of the previous chapter. This faltering of representation is what Stramm, and many Expressionists, sensed but struggled against in their writing. The war made it historically manifest.

Fort/Dada

1916 was the year in which the cultural event 'Dada' occurred. It was an act of negation. This chapter is called 'The Literature of Negation' because it looks at those elements in literature in German in which the impact of the barbaric surprises of the twentieth century is registered, even if not always directly represented. In relation to these elements, the moment of Dada marks a beginning and immediately also a limit.

Dada is relevant to the cultural history of German literature because its legendary founding performances took place in a German-speaking but neutral city, Zurich, and, while being proudly cosmopolitan, was largely inspired by German individuals (Hugo Ball, Emmy Hennings, Richard Huelsenbeck, Hans Arp and Hans Richter were all Germans opposed to the war; Sophie Taueber was Swiss). They were soon joined by Rumanian publicists Tristan Tzara and Marcel Janco, and many others. Dada became a slogan for the international avant-garde for the subsequent ten years or so. It was thus also a genuinely European event, an example of symbiosis between German and European culture, and, crucially, an effect of revulsion at the war.

Peter Bürger, in his *Theory of the Avant-Garde*, considers the special significance of Dada to lie in the assault it mounted upon what he calls the 'institution of art'. This is a valid way of differentiating the struggles of the Expressionists to express themselves from the seismic impact of the war, which crystallized and confirmed for culture the possibility of (indeed, the need for) significant negation. What the Dadaists objected to in Stramm, for instance, seeing in him less a precursor (he was killed in September 1915) and more a subject for parody, is that, for all the splintered immediacy of this diction, it is still based on the assumption that there is such a thing as a unified self to have feelings, an underlying historical narrative in which meaning, by extreme efforts of language, might be discerned, and a practice (or 'institution') of art in which these ambitions to capture and convey experience are justified and feasible.

If it is legitimate to liken pre-war Expressionism, as I did in the previous chapter, to an animal roaring in a cage (in other words, dependent upon the institution of the zoo, funding, and a civilized public in order to appear to threaten all those things), then Dada wanted to let the beast free.

Like explaining a joke, there is something self-defeating in rehearsing the antics of the Dadaists. An excellent account of them, and the implications of giving such an account, can be found in Greil Marcus's history of punk, *Lipstick Traces*. In one of cultural history's most memorable sound bites Dada announced that Art was Shit, and, in saying it, (de)posited its own cultural performance as something else, something taking place outside Art ('shitting in several colours'). The unplanned destruction of a significant proportion of the young male population of Europe that was taking place at the same time was also happening outside the frame of the institutions bearing responsibility for leadership and government in what had appeared a flourishing and progressive modern civilization. The event of Dada and the event of the Western Front were both meaningless in a strong sense, significant negations, and the former 'expressed' the latter in the way in which, according to Nietzsche in Section Nine of *Die Geburt der Tragödie*, Sophoclean heroes expressed the tragic core of existence, as 'radiant patches [...] to heal a gaze seared by gruesome night' (trans. Speirs; Geuss and Speirs 1999).

Bürger's argument about an avant-garde end to the bourgeois institution of art, which he equates too narrowly with aestheticism and the philosophical catchphrase 'autonomy of art', while claiming to define a sociological mutation, is curiously blind to the defining impact of the war. In fact, the integrated institution of German literature as distinct from the other arts came apart, as we saw, in, or at the latest, after Naturalism. The stylistic and political divergences that ensued were only apparently overcome by the supervening 'reality' of the advent of war. Very soon, reality revealed itself as a negating effect in relation to the existing plurality of resources for representation. This in turn brought about the urgent need to find new resources or reaffirm the old ones. The pre-existing divergent factions within what once had been an 'institution' (and enjoyed the recognition and influence of institutions) were thereby significantly amplified, although their authority in society at large was diminished (see chapters 5 and 6).

Dada's founding moment of refusal, lost in unrecorded performances at the Cabaret Voltaire, and recalled only in endless anecdotes, memoirs and increasingly tedious reruns, could not last by definition without becoming self-defeatingly familiar. Yet it was still a deeply significant intervention in culture. Sigmund Freud's thoughts at the time of the war offer a way of explaining the importance of Dada.

In 1915, Freud wrote an essay called 'Zeitgemäßes über Krieg und Tod' ('Reflections on Death and War'), in which he said that, while illusion is necessary for socialized existence for all sorts of reasons, it can become counter-productive when, as in the surprise return of barbarism among the peoples of culture, it leads to disappointment of a severity that threatens to be disabling for individuals and the nations of culture alike. His recommendation is that we should move a little closer to the primitive familiarity with death, which persists, he says, unaffected by history and civilization, in the unconscious mind and which emerges in time of war, as if the advances of culture had never happened. With the closing words of the essay he prescribes a dose of death if one is to face life as it has revealed itself again in history: 'If you wish to endure life, prepare for death.'

Exactly how Freud thought one might do this was not clear from the 1915 essay. However, by 1920, when *Jenseits des Lustprinzips* (*Beyond the Pleasure Principle*) was published, he had adjusted the model of the mind upon which the socio-medical practice of psychoanalysis was based to include an admixture of death. Affected by medical evidence from soldiers traumatized by modern warfare, Freud proposed that the instinctual economy of the psyche was based not only on Eros and survival instincts, the life-affirming drives, but that folded within these, and refracted in the various circumstances of an individual life, death was active as the individual's deepest instinctual orientation. In other words, he was administering the dose of death for which he had expressed the need in 1915.

One of the main clues to the existence of a drive beyond the pleasure principle and its derivatives was the existence of a compulsion to repeat that could not be explained by pleasure, since what patients were repeating was unambiguously unpleasurable. And one of the main clues to the existence of this role of repetition in the socialized life and identity of human beings (and not just in the mental damage sustained by trench survivors) was what is now universally called the 'Fort/Da' game. This was a game Freud reported observing his infant grandson play, in which the little boy throws away and retrieves a cotton reel attached to a piece of string, accompanying his actions with the words 'fort' ('gone') and 'da' (there'). The reason this practice of repetition seemed to Freud to be a piece of evidence in support of a major new dimension to the economy of the psyche beyond the pleasure principle was that it could be read as the repeated enactment of loss ('gone') in order to make it endurable by the individual subject. The absence of the mother, in which the individual subject comes to consciousness of himself as a separate entity through suffering and irrecuperable loss, is built into a rhythm of experience upon which a coherent and viable self can be based.

Freud tended to have a traditional view of aesthetic pleasure and explicitly denies, at the end of the second section of *Jenseits des Lustprinzips*, that the Fort/Da game (which is not played for spectators) can be seen as the model for the paradoxical pleasure derived by adults from tragic representations. Since I see a link between Dada, on the cultural level, and Fort/Da on the individual, Freud's aesthetic view cannot be squared with my parallel, earlier, between Dada and Sophocles. The answer to this is that the parallel was between Nietzsche's Sophocles and Dada, and Nietzsche, although also culturally pre-modern, is as we saw emphatically a precursor of that Modernism that responds to the need to find a new mask for the inevitable universality of suffering.

Nietzsche's ruminations upon the aesthetic, touched by the all-dissolving energy of Dionysus, as the only justification of life, and Freud's on the Death Drive (whether you believe him or not), are both attempts to help a disappointed enlightened modernity cope with hard truths once given meaning by religion. Until the Holocaust, the Western Front was the hardest truth European civilization had had to confront. Dada demonstrated in cultural practice how to administer a homeopathic dosage of negation in the interest of the survival of culture: 'man sagt ja zu einem Leben das durch Verneinung höher will. Ja-sagen – Nein-sagen:

das gewaltige Hokuspokus des Daseins beschwingt die Nerven des echten Dadaisten ...' ('one says yes to a life with the will to go higher through negation. Yes-saying – no-saying, the mighty hocus-pocus of existence excites the nerves of the genuine Dadaist') wrote Huelsenbeck in the Berlin manifesto of 1918. This is the twentieth-century version of the 'profound shallowness' Nietzsche attributed to the ancient Greeks in the foreword to *Die fröhliche Wissenschaft*.

The broken subject

Dada was publicity taken to an extreme. Huelsenbeck had been contemptuous of the Expressionists' disdain for the press and advertising, and what he and his companions were doing was openly acknowledging the very rivalry for public attention that, implicitly, had driven, and continued to drive, a lot of the old-world Wilhelmine Expressionist pathos.

Far from putting an end to 'aestheticism' as Bürger argued, the establishment of a radically oppositional practice of culture created the environment in which the historically most finely attuned aspects of modern literature, to whit language consciousness and a sense of the divided nature of the human subject, could enter public consciousness with a new weight.

Our argument is that it was the war that gave these things historical substance and created the need for their public acknowledgement. It brought out in events tendencies that pre-existed it. This was particularly true of the crisis in the relationship between subjectivity and technology. Ernst Jünger, about whom we will have more to say below, wrote of the experience of modern warfare: 'Da merkt man erst, wie wenig man in sich zu Hause ist' ('That's when a man realizes how little he is at home in himself'; quoted in Theweleit 1977–8: I, 307). This is exactly the experience of Rilke's *Malte*. We have seen how Stramm was brought to a sense of language crisis in the manner of Lord Chandos by the widely held perception that there was an unacceptable mismatch between lived events at the Front and their public appropriation. In Rilke and Hofmannsthal, these tendencies were masked by what Bürger would call 'aestheticism' (but nonetheless real for that). Expressionism was dedicated to a high public profile, but philosophically affirmative, haplessly positive. Dada staked out the public space for this 'negative' finding in art.

Franz Kafka (1883–1924) was to become the most internationally acknowledged and influential writer of German Modernism. Although he became famous as the author of the unfinished novels *Der Proceß* (*The Trial*, published in 1925) and *Das Schloß* (*The Castle*, published in 1926), his skill was perhaps best suited to the short form; the parable, the anecdote, the paradoxical aphorism. This conciseness was an important element in his subsequent global and epochal resonance: Kafka is short enough to be read and 'understood' in the modern world of metropolitan shocks and banal distractions. Yet there are profounder reasons also.

If we are to believe the gist of Gustav Janouch's account of his conversation with Kafka on the matter, he would have been surprised to be identified as a post-Dada writer. Janouch reports that Kafka thought their activities 'ein Gebrechen', a word that can mean moral weakness or physical infirmity, and that occurs in one of the most famous quotations in all German literature in which Goethe glosses the substance of his *Iphigenie auf Tauris*: 'alle menschlichen Gebrechen sühnet reine Menschlichkeit' ('pure humanity atones for all human weaknesses'). Kafka, according to Janouch, went on to opine that the fact of Dada was a sign of the times: 'Der geistige Rückgrat ist geknickt. Der Glaube ist gebrochen' ('The spiritual spine is bent. Belief is broken'; Janouch 1951: 97).

But this proves our point. Whether Kafka said these things or not (Janouch's account is not reliable), what is clear is that he cannot align himself with the moral and aesthetic authority that speaks so clearly through the celebrated line just quoted. He finds himself on the side of the 'broken' subject (Kafka himself, as remembered by Janouch, made the etymological link between 'Gebrechen' and 'gebrochen'). He does not have the benefit of access to pure redemptive humanity. In this sense, he is on the side of Dada.

In another anecdote, Janouch conveys the ambivalent reluctance with which Kafka entered the published world at all. On receiving his author's copy of one of his stories, he explained that it was his friends, and especially Max Brod, who were behind the publication. I am too weak and too polite to prevent them, said Kafka, and so things are published that were really only meant as private: 'personal evidence of my human weakness ... documents of my solitude' ('persönliche Belege meiner menschlichen Schwäche ... Zeugnisse meiner Einsamkeit' [Janouch 1951: 48]). It is the same legend that surrounds Kafka's whole oeuvre: it was supposed to be destroyed on his death by the author's executor, Brod again, but instead came to the world, as it were, negated by its author.

In both cases, no doubt, Kafka was being disingenuous. Janouch has him say as much in the next paragraph. But there is something symptomatic about the image of Brod, the Expressionist publicist, taking responsibility for turning documents of negation into literature.

The just-published story involved in Janouch's anecdote was 'In der Strafkolonie' ('In the Penal Colony'), which was published in 1914. It illustrates how Kafka's 'weakness' was really the function of being situated 'outside' the institutions of authority whose function had been to confer strength. These institutions collapsed on the Western Front, where their technological might imploded. What Kafka's parable explores is an analogous mutation in the relation between technology, subjectivity and language.

An explorer visits a 'punishment colony', to give a literal translation of the title, the exact location and purpose of which is, as is typical for Kafka, not given. French is spoken there (though not by all) and there is rationalized colonial brutality in the air, but naturalistic details in Kafka do not add up to Naturalism. Instead, they make it strange, creating an uncanny sense of unfamiliarity by virtue of their decontextualized precision. The story concerns an apparatus, a machine, described in circumstantial detail, the purpose of which is to embody the execution of justice, by physically inscribing the words of the transgression for which the condemned criminal must make penance, on his back. The torment lasts twelve hours, but after six of them the victim in the machine comes to understand the words, the inscription of which upon his back is slowly killing him, and has an experience of redemption. At this point, in other words, he grasps the meaning of his suffering and this is enough, as Nietzsche had said, to make suffering bearable. The story goes on to relate, however, that the apparatus neither works properly any longer nor is it securely embedded in the regime of the colony. Its only surviving advocate, who is also the source of the narrator and the reader's knowledge of the apparatus and its history, recognizing this, climbs into the machine himself and is destroyed by it, but without experiencing the promised redemption. Not only by this, but by the story as a whole, the reader is left bemused and perhaps resembles the explorer, who, not surprisingly, has felt acutely uncomfortable about his whole visit and at the end can only make a swift getaway in a state of moral bewilderment.

It is hard to imagine a more graphic parable for the suffering of which Nietzsche (and Schopenhauer) spoke as the basic experience of individuated human particulars against the ground of the *bellum omnium contra omnes*, a suffering for which there was now the want of a meaning. But Kafka's writing turned the deficit in meaning to aesthetic advantage.

First, his writing specifies how the suffering of human beings is dialectically inseparable from the very meaning which came about in order to alleviate it in the first place. We now see language as a metonym for the technology of all human institutions, from outside, as it were; a gruesome secularized apparatus that mangles the individual subject to no moral or metaphysical purpose.

But, second, Kafka's text is open to the abject, marginal, creaturely and defeated. A new solidarity is created between explorer and reader in their moral perplexity. Like the soldiers at the Front, as it is reported, who formed very deep bonds of affection with one another precisely because the objective institutions had failed and abandoned them ('we're here because we're here because we're here'), Kafka's texts offer incomprehension, paradox, as a starting point for a new form of shared cultural experience.

Kafka is the pivotal figure for the idea of a Literature of Negation because his mode of writing and the cultural exchange implied was effective not just in relation to the negation embodied in the First World War but to that embodied in the Holocaust as well. This is precisely because he wrote from the midst of the ruins of the nineteenth-century psycho-social order, and, once he hit his stride, and despite his hesitation about emerging into a sphere of publicity that he may well have felt was still informed by that order, he wrote from that place of desolation with assurance and artistic skill.

The moment at which this assured discourse emerged from the wreck of the old form of paternal authority is famously recorded in his diary entry on the morning in 1912 after he had stayed up all night writing 'Das Urteil' ('The Judgement'): 'Nur so kann geschrieben werden, nur in einem solchen Zusammenhang, mit solcher vollständigen Öffnung des Leibes und der Seele' ('Only in this way can writing be done, only with such coherence, with such a complete opening out of the body and the soul'; 23 September 1912).

Dominick LaCapra, one of the most intelligent and balanced writers on the formidable difficulties entailed by representation of the Holocaust (whether in theory, history or art), explains how it is beset by two symmetrically opposed hazards. On one side, there is what nowadays is called the danger of 'normalization', in relation to which the traumatic rupture of civilization is smoothed over and becomes part of continuous narrative, and therefore, however terrible the story, less problematic, less intractable and less morally challenging. On the other side, there is the problem of celebrating, as it were, unsayability, falling in love with the symptoms of trauma and 'sugar-coating' what cannot be incorporated into continuous narrative (LaCapra 1994: 198–200).

Kafka avoided this double-bind because he knew nothing about the Holocaust. The historical context of this illogical and anachronistic claim is to be found in the details of the fate of his sisters: Gabriele ('Elli') (1889–1941), Valerie ('Valli') (1890–1942) and Ottilie ('Ottla') (1892–1943). Kafka himself died of tuberculosis of the larynx in 1924. His sisters' dates of death reflect the fact that they and their families, as Jews, were taken away by the Nazis and died somewhere in the unredeemed reality of the Holocaust.

'Das Urteil' (like almost all of Kafka's mature writing) positions readers between the authority of a father who is dying, and the inability of the writing subject to succeed him and assume, or take up his place in, the same structure of authority. When Kafka had finished writing it, in his euphoric and presumably sleep-deprived state, he went through to his sisters' room to read it out to them, as he tells us in his diary. Reading to them (whether his own work or that of others, for instance Franz Grillparzer's *Novelle, Der arme Spielmann* [*The Poor Fiddler*]) clearly meant something special to him. It suggests to us a writing of self-exposure, touched by the asocial intimacy of incestuous desire, a testimony to the absence of shelter once provided by fathers. It is the consummation of Hölderlin and Rilke's dreams of the poetic language without a 'third person'. His writing is the bodying forth of the collapse of a certain order of meaning, namely one that can be passed on from father (whether Freud or Zarathustra) to son.

The authority that killed his sisters and their families, and would have taken him too had he survived, was of a different order. As Theweleit suggested in his justly famous study of the writing of members of the fascist Freikorps (see chapter 5 below), it was an authority born of pathological terror of intimacy that, likewise, came about with the collapse of the old, protective patriarchal system. As depicted in *In der Strafkolonie*, it was a pure physical mangling, an operation of technology untouched by the spirit of love or reason.

Although Kafka was not unknown before the 1940s (W. H. Auden claimed in 1941 that he captured the spirit of the times much as Dante, Shakespeare, Goethe had of theirs), his worldwide fame began among French existentialists and US and émigré academics in the late 1940s and 1950s. We would argue that this post-war appeal can be attributed to the 1912 'breakthrough' moment, in which Kafka found the way to write about something that, because it was so terrible, would be gravely difficult if not impossible to address by those who did know about it without falling into the traps so lucidly set out by LaCapra. By a small miracle of literary history, a German-speaking Jew had found the right homeopathic treatment for a civilization in dire need of help in coming to terms with its boundless 'disappointment' with itself, as Freud had mildly put it when speaking about the First World War.

Fascist negation

Before 1933, writers on both the left and the right of the political spectrum in Germany produced work which can be classified as 'Literature of Negation' in the sense we are using it here. On the right, the most important figure was Ernst Jünger (1895–1998) who, perceiving the need to reconfigure radically the damaged relationship between man and machine, saw the war as the forcing ground of a new kind of mechanized human subject.

Jünger's writing springs from his exceptionally distinguished military service, and there is no doubt that his experience of the war was that of a negation of the institutions of civilized Europe. For that reason, his work belongs in this chapter. His is an anomalous case, however, because much of his famous early writing, for instance *In Stahlgewittern* (*Storm of Steel*, 1920) and *Feuer und Blut* (*Fire and Blood*, 1925), directly describes the war, rather than matching negation with negation as the Dadaists had done or adumbrating modes of writing of the sorts that creatively avoid direct representation of modern technologized combat in recognition of the inability of realism or Naturalism to do justice to it. Jünger recognized this difficulty perfectly but derived aesthetic gain from it, since to render the experience as it happened was to challenge the submerged conventions within the superficially 'natural' style of realism. He turned the collapse of civilized values into a programme for renewal.

Jünger was certainly not alone in his view that democratic regimes were out of touch with the core truths of existence, although there may not have been many who felt as genuinely as he did that this core was tragic. But there can have been no other author – indeed, Jünger is a unique embarrassment in German literary culture, as a writer whose Modernism and whose fascism are integral to one another – who applied Nietzsche so literally as to see in the limit situations (*Grenzsituationen*) of the Western Front the aesthetic revelation of the way forward.

At the end of the second essay (in §24) of *Zur Genealogie der Moral*, Nietzsche reflects upon what kind of person would be strong enough to affirm the instincts against the habits of self-denial embedded by millennia of repression: 'For this purpose, we would need a different sort of spirit than those we are likely to come across in this age: spirits which are strengthened by wars and victories, for which conquest, daring, danger and even pain have actually become a necessity ...' It is exactly this sort of person that Jünger, in his idiosyncratic fusion of autobiography and poetic narrative, imagined. He felt that he and his surviving fellows had come through something in the trenches of the Western Front that made of them candidates for Zarathustra's approval. Even if, of course, 'victory' had been denied them, this was scarcely relevant since, as he said in the foreword to *In Stahlgewittern*, the struggle itself had been 'übermenschlich' ('superhuman', picking up Nietzsche's famous term 'Übermensch'), and the old world, the world Nietzsche had hated and wished dead, had now destroyed itself in fact.

A significant addition to Nietzsche's programme in Jünger is the importance he attaches to technology. If language consciousness is indeed, as we argued in the previous chapter, literary culture's attempt to grasp the impact of technology upon subjectivity, then Jünger saw in the hypertrophy of technology disclosed by the war the opportunity for a radical solution to the problem. He argued that the war was the expression of the domination of machine over man, of the slave over the master. The triumph of machines over values provided Jünger with a historical realization of the fallen state of civilization, as Nietzsche had seen it, but thus also objective circumstances in which Nietzsche's new kind of post-human subjectivity could come about. Like Dada, but unlike the Expressionists, Jünger acknowledged the moment of negation immanent in the war by siding with the very technology that had destroyed the civilization that developed and used it.

The way Jünger seized this opportunity was to a significant extent a literary one. His writing rises to the challenge by means of extreme stylistic impassivity. This is exemplified in the deadpan way in which physical mutilation is described, a documentary exactitude that would previously have been considered inappropriate in literature. The account of the physical effects of modern warfare, he reasoned, were only repugnant to those who were themselves afraid of pain and wished to turn away from the universality of suffering that Jünger, with Nietzsche, saw at the core of existence. Jünger creates a discourse that provides a new aesthetic for this invigorating reality of pain. Like the war itself, its meaning resides in toughening individual subjects 'like steel in a furnace'. Precisely by dint of the now manifest inhumanity of modern technology, the false humanity of the bourgeois age can be surpassed. In Jünger's idiom, the war is not dressed up in anachronistic tropes of heroism and chivalry but nevertheless affirmed and transcended. The post-human subject trumps the machine by becoming machine-like itself.

In challenging language to shed its complicity with psychology, Jünger contributes to the Literature of Negation in a significant way. His revision of what it means to be a subject is in its way as radical as that of other writers. His attitude departs from the cultural strategy of negation, however, when he reads the negation brought by the war to nineteenth-century civilization as something that is susceptible to conceptualization as positive. What he and the like-minded colleagues with whom he published the volume *War and the Warrior*, reviewed in 1930 by Walter Benjamin in a piece headed 'Theories of German Fascism', posited as the 'worldly-real' was 'real' in the sense that it showed the precariousness of human institutions (see Benjamin 1979).

Dada indicated the contemporary failure of institutions by making an intervention, as Peter Bürger argued, at the level of the institution of art. Insofar as the negation they enacted was more than a negation, a 'da' as well as a 'fort', it was such on the level of culture, and it had a powerful revivifying, even transformative, effect upon the institution it attacked. Jünger went far beyond literature in the construction he placed upon the historical negative that was his starting point. In his reflections, he projected his compensatory aesthetic pattern or form (*Gestaltung*) into social and political praxis. He went on to develop a whole theory of the mechanization or total mobilization of society. To see the (negative) tragic core as the orientation point of public affairs is to seek 'inside the political and economic arrangements of a society that which man must face outside organized society, alone)' (Stern 1953: 40). What Jünger 'is groping to express is life on the other side of individuation' (Stern 1953: 40), that is to say, he wishes to base a programme of social and political reform on the aesthetic of the Dionysian. While these concerns are at the heart of serious modern literature, as we understand it, J. P. Stern was surely right to insist that they have no place in the theory and practice of social or political institutions.

One could disparage this sagely as a category mistake on Jünger's part if it were not so close to the fascist ideology that became political fact in Germany in 1933. Jünger himself, though ideologically a fascist, did not align himself with the Nazis. His version of the 'negative sublime' of Front experience and its representation, which for him was the threshold to the brave new world, is not the same as that invoked by Himmler in his notorious and appalling Posen speech. Himmler praised the ability of the SS Officers whom he was addressing to witness (indeed commit) the mass murder of Jews and still remain 'anständig' ('decent'). As in Jünger, this experience of the negation of social behaviour, said Himmler, had served to toughen the soldiers and make them equal to their historical task. Jünger's programme was neither anti-Semitic nor banal. Nor was it monstrously uncaring; indeed, it proposed that the sublime encounter with mass destruction should potentiate a new order in which, in some sense, those who died are redeemed. Like Nietzsche, he identifies with the suffering for which he seeks to find a compelling modern meaning.

Nevertheless, Jünger is an important warning of how questionable it is to draw an analogy between a quasi-religious view of, in Dominick LaCapra's words, 'apocalyptic conversion' and any political and social practice. 'The view that only by acting excess out to the end (or succumbing to the abyss) can one reach the end of excess or attain the heights' (LaCapra 1994: 15) is a dangerous aestheticization of public life, and the danger extends to literature, which is part of public life. The Literature of Negation can only function as a homeopathic dosage of death if it does not encourage us to fall in love with our own symptoms or lead us to believe that cultural practice and social practice are not categorically distinct.

Negation in the dialectic

On the left, Erwin Piscator (1893–1966), alongside Bertolt Brecht (1898–1956) the most celebrated theatrical innovator of the Weimar Republic, dated his theatrical mission from his experience of the Western Front and, as a corollary, from his association with the Dadaists, from whom he learned what radical negation in the arts might mean. He went on to create a practice of political theatre which, in its disregard for the importance of the individual author, emphatically denies that it is art and only marginally qualifies as 'literature'. Although in those ways it has aspects of negation, it nevertheless moves more in the direction of journalism, information, propaganda, political rally, which is why we shall return to him under the heading of 'medial hybridity' in chapter 6.

Brecht himself, as we will argue, also fits more naturally under the heading of medial hybridity as it impacted upon literature in the Weimar Republic, exile and the Federal Republic, to which we turn in chapter 6. However, towards the end of the 1920s and in the early 1930s, as he moved towards explicit support for the revolutionary cause, he left what David Bathrick calls the market-media 'buffer-zone' that, in capitalist democracies, separates the artist from state power (Bathrick 1995: 231), approaching the icy region where the system to come impinges upon the system in place, as its 'outside'. Heiner Müller (1929–1995), Brecht's problematic heir in the DDR, to whom we turn in a moment, put it like this in the

'Anmerkung' ('Note') that he appended to his play *Mauser* (1970): 'SO THAT SOMETHING CAN COME SOMETHING MUST GO THE FIRST SHAPE OF HOPE IS FEAR THE FIRST MANIFESTATION OF THE NEW IS TERROR' (Müller 1976). This is thus the attempt aesthetically to instrumentalize 'negation', acknowledging it as radical historical reality (the French Revolution, the First World War, fascism), but mobilizing its affinity with death in order to enhance the 'life' of that which will replace it historically. Out of the collapse of the old and the horrors that will necessarily accompany such a collapse comes the redemption of a new social order.

Brecht's activity in the early 1930s was radical in that it broke with his earlier strategy of subverting from within the contemporary entertainment idiom (as with *Mahagonny* [1927 and 1930] or the *Dreigroschenoper* [1928]). This strategy was hard to distinguish from sophisticated, cynical entertainment. In the politically polarized circumstances of the end of the Weimar period, Brecht and his co-workers moved right outside the bourgeois institutions of entertainment or information and aimed to induct individuals into a new collective identity. The theatre became a rehearsal site for the revolution itself.

In the Federal Republic, Brecht's scattered theoretical remarks concerning this kind of theatre, which he had called 'Lehrstück' ('learning theatre'), became a 1960s rallying point. An influential book by the academic Reiner Steinweg (1972a) argued that Brecht had been working on a kind of theatre so radical as to eliminate the role of spectator altogether. Heiner Müller in the DDR took up this theoretical resurrection of (palpably unsuccessful) pre-revolutionary practice and thought about how to apply it in the post-revolutionary situation. Once that situation ceased to feel as if it had much to do with revolution one way or another, Müller wrote to Steinweg to say that he was renouncing the experiment 'until the next earthquake' (quoted in Wright 1989: 125).

The most unequivocally communist, pro-Soviet and controversial production with which Brecht was associated was the oratorio *Die Maßnahme* (*The Measures Taken*; but there have been many translations of this title), co-written with the avant-garde communist composer Hanns Eisler, a pupil of Schoenberg and Webern. It was conceived as a contribution to a festival of new music in 1930, but rejected, probably on political grounds, although it would not have been appropriate to admit this. It became instead a more explicitly political event, involving a choir of over 400 voices drawn from the German Workers Choral Movement and others. It was a spectacular evening; a mirage of what socialist high art would look and sound like.

The action represented by *Die Maßnahme* can be summarized brutally as follows: it is the enactment of the liquidation of a young agitator by his comrades for the greater good of the revolutionary cause. The anti-bourgeois frisson of the earlier play, *Mann ist Mann* (1926), in which a character is dismantled and reassembled like a motor car, is pushed here to the extreme point at which the entertaining, knowing frisson transforms into a threat to the bourgeois world as such, becoming a kind of cultural terrorism.

At the same time, and here we see a difference between Brecht and the consistent propagandist Piscator, Brecht and Eisler's extraordinary work was bad propaganda and recognized as such by the party functionaries. The reason for this is that the aesthetic values of the representation at certain points go beyond what is required for propaganda. Brecht and Eisler dwell upon the negation more than necessary for party political purposes.

The most remarkable moments in the oratorio have to do with the putting on and taking off of masks (a device used brilliantly within a more conventional format in the play *Der gute Mensch von Sezuan* [*The Good Person of Setzuan*, 1943]). In order to understand the force of these passages, it is necessary to recall that the motif of the death of an innocent individual had its origin in a fifteenth-century Japanese No play, an English translation of which Brecht's co-worker, Elisabeth Hauptmann, came across and trans-lated into German in 1928. The stylized ritual of the traditional Japanese theatre provided an edge of contrast to European character-based theatre of identification, leading to the devising of two stylized learning plays, *Der Jasager* and *Der Neinsager* (*The Yes-Sayer* and *The No-Sayer* [1930]). *Die Maßnahme* is an alloy of this non-European style with a more or less specific naturalism: the action is now set in what is presumably the Soviet Union in roughly 1919, where four agitators, having returned from a successful propaganda mission to China, appear before the central control commis-sion of the Party in order to justify the killing of their comrade.

The action concerns the excessive sympathy displayed by this young comrade, who is unable to restrain himself from intervening to help the oppressed. The reason he must be killed is that, by blowing his own cover and that of his fellow *agents provocateurs*, he endangers the long-term consciousness-raising exercise that will eventually permit the Chinese to liberate themselves. The message is thus perfectly clear, if provocatively brutal.

The fault line between old-style bourgeois individual feeling and new-style collective identification is indicated by the donning of masks (in the scene called 'Die Auslöschung' ['The Obliteration']), which naturalistically is a step into disguise and stylistically a move from one form of theatre (the traditional European one) into an unfamiliar, ritualistic one (the Japanese No play). This scene is affecting in itself but its resonance is only complete when, in the climactic moment of the drama, the young comrade removes his mask ('Der Verrat' ['The Betrayal']) in a gesture that, given the context, has the effect of exposing the human individual, finding means, by switching back from the unfamiliar idiom to the familiar one, 'defamiliarizing' it, or showing it from the outside. As Brecht put it, talking about all the learning plays, 'individual or unique characters don't occur in these plays, except in the case where the individuality or the uniqueness itself is the learning problem.' (quoted in Steinweg 1972b: 252). Here a character, who is absent by the ordinary conventions of European drama (in other words is impersonated by an actor), and is doubly absent because he is only ever represented by his comrade/killers, becomes unbearably present: 'and we looked and in the half-light we saw his naked face, human, open and guileless.'

These words are marvellously poised and far too ambiguous for the uses of propaganda, since the three attributes mentioned are all bad and good at the same time, especially the first, 'menschlich'. 'Der Mensch' at once evokes Enlightenment universality, behind which the capitalists hide their own interests and the ultimate goal of the revolution; as Heiner Müller put it in the play we discuss below, *Mauser*, with characteristic brutal irony: 'Ein Mensch ist etwas, in das man hineinschiesst / Bis der Mensch aufsteht aus den Trümmern des Menschen' ('A human is something to shoot into / Until the human rises out of the ruins of the human'; Müller 1976: 140–1). The life of the young comrade flickers between two realities that are mutually exclusive in these concrete circumstances: his own embodied existence and the social and political challenges that face humanity.

The final turn in the representation of negation comes in the scene of the actual execution ('Die Grablegung' ['The Burial']). The young comrade does not go to his death before he has declared himself 'einverstanden' ('consenting', 'acquiescent') with his fate. He thus confirms the message of the play and commits himself to the collective, even though his own life is sacrificed to it. But Brecht's anti-bourgeois style of staging assumes a surprisingly deep meaning. Because the young comrade has only ever been present as acted out for the benefit of the control chorus by the agitators, it is now possible – and this is what the stage directions require – for him quite literally to disappear in the embrace of his killers. The self-conscious alienated style of the performance (the acting of a character by other characters) comes to body forth the passage back of the 'dead' individual into the living collective.

Perhaps most powerful of all is the repetition of the party slogan, '... saying "yes" to the revolutionizing of the world', as it had been spoken in a triumphalist context, after the initial masking sequence. Now they are the young comrade's dying words, they are what revolutionary history has written on his body. The bitter ambiguity of the repetition is poised between triumph and emptiness; the negation swings together with the affirmation in an aesthetic ambiguity that exceeds the needs of propaganda but expresses the pathos of revolution.

The young comrade's *Einverständnis* with his own destruction indicates that this play is written against the horizon of a post-revolutionary future. The negation is given a historical meaning (it is the end of bourgeois capitalism) which entails a positive, embodied, equally concretely, in the Soviet Union and the Comintern's project to bring proletarian revolution to the workers of the world. Heiner Müller has a claim to being the only genuine artistic heir to Brecht, in the sense of one who is both concretely identified with the communist cause and a serious, radically innovative dramatic artist. But, as a citizen of the DDR he did not enjoy the same perspective in relation to either the Soviet Union or the future.

Like Brecht, Müller rewrote and adapted material. So too with *Die Maßnahme* which Müller reworked for the new circumstances as *Mauser* (1970). As he was to say in 1980, 'Brecht zu gebrauchen, ohne ihn zu kritisieren, ist Verrat' ('To use Brecht uncritically is to betray him'; Müller 1982: 149). Müller's text is still conceived as a learning play but it aspires to be truer to the idea of the learning play than Brecht had himself been. By achieving even greater abstraction, he hoped to increase the concrete, historical yield in consciousness for those involved with it, and therefore work in a more truly dialectical way. This emphasis upon process rather than outcome was the result of the fact that the play was not written against a post-revolutionary horizon but in a post-revolutionary present in which the horizon threatened to vanish behind historical circumstances. As the chorus says near the end of *Mauser*: 'Nicht eh die Revolution gesiegt hat endgültig [...] Werden wir wissen, was das ist, der Mensch' ('not until the revolution has triumphed finally [...] will we know what that is, a human').

The most striking variation Müller makes is that the central protagonist or subject of his drama is not 'einverstanden' with his liquidation. As with the Brecht/Eisler oratorio, the action is filtered through a tribunal performed by a chorus. This ritual aspect once again conveys the sense of a collective defining its own moral consciousness. In the play's abstract idiom, character B (conveniently Brecht's initial) has been eradicated for the trangression of pity, as in the original, while Müller's version concerns the example of the executioners.

Character A is such an executioner 'licensed to kill' in the service of the revolutionary struggle. He, however, has transgressed in two distinct ways, neither of which resembles the sentimental weakness of Brecht's young comrade or character B. First, he has desensitized himself too much, identifying himself with the machinery of death, the 'Mauser' of the title (a make of pistol), and becoming a 'killing machine' reminiscent of Brecht's hero Galy Gay in *Mann ist Mann*. Realizing this, character A asks to be relieved of this duty, but is refused since the revolution continues to require his services. Thereupon he finds excessive delight in the killing, identifying with his task in a way that affirms cruelty beyond moral consciousness, simply as a bodily experience. For this sadism he is condemned by the tribunal. This excess goes in the direction of Antonin Artaud's hugely influential Theatre of Cruelty, an avant-garde theatre based on a mode of a perfomance which 'cruelly' strips off the defences and pretences of socialized existence.

Character A must be eradicated because he cannot maintain himself within the zone of collective consciousness that distinguishes between means and ends. What makes this consciousness so precarious is that it has no clear sense of the end of the brutal region through which it must pass. The moment of 'negation' in Brecht's learning plays had still been offset by the promise of revolutionary emancipation (in other words, the negation was legible as the catastrophic collapse of capitalism). In the reality of the DDR, with the experience of the Holocaust and Stalinism to contend with theoretically, negation now regains an ahistorical resistance which can only be overcome, if at all, when it becomes understood that the integration of the individual subject in the collective cause cannot proceed without loss. The function of such drama in the DDR would then recall the Freudian notion that societies sometimes require a dosage of 'death' if they are to be able to live with the disappointment inseparable from the inevitability of illusion.

If we return, thus, to our account of the First World War as the 'moment' of negation to which culture responds with a negation of its own, Müller, more than the Brecht of the *Lehrstücke*, was addressing the fundamental truth laid bare by the Great War: that there is a lack of fit in modernity between technology and human suffering. This truth seems, of course, all the more difficult to overlook after the monumental cynicism of the

Holocaust and Stalin. The 'development of industrial production, technology, and science', it now seemed to those on the left, did not 'inevitably lead to the emancipation of society as a whole' (Bathrick 1995: 226). This is the significance of character A's inability to integrate the roles of *Mauser* revolver and Artaudian-Nietzschean asocial desire-bomb.

Put at its most abstract, the technology of socialization will always be written into the flesh of the embodied individual. This is not the only affinity between Müller's Literature of Negation and that of Kafka. The position from which Müller was writing resembled the kind of position Kafka described by his figures of negation. Müller, in his unsuccessful attempts at artistic dialogue with power became 'a performer of his own abjection' (Bathrick 1995: 233). Kafka, Jünger and Müller all write during a dark night of the soul: belief tested beyond despair in order to found the redemptive moment, as in the story of Abraham and Isaac. For Kafka this belief was some variant of theology, for Jünger some variant of Nietzsche, for Müller some variant of Marx.

The core belief of the hard-nosed *Mauser* is surprisingly sentimental to twenty-first century post-Cold War ears: 'Der Mensch ist mehr als seine Arbeit' ('a human is more than his work'). The connection of the word 'Arbeit' with the 'job' of killing in the discourse of the play makes this assertion into the clear expression of a hope beyond the negation, a dialectic in the material. The cynical morality that prevails in capitalist democracy (see chapter 6) is hard put to it to say what the 'mehr' might consist in (leisure?).

The chorus goes on: 'Oder er wird nicht sein' ('Or he will not be'). For Müller, more than for the early 1930s Brecht, the negation remains properly implacable. What is implied is either apocalypse as a result of the hypertrophy of technology, an outcome only the optimistic or the complacent will even today rule out completely, or less apocalyptically, simply that the pathos of 'der Mensch' as something distinct is finally played out. For contemporary information theorists and neuroscientists, human beings are indeed functions of technological systems, and none the worse for that. It is some consolation that character A, like Brecht's amoral post-Romantic hero Baal (versions 1919, 1922, 1926, 1930), experiences no diminution in the will to live simply because there is no meaning to inform it with shape and direction. This is the force of his refusal to acquiesce in his own obliteration.

This aesthetic extremism of 'negation', as we have described it, has the sort of value it has for Freud if it operates in a context like that of Kafka or the earlier Müller, that is to say in a context of belief threatened, or, in

Freud's scientistic yet still paternalistic perspective, if it operates in relation to a life-affirming illusion that it shores up against the effects of excessive disappointment. Without it, negation is easily appropriated by what the 1960s radical Guy Debord (1967) memorably defined in §16 of *Society of the Spectacle* as 'no more than the economy developing for itself'. Now, since the failure of communism in Europe, this economy develops unchallenged in the hands of what Debord, again, called the first 'class power which admits itself stripped of any ontological quality' (§189). With Müller's later development, when his belief in the possible success of this particular historical revolution is no longer really present, and the learning play project has been abandoned, it is possible to observe how the border between negation and the realm of high Modernist or Post-Modernist performance art becomes permeable. It is hard to be sure where the serious psycho-social function ends and the high-end entertainment for complacent theatregoers begins.

In works like *Germania Tod in Berlin* (*Germania Death in Berlin*), which dated back to 1956 but was not published until 1977 (in the West), and not performed until 1989, Müller's effort to blast out awareness of the fascist mentality compacted within the stagnation of the DDR became more of an aesthetic end in itself and less a contribution to a realistically evolving social experiment. In *Die Hamletmaschine* (*The Hamlet Machine*, 1977), the cultural evocation of negation, once touching the real horror of history, is indistinguishable from the demonstration that all media are in fact media, or, put another way, that the Symbolic Order can make mistakes and not serve the broader interests of humanity.

In one way, this radical work on the theatre as a medium (Müller worked with the avant-garde director Robert Wilson on a remarkable production of *Die Hamletmaschine* in 1986) powerfully performed the disassociation between the suffering body and the technologies of meaning. As we suggested above, it is possible to trace a genealogy of Müller's work not only to Brecht, but also to Artaud, whose Theatre of Cruelty carries much of the original Dada gesture of negation. It is not an accident that the émigré German-language author, Peter Weiss (1916–1982), who like Müller identified both with the avant-garde and with communism, caused a cultural sensation in 1965 with a play, *Marat / Sade*, that aggressively combined Brechtian with Artaudian elements.

Yet in another way the meaning of Müller's 1980s theatrical brilliance is exhausted in the demonstration of its own mediality (since the only other meaning it has to convey is the negative one that the suffering body is always in excess of meanings). There is something disturbing in the capitalist West taking sophisticated delight in Müller's figures of Artaudian negation. This is because these figures originally drew their justification from their combination with Brecht's political aesthetic to administer a 'dosage of death' in the service of the socialist project of the DDR. It is as though the 'disappointment' of the East was packaged and marketed for the West.

The DDR was built on a bedrock of anti-fascism and considered its very existence a refutation of the crimes of the Holocaust. This was the orthodoxy that Müller questioned in order to refresh and strengthen it. His representation of the failure of the DDR to some extent cushioned what remained, in the West, an unmediated historical trauma. There, one can argue, the Literature of Negation had a more clearly meaningful psychosocial function. While Kafka was welcomed as uncannily familiar in the West, he was highly controversial in the East. There, the cultural authorities were reluctant to allow that alienation was a psychological issue any more in 'real existing socialism'. We turn now to the kind of resources the Literature of Negation had in response to the most challenging historical negations of the century.

Negation and the Holocaust

The post-1918–19 political reorganization of Germany during the Weimar years was undermined by the unfinished business of the First World War. Whereas 1914–18 had surprised responsible governments, resulting in the unprecedented destruction of soldiers, the second phase, from 1939 to 1945, of what the historian Eric Hobsbawm called the 'thirty-one years' war', brought forth more appalling surprises for European civilization: this time the unprecedented destruction of civilians, particularly the attempted genocide of European Jews in death camps and the strategic option of destroying entire cities by means of aerial warfare.

German writers in the West faced peculiar difficulties with this poisonous legacy, and we will return to these in chapter 6. Evasion was natural, but also morally unacceptable. It is sometimes maintained that German writers avoided the topic of the Holocaust completely but this is not really so. It is, however, clear that even more than those of the First World War, the moral crimes of the Second World War defied naturalistic treatment (exceptions, such as texts by Anna Seghers or Bruno Apitz, to whom we come in due course, relied upon the anti-fascist perspective). The skilled novelist Wolfgang Koeppen (1906–1996) made an honest attempt with *Der Tod in Rom* (*Death in Rome*, 1954) to devise a story that would hold the issues not just of the shameful past but also of the prospect for moral and aesthetic survival. Koeppen approaches 'negation' in our sense, as his title implies, and by way of his representation of the unreconstructed Nazi, Judejahn, as a personification of death, and in the deployment of a kind of narrative discontinuity and plurality of perspective, that could be termed 'modernist' in a superficial sense. Yet the title is an adaptation of the distinctly conservative *Der Tod in Venedig* (*Death in Venice*) of Thomas Mann, and the bid to reduce the post-war situation, in which unredeemed and unexpiated crimes are overlaid with sudden prosperity, vestiges of religious belief and a complacent faith in the old culture, to a conventional economy of themes can lead only in one of two directions. Either towards *Kitsch*, as is sometimes the case with Heinrich Böll (1917–1985), who tried something similar to Koeppen in his ambitious stream-of-consciousness novel *Billard um halbzehn* (*Billiards at Half Past Nine*; 1959), or towards melancholy, as is the case with Koeppen, who despite his evident gifts fell silent for decades soon after the publication of his immediate post-war novels.

Austria, unlike the Federal Republic, denied until the late 1980s that it had been complicit with the Holocaust, claiming that it had been a victim of fascist aggression. Several writers of outstanding gifts wrote prose and drama that reflected, in accomplished and bitter stylistic distortion, the moral deformation wrought upon culture itself by the crimes of the war years, compounded by the public disavowal specific to Austria. Thomas Bernhard (1931–1989) and Elfriede Jelinek (born 1946), who was the Nobel Laureate for literature in 2004, represent contemporary Austrian society with a sarcastic viciousness that carries the Holocaust in its very disgust (not always distinct from self-loathing). Bernhard and Jelinek's cultural prestige, however, inevitably dulls the edge of their satire and softens the bitterness of their discourse in a way that begins to move them towards that middle ground of literature to which chapter 6 is dedicated, co-opting it as Post-Modernism and drawing its radical teeth. Perhaps Ingeborg Bachmann (1926–1973), another Austrian author who was a lyric poet first before she turned to prose, offers a 'purer' example of the Literature of Negation.

Bachmann was prominent among the small number of authors who took up the challenge of facing the past as still effectively present in the post-war period. This was an unfashionable thing to do; yet she did it twice, first in her lyric poetry in the 1950s, and then with a series of prose works published in the 1960s. Her lyric poetry, showcased in the seminal Gruppe 47 (see chapter 6) in 1952, was, alongside that of Paul Celan, of whom more below, the first to bring literary strategies for dealing with 'the unsayable' to bear upon the task of writing 'the unspeakable' ('Das Unsägliche geht, leise gesagt, übers Land' ['the unsayable, quietly said, goes through the land']; 'Früher Mittag' ['Early Midday']). Her one completed novel, *Malina*, which was published in 1971, was derided by pundits as a throwback to outdated High Modernism at a time of politically engaged literature.

Bachmann's turn from poetry to prose in the early 1960s coincided with the trial of Adolf Eichmann in Jerusalem and the Auschwitz trials in Frankfurt that focused attention on the Holocaust. Bachmann embarked on an ambitious project for a series of novels under the general title of 'Todesarten', or modes of death. The conception of serious culture, in this case the Modernist novel, as a means of administering a dosage of 'death' in order to render civilization more compatible with the 'death' that Freud saw (whether you accept the hypothesis of the Death Drive or not) as underlying it, could not be clearer. In a book famous for the density of its high-cultural allusions, there is at one point mention in *Malina* of the German translation of a book of stories and essays by the crime writer Raymond Chandler, *The Simple Art of Murder*. In German, it is called *Mord ist keine Kunst*, which means exactly what Chandler's original title did, but which, if you read the idiom employed literally, says: Murder is not Art. Bachmann's novel ends with the enigmatic statement: 'Es war Mord.' The text closed by this rather emphatically final phrase is both murder and art, both 'Fort' and 'Da', a significant game for culture, accommodating the constitutive component of suffering and loss in human subjectivity. In the polyglot post-Joycean world of Modernist fiction, it is difficult not to see 'art' within the German compound noun 'Todesarten'.

Bachmann's narrative agent is an 'Ich', while the narrative space of the text is organized around 'Bezüge' that define this 'I' in relation to 'Instanzen' or agencies who, like the narrating 'Ich', are never allowed to become conventional novel characters. The text opens with devices calculated to confuse ordinary expectations about conventional narrative, establishing instead the kind of expectation of performance one would associate with a play or opera (idiosyncratic accounts of the dramatis personae, time and place settings). Like the eighteenth-century novel, before the form became homogenized, but also like the Modernism of Joyce and others, the text is varied, including sequences of dramatic dialogue, italicized fantasy sections, accounts of dreams and the text of unsent letters. When conventional novelistic characters appear, as they do towards the end of the first section, they are primarily functions of the suffering of 'Ich': their very existence 'out there' is an offence to the space of inward relations described by the text. The novel is divided into three sections, each one dominated by a different relation between the 'Ich', who is a woman writer with a public profile, and a different masculine other: Ivan, her lover; nightmarish father figures; and the eponymous Malina.

The inevitable suffering and sense of loss involved with being a human subject is conveyed by means of these relations which, by virtue of being relations rather than closed entities, are never complete (indeed, they divide one another: no one relation defines the whole subject). On one level, it is assumed in the devising of this writing that what matters most in individual experience is – inevitably – lost in language. As Bachmann wrote in the poem, 'Wie soll ich mich nennen?' ('What Can I Call Myself?'): '... Wie soll ich mich nennen, / ohne in anderer Sprache zu sein?' ('What can I call myself, / without entering another's language?'). The startling death with which her novel concludes has convincingly been read as the 'death' of the subject when it enters into language, a model of the technology of language in relation to subject construction in the tradition of Bachmann's Austrian forebears, and subsequently central to post-structuralist discourse (in Roland Barthes and Paul de Man, for instance). An extension of this is to say, as Sigrid Weigel (1999) has done, that the 'death' of the *Ich* is the birth of the author of autobiography. Malina, the figure who throughout has managed the hysterical chaos suffered by the narrator-*Ich* and brought it in line with the bloodless expectation of everybody else (apart from lovers), finally takes on full responsibility for (mis)representing subjective experience.

However, there is more to the structure of Bachmann's text than a proposition about the nature of subjectivity. The title of the remarkable middle section of *Malina*, 'Der dritte Mann', is an allusion to *The Third Man*, the 1949 British *film noir* set in a Vienna still physically and morally marked by the war recently ended. 'Der dritte Mann' makes the connection between the representation of individual psychology, that is, the rationale of the text as a whole, and history.

Like Kafka's mature *oeuvre*, the central section of Bachmann's novel concerns the role of the father, in the broadest sense possible. This is as the name for the point at which the individual human subject is inhabited, informed, by a Law that forges him or her into part of an identifiable historical community. Kafka's discourse flourished gloomily at the point at which this link between father and child failed for one individual subject, setting both subject and reader adrift in experiences askew in relation to this authority (but nonetheless still subject to it); experiences rich in literary and spiritual potential. For an Austrian of Bachmann's generation, the relation to the authority which oversaw the construction of her identity is fraught with the shame related to the collective guilt of genocide, a guilt attaching to, and staining, an entire polity.

Kafka was able to write himself and the reader free from an historically outmoded patriarchy and into the 'negative' space in which the passing of one social coding is recoded by means of hitherto unfamiliar artistic means. Bachmann's application of the literary negations she had inherited, namely the negation of language as an unproblematic social institution and of the unified subject, does not create the same possibility of a culturally purified artistic space, the very possibility of which was doubted after the Holocaust. Instead, she engages with profound transgression, unresolved guilt and an excess of unrelieved suffering. For this reason, the dream of redemption through poetry is now explicitly drawn into the thematic economy of negation, and thereby disappointed. The earlier lyric had read: 'Ein Wort nur fehlt! Wie soll ich mich nennen, / ohne in anderer Sprache zu sein' ('A single word is all that is lacking! how can I name myself, without entering another's language?'). The absence of this word is the burden of the failed legend in *Malina*, 'The secrets of the princess of Kagran', which cannot meet the demand of Ivan, the narrator's lover, for an affirmative literature.

In the narrator-*Ich*'s dreams, the father figure represents variations upon terrifyingly violent identity formations. Incestuous sex with him is a duty, annihilating cultural performance is demanded (staining the practices of culture themselves with this relation); there is a landscape dominated by a cemetery of murdered daughters. Moreover, this regime of brutal socialization is contaminated by Nazi associations appropriate to the father's generation: the father is identified with history's executioners (execution: the most efficient form of socialization) and the father condemns the daughter to be gassed (the 'gas chambers', like the term 'Auschwitz', and before the terms Holocaust and the Shoah came into currency, was the recognized metonym for the historical unspeakable).

These passages are perhaps not decodable. Yet they are clearly the mimesis of an unconscious network of associations (they are dreams; Malina, the personality manager, helps the narrator-*Ich* to deal with them when she is awake). What is important about them as literature is that they are the representation of a specificity. Unlike Kafka (or any of her other male predecessors), Bachmann combines representation of specifics of a gendered historical subject with a literary art fully determined by language consciousness and the consequent incompleteness that underlies subjectivity.

Bachmann's writing combines strategies of negation with the rhetorical demands of the post-Auschwitz situation for German-language writers. The psychology of shame and victimhood is represented in the circumstance that the relation to the father, a relation of identity-forming intimacy, is contaminated by the Holocaust. For Bachmann, writing as a woman, victimhood is part of the patriarchal structure, overlapping, but not identical with, the more drastic forms of victimhood suffered at the hands of her fathers, but also therefore in her name.

When the 'Ich' is murdered, and vanishes into the objective world, not only does the 'excitement' of her creative passion fall silent, so too do the excited agonies that inform her dreams. They too are taken up into the cultural game of Fort / Da that bids to acknowledge death in life. Each of the three sections ends with an emphatic negation: 'Wien schweigt' ('Vienna is silent'); 'Es ist der ewige Krieg' ('It is the eternal war'); 'Es war Mord' ('It was murder'), yet together they do compose art out of murder.

The Literature of Negation is life-affirming. *Malina* has lasted better than the engaged literature with which it was contemporaneous. Indeed, despite its dismissal at the hands of critics, it sold unexpectedly well for such a difficult text. Moreover, its 'autonomous' commitment to both art and to the never-absent facts of silence, war and death enabled the production of a text that spoke to other women who shared an identity struggle in the crisis of patriarchy (manifest in both its world wars).

Bachmann's 'Third Man': Rilke's 'third person': both authors devise ways of writing otherwise and scoring temporary victories over the authority. In *Malina* the Third Man is written about in three different guises but does not determine the writing, or, more precisely, his inevitable triumph (what could language ever be without the third person?) is deferred until the end of the text. By then, a possibility of communication has already taken place.

The parallel with Rilke's *Malte* can take us further here. In that text, Malte eventually recognizes his inner affinity with sub-social urban characters that he had initially perceived only as wholly other. I take it that Bachmann is alluding to Malte's experience of solidarity with the 'Fortgeworfenen' in a passage in the third chapter of the novel in which her narrator-*Ich* recalls her own time in Paris. Though without funds herself, she would sometimes anonymously donate bottles of wine to homeless men sleeping rough in the streets. She associates the French acknowledgement of the kindness 'que Dieu vous ...', with its English equivalent, 'bless you', and reflects that these muttered words of recognition tell something of the way 'the wounded' ('die Blessierten') talk among their own kind, and, like her, simply carry on existing, covered in all manner of wounds. The parallel 'bless you / Blessierung' both tricks language by virtue of being a polyglot pun, and, in so doing, links Grace with wounding. The mutual recognition takes place not between those who master language, or vanish into it, and can thus speak to each other, but between those who are excluded, multiply wounded, yet who live on unnamed.

This is a recognition made possible by the postponement of the Third Man's triumph. It is a recognition that can serve the feminist cause, certainly, and appears to have done so historically. It can also point to belief in a wider possibility of dialogue from subject to subject facilitated by poetry. It is significant that the legend 'The secrets of the princess of Kagran' contains a network of allusions to poems dedicated to Bachmann by Paul Celan. The failure of a literature of affirmation (the story is written to satisfy Ivan's demand for a positive literature) has a secret within it that suggests the redemptive possibilities of a Literature of Negation, even after Auschwitz.

The lyric of negation

Paul Celan (1920–1970) came from a multilingual part of Europe. His mother tongue was German but the milieu of his childhood, Bukovina (which became part of Romania after the First World War), contained a mixture of languages, including – besides Romanian – Ukrainian, Yiddish and dialect German. He was an outstanding linguist and active translator, working with Romanian, Russian, French, English and Hebrew. Yet his unremitting commitment to the serious calling of not just 'literature', but very specifically poetry, as in the case of Stefan George (see chapter 3) but in different historical circumstances, required him to work in German. The main different circumstance was that for Celan, as he said in his speech accepting the Bremen literary prize in 1958, the German language was 'todbringend' ('deathbringing').

Kafka and Celan are the two writers who typify what we mean by the Literature of Negation. They also have in common that they both came to the world in German, but not from Germany. Certainly among the greatest writers in that language, as Jews their writing is pitched against the historical results of the German nation's bid for unified and ethnically cleansed identity. Steeped in love for and emulation of German literature, they recoiled from the stiff spine of official literary tradition.

If Kafka 'represented the Holocaust' by chance, with Celan we reach the nub of the matter. His biographical experience placed him very close to the historical reality. His mother and father were deported, his father dying of typhus in 1942. His mother was shot soon afterwards when she became unfit for work (the exact date of her murder is not known). Celan himself survived nearly two years in labour camps. In 1947, he arrived as a young poet in Vienna, after a journey – typical for those days – outside the law (sleeping rough and helped by farmers; he was escaping a Romania that was about to become a Soviet satellite state), carrying with him a letter of introduction in which his poetry was described as 'the only lyric counterpart to Kafka's work' (quoted in Felstiner 1995: 51).

Celan's post-war literary career began in surrealist milieux in Bucharest and Vienna. In 1948, in a short introduction to a catalogue of surrealist paintings ('Edgar Jené und der Traum vom Traume'), he reflected upon the 'negation' worked by Modernist art in the general sense of the challenging of conventional discourse. In echoing Malte's 'great questions' about the possibility of a whole different order of meaning (see chapter 3), he remarks how, alongside the deep truths of human existence that have been distorted by what we called above in the context of Rilke and others the 'third person', there was also 'die Asche ausgebrannter Sinngebung [...] und nicht nur diese!' ('the ashes of burnt-out meanings [...] and not just that'). In other words, he renews the original Dada sense of a negation *in history* that requires a resonance in art, and their sense that this is not just a matter of style or even discourse.

Celan's renewal of the gesture of negation takes the form of a lyric idiom that acknowledges the historical contamination objectively proper to language. In the Bremen speech as we saw, he described his own relationship to the German language by saying that it had gone through the 'thousand darknesses of deathbringing speech', finding no words for 'that which happened', but nevertheless traversing it, emerging from it. It is hard to think of a better definition of what we mean by the Literature of Negation.

He achieved fame with the poem 'Todesfuge' ('Death Fugue', written in 1944 or 1945, first published in Germany in 1952), in which, as he claimed in 1960, he had tried to bring the monstrosity of the gas chambers into language (Wiedemann 2003: 608). Germany, present in its name 'Deutschland' (a word which appeared nowhere else in poetry Celan intended for publication) and in a series of deadpan references to music, Faust, the starry sky, blue eyes, hunting dogs and cruelty, is compromised and contaminated by juxtaposition with the experience of those about to be gassed.

The poem is marked also by a use of repetition that is at once poetically formative and a message from the death instinct. This, as we saw, was a psychic enchainment Freud deduced from observing the symptom of a compulsion to repeat which was categorically not connected to any kind of wish fulfilment (including aesthetic gratification). The opening phrase, 'Schwarze Milch der Frühe' ('Black milk of daybreak') asks to be read as a metaphor but fulfils itself in the poem not by yielding metaphorical sense, but, first, as one of the structuring, 'deathbringing', repetitions of the poem, and, second, as a version of the Fort / Da game, since it is a naming that negates the mother ('black milk'), thus bringing 'death' into culture, in the sense of the abandonment of all hope of gratification (what 'we drink' is death). The voice that the poem gives to the dead is not an antidote to the toxicity of the German contribution to twentieth-century history; on the contrary, it is testimony to the unconsoled nature of the last hours of their victims' lives.

'Todesfuge' is arguably the most famous poem in post-war German literature. But perhaps in confronting the gas chambers so clearly (albeit brilliantly), it came too close to 'finding words for that which happened'. Celan certainly felt that his poem was misappropriated by the Germans in their need for cultural renewal after the Holocaust. The academic critic Hans Egon Holthusen, in a long 1954 review of the volume *Mohn und Gedächtnis* (*Poppy and Remembrance*), in which 'Todesfuge' was published, first, failed to read the gap between Celan's idiom and that of the pioneering French Modernist poet Mallarmé (namely, that it bore the burden not just of burnt-out meanings but bodies too), and, second, averred that 'Todesfuge', in its direct treatment of the topic of topics, namely the gas chambers, had somehow purified or transcended the historical horror in poetry. The real point, however, was that the historical horror contaminated poetry which, somehow, survived.

The function of the Literature of Negation in the face of the technological calamities of the twentieth century, as we have argued, is to administer a homeopathic dosage of 'death' in order to help treat the psycho-social disappointment resulting from the failure of law and morality. In the case of the incipient post-war German literary culture, there is the opposing and inevitable risk that such art will serve as an alibi, a premature or false reconciliation for what has not yet been properly expiated. To put it in a paradox: to understand this poetry is to misunderstand it. Yet, on the other hand, what from Celan's point of view was a misappropriation can also be seen as a contribution nevertheless to a longer process of reconciliation. It is questionable whether the Literature of Negation can ever be understood in any other way than by misunderstanding, since to understand it perfectly would be unendurable.

At all events, while Celan did not wish his poetry to be misused, he wished it to be received. His impulse in writing, at least as he explained it in rare public pronouncements on the matter, was not only a gesture of exclusion but also one of address. It was a phenomenon of language and therefore essentially dialogic, as he emphasized in the Bremen speech. In this, it contested the dominant aesthetic of lyric poetry in the 1950s in German letters, that of Gottfried Benn, which was proudly monologic. If 'Todesfuge' was uncharacteristically 'accessible' for Celan's poetry, his poetry usually reflects and requires very acute attention: this is the only way to read it, since the words resist their usual meanings and uses, while conveying an urgent sense that they are real words (that is to say, words that have 'gone through' history) and, since they have been put together as poems, given to others to receive. Celan used the image of a message in a bottle ('Flaschenpost'). Perhaps one could say that his poems aim to purify language so that it may reveal its impurity.

A parallel and a contrast with Rilke may help to clarify what is at stake here. In the *Duineser Elegien*, written between 1912 and 1922 but with an extended hiatus around the First World War, Rilke wrote in such a way as to give voice to a position between two forms of life or orders of meaning. As the Seventh Elegy has it: 'Jede dumpfe Umkehr der Welt hat solche Enterbte, / denen das Frühere nicht und noch nicht das Nächste gehört' ('Each sluggish turn of the world has such disinherited minds, / to whom neither the past nor yet the future belongs'). This doubleness of purpose, lamenting the familiar old but affirming the unknown new, is later, in the Ninth Elegy, compressed into one line in which the resources of the German language are exploited to convey antithetical meanings simultaneously: 'wie selbst das klagende Lied rein zur Gestalt sich entschließt' ('how even the lamentation of grief might purely decide to take on form'). Here translation is hindered by the German double meaning to which we wish to draw attention. 'Entschließen' has the primary meaning of 'decide', and thus connotes the closure of a decision, but also contains elements that can yield the meaning 'unlock', that is, open (ent-schließen). So Rilke is characterizing the achieved form of lamentation ('elegies') as something that simultaneously opens jubilantly upon what will succeed or replace that which has been lost.

Rilke was certainly one of Celan's guiding poets, and he used the same stylistic device. Perhaps it would be more precise to say that he enabled the same kind of linguistic event to take place, since the double meaning is in the word already and is only set free by the poem. The difference between Rilke and Celan is not fundamentally stylistic, but historical.

Where in Rilke the gloom of the world from within whose ruins he writes enhances the glory of the world towards which his poem points but cannot speak about directly, the world to which Celan's poetry points, but has no words for, contains the extermination camps. Just after explaining, in the passage already cited, how his German has gone through the darkness and silence it cannot name, Celan adds: 'Ging hindurch und durfte wieder zutage treten, "angereichert" von all dem.' It emerges, not unscathed or triumphant, but 'enriched', the word for which in German, as Felstiner (1995: 115) observes, contains Hitler's 'Reich' within it. Another example from the prose, but this time with a specific relation to Rilke is the adjective 'tausendjährig'. This occurs in the essay for the surrealist catalogue mentioned above, and from the context is an allusion to the millennia ('Jahrtausende') invoked by Malte during which time the truth has never been spoken (and will now be spoken, or will soon). By the time of Celan's allusion, the word has acquired an association with the (thousand-year) Third Reich that it is impossible to overlook.

The poem 'Corona' from Celan's first officially sanctioned collection, *Mohn und Gedächtnis*, is also an echo of Rilke, this time of his famous poem 'Herbsttag' ('Autumn Day'). 'Corona', the reader will discern, is a love poem (Bachmann quotes it in *Malina*), and in that sense is a positive answer to Rilke's sweet melancholy about being alone. There is a tender and intimate erotic moment at which the poet's 'eye goes down to my lover's loins' (trans. Felstiner 1995: 54). The German phrase, 'Geschlecht der Geliebten', however, contains and releases another meaning: 'the beloved race'. The following lines, 'we gaze at each other / we say dark things', therefore allow the description of an encounter between lovers to resonate with an impossible turn towards the absent loved ones who have been murdered. In Celan's penultimate collection, *Lichtzwang* (*Light-Compulsion*, 1970), to cite just one more example, the following two lines occur together, concluding a short untitled poem beginning with the word 'Fahlstimmig' ('wanvoiced', trans. Felstiner 1995: 247) that touches upon a series of negations, affirmations and antithetical oblique references to a 'thou': 'wunder Gewinn / einer Welt' (II, 307). Possibly they are attributed to a voice that is mentioned in the first word, or maybe they describe what that voice says or knows. The point is that the poem ends with a 'result', a 'world', inhabited by a balance of meanings. The phrase 'wunder Gewinn' means 'wounded gain', itself a balance, suggesting with perfect economy the kind of balance we have argued inhabits the Literature of Negation. But beyond this, hidden in the adjective 'wunder' (wounded) is the noun 'Wunder', which means 'miracle'.

These are not poems 'about' the Holocaust but about the historical negation of civilized values that is the condition of their existence as poetry. As such, they also negate the kind of Modernist transport of Rilke's elegies, but they negate it in the service of a kind of address that Rilke strove for, as indeed had Hölderlin, that dispensed with the 'third person' in order to draw shamed, abject and excluded human subjects back towards each other in love and respect.

This defining mixture of negation and affirmation is reflected in the opening poem of the collection *Sprachgitter* (*Speech Grille* [1959]), 'Stimmen' ('Voices'). It concerns the trope of relationality or 'Bezug', the significance of which in texts of Hofmannsthal, Musil and Rilke we noted above (see chapter 3). The Celan poems begin again with mention of a voice, which is 'scratched' ('geritzt') into the surface of water. As with the poem beginning 'Fahlstimmig', the reader will tend to connect the voice with that of the poem. At the end of the poem, in a moment of negation (after a series of stanzas introduced by variations upon 'Stimmen'), we read 'Keine / Stimme' ('No / Voice') and are offered instead the adumbration of a reciprocal sign of life, including the passage: 'ein / Fruchtblatt, augen-groß, tief / geritzt'. Here an eye, or something like it, replies to the voice, reminiscent of the examples we cited in chapter 3 (and of others too, for instance in Rilke's *Neue Gedichte*). Yet this eye might be 'deeply scratched', as if Celan wishes to negate this very redemptive trope by scarring it. In the final turn of the poem, the wound itself (as in 'Fahlgestimmt'), becomes the substance of the response 'es / harzt, will nicht vernarben' ('It resins. It won't scar over'; trans. Felstiner 1995: 100).

This alternation between negation and affirmation, what Felstiner calls the struggle 'to keep No and Yes unsplit' (100) brings us on to the final point we have to make under the heading of negation, and this concerns tradition. We said above that Celan, and Kafka, had an ambiguous relation to German literary tradition. In one way, they distanced themselves from it; Kafka, in his diary entry for Christmas Day 1911, preferred to imagine a 'minor literature' distinct from the overbearing historical authority of official literary tradition. For Celan, his identification as a Jew entailed for obvious historical reasons revulsion at any talk of German identity. Yet the balance of negation and affirmation extends to the poets, including German ones, of the past as well. In the poem 'Psalm', from *Die Niemands-rose* (*The No One's Rose*, 1963), Celan speaks for the collective of the mur-dered, in such a way as to deny any cultural continuity: 'niemand bespricht unsern Staub' ('No one gives speech to our dust'). Yet the poem develops towards an affirmation of this 'Nobody', even towards identification with a nothingness which will nevertheless blossom like the 'No One's Rose' that gives the collection its title.

The rose is (once more) an echo of Rilke who composed the following epitaph for himself in his will: 'Rose, oh reiner Widerspruch, Lust, / Niemandes Schlaf zu sein unter soviel Lidern' ('Rose, pure contradiction, delight / in being nobody's sleep under so many eyelids'; trans. Hamburger 1981: 105). We cite this extraordinarily rich poem, not for its own sake but in order to establish a connection in gestures of negation between Celan and Rilke, and thus to affirm that, of course, Celan felt himself part of a lyric tradition in German.

If it is objected that Rilke was as much of an outsider in relation to the mainstream of German literature as Kafka and Celan himself, then one can point to the next poem in the same collection that is directed towards Hölderlin (while also containing a crucial allusion to Büchner, a writer celebrated by Celan on the occasion of the award of the Büchner Prize in 1960). The word 'Deutschland' and its variants did appear frequently in Hölderlin's poetry, and his patriotism and hopes for his fatherland (see chapter 1) were predictably co-opted by the National Socialists. Yet in 'Tübingen, Jänner' from *Die Niemandsrose*, the insane poet is implicitly merged with Jewish patriarchs who would be unable to find words to respond to the modern world, were they to return to it. The poem ends enigmatically with: '("Pallaksch. Pallaksch.")', words, which, according to Celan's source, Hölderlin was fond of using during his long years of madness, and which often signified his unwillingness or inability to commit himself to either 'yes' or 'no' (Wiedemann 2003: 681). Celan had himself written in 'Sprich auch Du' ('Speak You Too') in the collection *Von Schwelle zu Schwelle* (*From Threshold to Threshold*, 1955): 'Sprich – / Doch scheide das Nein nicht vom Ja' ('Speak – / But do not separate the No from the Yes'). The real and meaningful continuity between Hölderlin and Celan resides less in their common language than in their common insistence upon 'not being understood', on being read as open and wounded but still speaking. In this, they are related to Bachmann and Kafka, as well as to Dada, as we saw (pp. 119–20): 'Ja-sagen – Nein-sagen: das gewaltige Hokuspokus des Daseins beschwingt die Nerven des echten Dadaisten.'

5

The Fate of Affirmative Literature

This chapter explores the effect on German literature of the two non-democratic regimes to hold sway in German-speaking lands in the twentieth-century. Recent scholarship has tended to downplay the literary-historical significance of political regimes in favour of concentration upon the literature actually produced despite or against them. There is persuasive evidence for a conservative turn in German literature that preceded the accession to power of the Nazis and survived the foundation of the German Democratic Republic by nearly ten years. There are cogent reasons for looking at the later writing of the DDR as versions of Modernism and Post-Modernism. But in a cultural history of literature it is important to respond to those cases where politics and literature are in a real, rather than an imaginary or virtual, relation. The Third Reich and the German Democratic Republic, as the authors of one of the major studies marginalizing politics in favour of literature concede, are examples of the 'unparalleled political instrumentalization of German literature' (Parker et al. 2004: 8). As such, they are at once intrinsically interesting examples of literary environments, and instructive in defining *ex negativo* the kind of literary culture that comes about in an environment, our own, without clearly discernible substantive values but substantially determined by commercial ones, to which we turn in our final chapter.

The Third Reich

In 1933, the National Socialists gained power in Germany (Austria was annexed in 1938). The first cultural priority for the new regime was to establish the conditions for a return to an affirmative culture.

An affirmative literature is a discourse or array of discourses that serves a perceived common collective cause. This implies, at whatever level of distinctness, a 'reality' to affirm. It is best to imagine this reality less in terms of something objective 'out there' and more as a prevailing public and private concord about a network of values, including moral and aesthetic ones, that do not contradict or cast doubt upon one another. The lack of such structural homogeneity underlies, in differing (and productive) ways, the Literature of Negation, which was the subject of the previous chapter, and the unregulated literature of the modern culture market, which is the subject of the next.

The National Socialists drew popular support (as distinct from their ideological programme) from nostalgia. In seeing literature as part of 'culture', a sphere set apart from the uncertainties of everyday life in modernity, the cultural administrators were exploiting the reassuring familiarity of the post-Romantic identification of music, literature and art as timeless German values. Merely the existence of a specific sphere of national culture suggested that there was still a unified reality, inaccessible to the competing claims of the Soviet Union and the US to reconfigure the world according to their respective belief systems and economic agendas.

Nazi cultural policy had to negate the hated cultural model of Weimar, to which it denied all claim to having been real at all. The many innovative, oppositional and experimental cultural practices for which Weimar is justly famous were officially identified as *entartet*, which is usually translated as 'degenerate', but also has the sense of 'unnatural'. Rainer Schlösser, who advised the regime on theatrical matters, saw a 'mythical, universal, unambiguous reality beyond reality' (quoted in Schoeps 2004: 153) and called for a return of the arts to cult status in order to address this higher dimension. The messy circumstances, hardships and failed compromises of the Weimar period were seen as the piece of grit around which the pearl of a New Germany was destined to form.

This was the explicit and planned reversal of a cultural symbiosis. The reality the Nazis wished to promote was emphatically German and anti-Semitic, and there was thus a return to the sort of aesthetic anachronism of the first national phase in the previous century. In this sense, the aim was to put the lid back on the Pandora's Box of the Weimar Republic which, as we shall see in the next chapter, had embraced the cultural possibilities of democracy and capitalism enthusiastically. After 1933, the concentration was on the many and various national, anti-Semitic or (aesthetically) conservative elements on the heterogeneous literary scene, to the exclusion of anything redolent of Weimar modernity, bolshevism, Judaism, liberal democratic ideology and so on. In retrospect, it is easy to overlook how thick on the ground these sorts of elements were, eclipsed as they had been by the radical chic of Piscator and Brecht, the cutting-edge aesthetic prose of Döblin and Musil, the satirical brilliance of Kästner and Tucholsky, the flourishing post-Dada aesthetic extremism in France and the Soviet Union and so forth. Now, for instance, the historical balladeers of the Wilhelmine period, Börries von Munchhausen, Lulu von Strauss und Torney and Agnes Miegel, all still going strong, if rather out of the mainstream during Weimar, returned centre stage, with decent sales for their ballads, lyric poems, *Novellen* and novels, as well as many public acknowledgements in the form of prizes and, in the cases of Miegel and Münchhausen, prominence in the National Socialist version of the Prussian Academy of Literature.

A particular example of the triumphant turning back of the aesthetic clock was the *Novelle, Der Wanderer zwischen beiden Welten*, by Walter Flex. This basically nineteenth-century treatment of the First World War, aesthetically light years from the more or less contemporaneous fascist Modernism of Jünger, had already been a spontaneous best-seller in 1917 (when Flex had fallen in action) but, promoted by the cultural authorities in the new Reich, reached extraordinary sales figures (some say over a million) until and on into the Second World War. If one considers how out of date it seems looking back now, even for 1917, the incongruity of its best-seller status in mid-century is striking.

Nazi cultural pragmatism took the form of a juxtaposition of wilful anachronism with intensive affirmation of the modern world. In literature, there was no need to rely entirely on the nineteenth-century aesthetic time warp or the creation of modern *völkisch* epic poetry such as Hans Friedrich Blunck's *Sage vom Reich* (*Legend of the Reich*, 1941–2), or Josefa Berens-Totenohl's *Einer Sippe Gesicht* (*The Face of a Clan*, 1941), since there was a strong tradition of perfectly suitable best-selling novels to draw on, going back to Freytag's *Soll und Haben* and continued in other successful novels like Felix Dahn's *Kampf um Rom* (*The Struggle for Rome*, 1876) and Gustav Frenssen's *Jörn Uhl*. Herman Burte's *Heimat* adventure fantasy *Wiltfeber*, mentioned in chapter 3, was now seen as one of the most profound poetic treatments of 'real' German history. Indeed, after the First World War, this novel tradition was intensified by political circumstances highly favourable to the sort of disaffected right-wing constituency from which the Nazis drew their support. The anti-Semitic best-seller, *Die Sünde wider das Blut*, by Artur Dinter (*The Sin against the Blood*, originally published in 1917) sold many hundreds of thousands of copies after 1933. Hans Grimm's *Volk ohne Raum* (*Nation without Space*, 1926), a colonialist fiction described by the Weimar satirist Kurt Tucholsky as 'the Bible of Germanness', was a best-seller during the Weimar Republic but became an absolutely top-selling title once the Nazis came into power and promoted it (it could not have been more suitable for their purposes).

Many other authors who rose to prominence within the National Socialist apparatus, such as Erwin Guido Kolbenheyer and Will Vesper, were established well before 1933. Ernst Jünger's writing from the early 1920s on is *sui generis*, although it emerged from an environment in which right-wing war diaries were common. Towards the end of the 1920s, Werner Beumelburg, Edwin Erich Dwinger, Franz Schauwecker and others produced fiction and memoirs representing the Great War from a *völkisch* angle (in opposition to the pacifist message of Remarque's *Im Westen nichts Neues* [*All Quiet on the Western Front*] of 1927), and these authors went on to play important parts in the delivery of an ideological literature for the Third Reich.

By no means were all of these men and women fervent Nazis, anti-Semites or bigots. But their work was all available to the Third Reich as affirmative literature. It is as though a photograph of the rich and varied scene of Weimar culture is suddenly seen as a negative, so that all the features that seemed provincial and old-fashioned now appear illuminated in the light of the new German picture.

The pragmatism of the National Socialist regime in relation to literature, however, went further than adopting and encouraging material which chimed with its retrospective annihilation of Weimar and affirmed Nazi ideology. In some ways, Expressionism informed the Nazi attitude to culture, since Expressionism was a stylistic resource for conveying fervent dissatisfaction with ordinary reality (the one that had been a sort of bad dream) and the desire for a new order. Joseph Goebbels's protagonist in his novel *Michael. Ein Deutsches Schicksal in Tagebuchblättern* (*A German Destiny in the Pages of a Diary*, 1929) saw 'Expressionism' as the tendency of the century to project new worlds (which is what the Nazis claimed to be doing). Expressionists on the left had had the same view. Ernst Toller (1893–1939), a leading Expressionist playwright, had actively supported the revolution of 1918–19. Goebbels, who was the most important figure in Nazi publicity, whilst certainly a fervent ideologue nevertheless would have been able to envisage the Expressionist painter Emil Nolde as a suitably affirmative representative of Nordic culture, had other elements in the party (notably Alfred Rosenberg and Hitler himself) not insisted upon the blanket proscription of Expressionism as *entartet*.

In 1933, Münchhausen wrote a widely syndicated piece celebrating the passing of 'Expressionism' in literature, and musing on its nature, which he, predictably, found degenerate, market-driven, un-German and Jewish (although Münchhausen was not in fact an anti-Semite in the Hitler–

Dinter–Rosenberg mould). Gottfried Benn wrote a response to this, in which he sought to reconcile his deep artistic commitment to the Europe-wide Modernist spirit of Expressionism, with his current enthusiastic commitment to the New Germany. Benn's point is that what appears as distortion in these discourses and practices is merely the reflex, in true, serious, formally disciplined art, to the lack of 'reality' (here we have that theme again) of the period now drawing to its end. Although he is rather vague about how he intends to express his commitment to the New Order in his poetry, the implication is that this New Order is the affirmative expression of what Expressionism had registered authentically but, due to historical necessity, negatively.

Benn's sophisticated argument did not convince the ideologues, but in practice Nazi culture did have something intrinsically Expressionist about it. Modris Eksteins, in *Rites of Spring*, went as far as to argue that fascism itself was a popular version of the avant-garde attitude, a kind of institutionalized 'adversary culture' (1989: 305). Eksteins has some difficulty in sustaining this argument, given the anti-intellectualism and appalling artistic taste displayed by the Nazis, but there is something in the perception, to use Jeffrey Herf's phrase, that the convergence of right-wing politics with the imperatives of modern technology produced a 'reactionary Modernism'.

Hanns Johst (1890–1978), who became without question the leading literary functionary in Nazi Germany (he was president of the Reich Chamber of Literature from 1935 until 1945, as well as president of the German Academy of Literature), was an Expressionist playwright during the years of the First World War. His play *Der Einsame* (*The Solitary Man*, 1917) was pathos-filled and idealistic enough to serve Brecht as the starting point for his pastiche of Expressionism, *Baal*. Although Johst forswore cosmopolitan idealism in favour of German nationalism, his famous drama *Schlageter*, premiered on Hitler's birthday in 1933, caused a sensation, employing theatrical techniques and pathos unthinkable without Johst's earlier affiliation. The closing tableau in particular was reminiscent of Expressionist staging and dramatic address: the German martyr (about to be executed by the French for his part in resistance to their occupation of the Rhineland) stands with his back to the audience, so that the salvo passes through his body, and with suitable lighting, into the audience as the spark of retribution. Here the vague ecstasy of Expressionism is put to expert ideological and propagandistic use.

Schlösser, when evoking in 1935 the 'higher reality' that National Socialist art must serve, was referring to the programme worked out by himself, the youth leader and poet Baldur von Schirach and the dramatist Eberhard Wolfgang Möller (1906–1972), for the *Thingspiel*. This was a multimedia concept, a mixture of oratorio, pageant, drama and dance; a total work of art for the *Volk*, set in open-air amphitheatres with the seating capacity of football stadiums. Very grandiose plans for the construction of hundreds of *Thingplätze* were made, and many events did in fact take place between 1934 and 1937 before audiences of thousands. Henning Eichberg (1977) has shown that, far from being the quintessence of specifically Nazi manipulation of culture for ideology, the mass open-air event was a feature of culture across the ideological spectrum in the 1920s. There are also clearly echoes of Wagner, Hofmannsthal and Max Reinhardt, all of whom had experimented with ways of transcending the bourgeois stage (as did the communist director Erwin Piscator and the Modernist architect and theatre designer Walter Gropius). Möller cited Georg Kaiser and Igor Stravinsky among his influences. Here once more is an example of a pragmatic co-optation of existing practices. It is interesting to note that there were many spontaneous 'bottom-up' events of a similar kind, but not necessarily ideologically entirely sound, after 1933 alongside the officially promoted ones. The most famous of these latter was Möller's own *Frankenburg Dice Game*, put on to coincide with the opening ceremonials for the 1936 Olympics in Berlin. Lest we are too ready to regard the *Thingspiel* as a phenomenon from a different ideological planet, Eichberg points to the continuity between this twentieth-century tradition of mass open-air spectacle and the torch-lighting flag-bearing pageantry still inseparable in the public mind from the Olympic Games.

There was no official censorship of literary output during the Third Reich before the outbreak of war. It would have been self-contradictory to admit that any legitimate member of the classless *Volksgemeinschaft* (community of the people) could wish not to contribute to the common cause. This would not have been consistent with the notion of a higher collective reality. In practice, there were extensive official controls of literature in its various manifestations. The trade organizations for authors that had grown up since the late nineteenth century to protect the interests of creative writers in their negotiations with publishers and distributors (such as the Schutzverband deutscher Schriftsteller [Association for the Rights of German Authors], founded in 1909), were swept up into the Reichskultur-kammer (Reich Chamber of Culture), headed by Goebbels. This effectively turned the protection around since anybody ideologically unsound was not permitted to pursue a profession in the arts. All established writers, who did not fit the new reality (such as Heinrich Mann, until 1933 the president of the Literature Section of the Prussian Academy) were excluded immediately the Nazis came to power.

As we saw, the regime had a propagandistic and ideological investment in culture, echoing in this the late nineteenth-century invention of a German classical tradition. They emphasized Hölderlin and Kleist, patriotic writers at the edge of reason, and downplayed or qualified Goethe, Schiller and especially Lessing (whose *Nathan der Weise* was banned from the stage during the Third Reich) who were uncomfortably closely identified with the Enlightenment. The desirability, mentioned above, that there should be a self-evident sphere of culture provided another motive for disavowing censorship publicly. Yet the exclusion of so many talented writers on grounds of ideology and especially race, plus the manifold forms of unofficial coercion in literary matters, stifled the development of serious literature, sending writers unable or unwilling to make a creative contribution to the cause into inner or actual exile.

It has recently become clear to historians that there was never anything like total control of what people in the Third Reich actually read and enjoyed. It is notable that only a quarter of the best-selling novels of the period were unambiguously ideological in nature, and these were mainly grouped at the beginning of the period, while enthusiasm for the new regime was still fresh, and there was a gap in the market for ideological material. Moreover, where politically correct texts did achieve high sales figures, as with the works of Hans Zöberlein, this was with the heavy support of the Party and the media, which it controlled. Hitler himself wrote the foreword to Zöberlein's *Der Glaube an Deutschland* (*Faith in Germany*, 1931), an affirmation of the Front experience, which is reputed to have sold 800,000 copies.

Otherwise, writers like Karl May and Ludwig Ganghofer continued to enjoy enormous sales figures (although Courths-Mahler's success dipped during the period, picking up once more in the Federal Republic). Ehm Welk's *Die Heiden von Kummerow* (*The Heathens of Kummerow*, 1937) was the third best-selling novel of the period (Schneider 2004: 81). Welk had worked with Erwin Piscator during the 1920s (although without approving of his propagandistic practices), had been interned in 1934 for criticizing Goebbels, and Welk's novels (including this one) later became classics of the DDR. He was, then, in no sense, a Nazi author, but rather a humorist, whose narrative angle through the eyes of children permitted muted social criticism and appealed to readers. Another apolitical humorist, Heinrich Spoerl, became the best-selling author of all during the period, and continued, with minor editing, to be widely sold in the Federal Republic. In some prominent instances, the authorities' interests and those of readers went hand in hand. This was the case with a novel about the history of German industry by K. A. Schenzinger, *Anilin* (1937; with 920,000 copies the best-selling novel of the entire period [Schneider 2004: 80]). Schenzinger had published *Der Hitlerjunge Quex*, a propaganda classic, in 1932, but his later fiction was not stereotypically National Socialist. It was entertaining fiction with a strongly affirmative message about Germany but, in its central theme of modernization, not what one might expect from a specifically Nazi literature.

This is less to say that the way the National Socialists policed literature was ineffective but rather that literature did not really matter that much to them. Ensuring that what literature there was was affirmative was less pressing than what was being affirmed. In a system that had an ideological (anti-Soviet) stake in claiming that free enterprise was not subordinate to state control, the key was to neutralize rather than to co-opt the commercial media. In what was, despite the atavistic ideology (which required lip-service to German culture, including literature) a modern technological state, the really effective mass media were cinema, press and radio, all of which were skilfully manipulated by Goebbels's propaganda regime. In the sphere of cinema, for instance, the Propaganda Minister's policy of allowing concessions to public taste emerges even more clearly than in the sphere of literature. Although there were high-profile anti-Semitic films (most famously the costume melodrama *Jud Süß* [*The Jew Süss*, 1940]), until 1939 or thereabouts, when it became less easy to screen US films, the German cinema-going public had free access to contemporary American cinema (the parallel to this in the case of literature is Margaret Mitchell's *Gone with the Wind* [*Vom Winde verweht*], which was among the top-selling novels of the period). The nominally independent German movie industry was in competition with Hollywood films, producing a recognizably domestic version of modern entertainment cinema, not much more or less propagandistic, in subtle ways, than the Hollywood films themselves, which likewise embedded certain values, if different ones.

The single most famous literary event of the period was not to do with the publishing of books but with the burning of them. The main message of all the propaganda, as well as of the serious ideological material itself, was that words were not enough. This was a period for men to be men, and literature was still, as in the mindset of the nineteenth century and the *Gartenlaube*, basically for women (the second best-selling novel of the period was Kuni Tremel-Eggert's *Barb* [1933], a propaganda novel on the ideal of National Socialist womanhood). The prevailing Hitler myth was that of a simple war veteran from the ranks who moved from the spoken word (his early rhetorical brilliance), through the written word (*Mein Kampf*), to active effectiveness on the stage of history. The excessive pathos of Expressionism had always been urging 'these words, or these actions on stage, are "not enough" '. The most famous line in Johst's *Schlageter*, if not in all Nazi literature, is 'when I hear "culture", I undo the safety catch on my Browning'.

The National Socialist regime, then, encouraged bombastic nonsense, acquiesced in popular novels and effectively discouraged the production and dissemination of serious complex dissenting or critical writing through its benighted procedures of exclusion. In other words, it successfully subordinated literature to the propaganda operation overseen by Goebbels and the *Reichskulturkammer*. But there is another aspect to the 'fate' of affirmative literature that is less a question of practical propaganda or opinion management, and rather one of ideology. The resurrection of the notion of an affirmative literature, an anachronism in modernity, could only flourish within the project of the 'common cause' in which the Germans were engaged from 1933, and this common cause was an ideological fiction.

Nazi ideology placed the opposite construction upon the First World War than that implied by the Literature of Negation. It filled the epistemological vacuum with an imaginary narrative. The story went: a Germany, destined for European leadership, betrayed and cheated of its rightful accession to dominance by modernity (that is, the Jews), was now at last girding itself to make amends, willing to risk annihilation in the process. Defeat in the Great War was a profoundly significant stage in the process of national renewal. The closing words of Franz Schauwecker's novel *Aufbruch der Nation* (*A Nation Awakes*, 1929) became famous: 'we had to lose the war in order to win the nation. ...'

Components of this narrative pre-existed the war, but only the trauma of the war could have converted anti-Modern *Heimat* sensibilities and anti-Semitism into a coherent myth of the German nation with enough authority to occupy a determining place in public life, which was now organized as if it were the expression of the world according to Germany. In German lands in 1918, the institutions of responsible government had actually collapsed rather than simply exposed their haplessness in the face of the logic of technology. This intensified the need to convert the experience of the loss of meaning into an excess of meaningfulness.

In the 1970s, Klaus Theweleit published a celebrated study of a certain body of writing that forms the bridge between this traumatic context and the fascist ideology informing the Third Reich. The texts he analysed in *Männerphantasien (Men's Fantasies)* – for instance by Dwinger, Jünger, Schauwecker, Zöberlein – are fictions and memoirs written by men associated with the Freikorps. These irregular military units were made up partly of units of the defeated German army and partly of bands of volunteers in ad hoc groups. In the aftermath of the defeat, they continued the struggle, twitching like an amputated limb of Wilhelmine German national ambition, helping to defeat the communists in Bavaria, the Baltic and Upper Silesia, but left betrayed and disenfranchized by the Weimar Republic. Theweleit analyses their literature in such a way as to bring out the pathological deformation effected by this combination of unplugged imperial ambition, brutalization as a result of the experience of modern technological warfare, and transition through a state of anarchy. Although he had a specific agenda (he wished to link fascism with patriarchy and capitalism and promote the concept of free-flowing socio-psychological energy expounded in Deleuze and Guattari's *Anti-Oedipe* of 1972), his reading of these texts demonstrates how the mixture of a strong sense of military hierarchy, the disinhibition occurring in combat and the experience of the historical collapse of authority, led to a dehumanizing hypertrophy of psychological defence mechanisms.

This writing, often in the form of memoir or diary, is tormented testimony to an injustice that exceeds the ability of the sufferer to comprehend it. The empty space where the source of justice should be located is filled with an excessive structure of control deeply complicit with destruction and death, with sacrifice as ecstatic fulfilment and the only surviving wellspring of true meaning. It is 'heroism of the absurd' (Eksteins 1989: 314). This psychotic energy was anti-literary in that it was impelled to bear true autobiographical witness to the source of meaning residing in the heart of darkness. It therefore needed emphatically to distinguish itself from what Goebbels was to call 'bloßes Artistentum' ('mere artistic facility'). Zöberlein regarded any attempt to clothe his testimony in literary art to be 'effete posturing' (Baird 2008: 99). Nevertheless, in the value it attached to documentary authenticity, quite distinct from the traditional values of literature that contributed to the propaganda interest of the Third Reich, this writing is an important forerunner of the autobiographical fiction that became a prominent feature of post-Second World War writing.

This discourse was useful as propaganda during the Weimar Republic, but, since it was intrinsically impractical due to its inebriation with death, needed pragmatic restraint once the National Socialist state was in power; hence Goebbels's much lighter touch with literature. He separated ideology from propaganda. Ideology was officially approved of and supported but not foisted upon readers. However, the kind of compensatory defensive structures disclosed by Theweleit in the Freikorps literature came to inform the national myth. This externalized the defensive 'character armour' developed in the poisoned matrix of Freikorps subjectivity and posited it as both subject and object of a redeemed and just reality.

Möller's *Thingspiel*, *The Frankenburg Dice Game*, was the embodiment of this (although Goebbels was in fact extremely enthusiastic about the performance). It represented the affirmative version of the unbound lust for justice of the Freikorps authors. The ritualistic enactment of the action, namely the reversal of a famous injustice perpetrated by the highest authorities of the Catholic Counter-Reformation upon Protestant Austrian peasants during the Thirty Years' War, put the audience (20,000 strong at the premiere) into the position of participating, by force of their massed spectatorship, in this performance of justice, countermanding the historical abuse of authority by the once-sovereign Emperor and his officials.

Despite Goebbels's aesthetic appreciation, the *Dice Game*, which has been described as 'a nationalist high mass' (Baird 2008: 182), clearly did not respect the distinction between ideology and propaganda. It marked at once the high point and the beginning of the decline of the *Thingspiel* movement. The event was held to be too religious by some factions in the circles vying for control of the Nazi cultural sphere, notably that around Alfred Rosenberg, which opposed the more aesthetically informed and nuanced direction of Goebbels. Möller himself, though a completely dedicated National Socialist, began to attract hostility for his uncompromising commitment. It is as if when a serious artist, as Möller assuredly was both by background and by influence, addressed the kind of desperate ideology that drove the Freikorps and Hitler himself, the pathological nihilism from which it sprang was revealed. There is an attachment to sacrifice for its own sake (this became explicit in Möller's controversial next play, the *Fall of Carthage*). The pervasive presence of 'blood' in the ideological reaches of *völkisch* and then Nazi discourse hardly distinguishes between the blood shed by those who oppose, or who are simply not part of, the chosen race, and the blood that courses in its veins, guaranteeing its racial purity. In the midst of the actual carnage of the war, Möller had to confront the fatally imaginary quality of the preoccupation with blood, death and sacrifice that he had once celebrated.

The famous public theatricality of the Third Reich (annual week-long Party rallies in Nuremberg, torchlight processions, forests of flags and massive phalanxes of uniforms, etc.) leapfrogged other forms of representation, including the *Thingspiel* movement, as manifestations of Schlösser's 'higher reality' and was itself merely a stage towards the enactment of the German mythical narrative of just retribution upon the stage of actual history. These circumstances go beyond the purely literary but are relevant because they situate literary culture, as we know and esteem it as a social and aesthetic practice, in a subordinate relation to a monstrous deformation of imaginary representations. This monstrous deformation, a transgression of the border between art and politics, is perhaps best exemplified in Hitler's own obsession with Wagner. Joachim Köhler (2000) has argued not only that the Wagner circle was influential in relation to the ideology and politics of National Socialism, which is beyond doubt, but further that Hitler confused the pleasure and subjective empowerment he experienced when listening to Wagner's music, of which he had been a fanatical devotee since 1906, with objective insight. According to Köhler, Hitler found in Wagner the higher reality, the mythic narrative that licensed his disregard of civilized and rational standards in public life.

Whether this is true or not, and whether or not Hitler did go to his death imagining himself the tragic hero of a Wagnerian music drama, the upshot of this fiction inflicted upon Europe and the world was that the curtain was once again drawn aside, as it had been between 1914 and 1919, not upon a metaphysical landscape of meaning and justice but upon the brute materiality of the world when it is without the benefit of either reason or love.

The German Democratic Republic

The German Democratic Republic was one part of the divided Germany that resulted from the outcome of the Second World War. It lasted from 1949 until 1990. Apart from the absence of what we would understand as a democratic government and the eventual historical failure of its project, it bore little resemblance to the previous regime. It lasted longer (the Third Reich lasted just six years before the beginning of the war which ended in its total collapse), it was much less murderous, it was largely dominated from outside (by the Soviet Union and by rivalry with the Federal Republic), and it was (distantly) based upon Marxism, which is an informed analysis of economic history, especially capitalism, and not a racist myth nourished by ignorance, prejudice and modern mass media. The common cause informing this authoritarian state had deeper roots in historical causality than the death-obsessed Third Reich, as well as a theoretical concern for the welfare of the whole human race, and not just one part of it.

Nevertheless, it was, like the Third Reich, a regime that considered it necessary to extend its influence to the spheres of public representation. Here too there was an official reality that literature was called upon to affirm. But there is something in Marxism about the sense of what reality is that confers upon literature a potential importance it could not have had under National Socialism. This is the question of whether human consciousness plays an active or a passive part in history. At the very heart of Marxism there is a hesitation about this, which had crucial consequences for the way literature was practised in a state claiming legitimacy from Marx.

That is why for the purpose of this chapter on the fate of affirmative literature we do not follow the otherwise very sound counsel of the DDR's leading literary historian, Wolfgang Emmerich. His advice was that, after the end of the DDR, its literature should no longer be treated as an epiphenomenon of the central historical phenomenon of a failed socialist state. Although we can see through the propaganda term 'real existing socialism' to the state of 'petrified hope' (in the words of the dissident intellectual Kurt Bartsch) that became of it, the writing that came about because of this ideological and economic context nevertheless offers a significant contrast to the literary culture in the capitalist democracies of the Federal Republic, Austria and Switzerland. This literature is often indifferent to its own lack of access to objective meaning and to its subliminal dependence upon market forces.

On the other hand, because it is based upon a dialectical view of history, or, to put it another way, upon a constitutive uncertainty about the priority of theory and practice, DDR literature tends in the event to outgrow the – artificial – boundaries of reality as defined in the DDR and approach the limit-writing of the Literature of Negation (Heiner Müller) or the serious middle-brow literature of capitalist democracy (Wolf Biermann, Stefan Heym, Ulrich Plenzdorf, Christa Wolf), or the elitist post-modern cultural landscape of the 1980s (Müller's work with Robert Wilson, the poets of the Prenzlauer Berg).

The entity that DDR literature was required to affirm was the result of a historical pincer movement. What had begun in theory in the tradition of German Idealism, in Hegel, if not already in Kant, returned in practice in the form of the dictatorship of the Marxist-Leninist Communist Party (called the SED, *Sozialistische Einheitspartei Deutschlands*, in the DDR) to impose itself upon one part of the country of its birth, but now unrecognizably pragmatic, not to say brutal, in its Stalinist variant. On the other side was a specifically German cultural consciousness. Although in retrospect the nasty farce that the DDR became looks like the revenge of history upon Hegel, at the time there was a justifiable temptation to see an historical dialectic at work. The new German state, notwithstanding the traumatic circumstances of its birth (but what birth is not traumatic?), was the continuation and completion in historical reality of a process of enlightenment and emancipation that had begun with the French Revolution and found its theoretical formulation in the German Idealist tradition. It was tempting to hope that these things, having emerged from a single source to become thesis and antithesis, might achieve synthesis in the return to their land of their origin. A body of Marxist thought, notably that of Karl Korsch, who influenced Brecht, the younger Georg Lukács (1885–1971), whose *Geschichte und Klassenbewußtsein* (*History and Class Consciousness*, 1923) is the classical exposition in Marxism of the historical agency of consciousness, and Ernst Bloch, whose work was important to Christa Wolf, lent theoretical support to this hope.

The promise of interaction between theory and practice was, as it were, embodied on the empirical-historical level in the convergence of Stalinist Germans returning from the Soviet Union, and émigré artists coming back from exile in other places who did not identify fully with the calcified Leninist view that the Party has a monopoly of historical consciousness and agency. Johannes R. Becher (1891–1958), the Hanns Johst of the DDR, exemplifies the former. He had been one of the most vocal and active Expressionists, and there can be no doubt about his identification with serious literature and – some version of – the German literary inheritance. But at the same time, he was a member of the 'Ulbricht Group', a government-in-waiting made up of German communists exiled in the Soviet Union who arrived in Berlin in 1945. Becher became the most prominent cultural bureaucrat in the government until his fall from favour in 1956, wielding actual and considerable power in the important field of cultural policy. He continued to be officially revered throughout the life of the Republic. Brecht, on the other hand, the most influential author in the DDR, both before his death (in 1956) and afterwards, had assiduously avoided residence in the Soviet Union during the years of exile. At the same time, he had been a convinced if heretical Marxist since the mid-1920s, and his work in the cultural sphere was clearly committed to the revolutionary overthrow of capitalism and the establishment of a socialist society.

Both Brecht and Becher believed in the historical significance of culture, the political cause of socialism, and their necessary interdependence. Becher, the bureaucrat, wrote in the journal *Sinn und Form* (*Meaning and Form*) about the philosophy of the sonnet, and Brecht, the maverick practitioner, received institutional recognition in the shape of his own theatre and ensemble. They supported one another, even though they were far apart in their aesthetic positions: for instance, Brecht's *Berliner Ensemble* staged Becher's play *Winterschlaf* (*Hibernation*) in 1954, while Becher extended official legitimation to Brecht, and the two of them often appeared together as the public representatives of culture in the early years of the DDR.

More generally, in word and deed, the Party sponsored authors and encouraged them to support the common socialist cause, while many authors, for their part, were enthusiastic about influencing the consciousness of the kind of individual who would populate the new society. Yet the indeterminate relation between history and consciousness, practice and theory, left fundamental questions open: were authors merely supporting a regime, or helping to realize it in history? Did playwrights, novelists and poets hope to confirm the new consciousness, generated by the change of the relations of labour and production under socialism, or did they hope to shape that consciousness? Were they required to speak to and for the new individual populating the new society, or cooperate on a future model of subjective identification which, when realized, would make the new society possible?

These imponderables translate into roughly three aesthetic positions which offer a schema for defining and exploring the fluctuating relations between the politicians (and academics) of the SED and the actual writers of the DDR. In essence, the discussion went back to the late nineteenth century when socialism had first become a party political reality in Germany. The question of the role of literature before, during, and after the revolution was the subject of much debate on the left during the Weimar Republic, and many individuals, such as Becher and Brecht, but also Georg Lukács, Anna Seghers (1900–1983), Peter Huchel (1903–1981) and others, participated then and continued to be involved in the post-war situation.

These three positions are, first, the adaptation of the bourgeois institution of literature of the preceding two centuries insofar as it can be useful in the new situation. Second, the idea that, with the end of the bourgeois era and its replacement by the proletariat on the way to the classless society, a specifically popular literature must develop, so that the division between intellectuals and workers may eventually be overcome along with the other injurious splits in consciousness systemically entailed by capitalism. And finally, the idea that neither of these, somewhat mechanical, 'reflections' of the new social order can be sufficient to the raising of a new consciousness and that the 'vanguard' political consciousness of the Party, if it is not to become simply coercive and arbitrary, must be matched by an avant-garde in art, that is, a practice that operates at the edge of the areas mapped out by institutions, like a pioneer exploring new territory.

At the time just before the founding of the DDR, the effects of the first view obtained for the practical reason that, immediately after the war, the issue was how to deal with the ideological-psychological aftermath of fascism. The model to hand for this was the broad coalition of left-wing parties that had been formed rather belatedly in the 1930s under direction from Moscow as the Popular Front (*Volksfront*), in order to oppose fascism. The form of culture fit to this task was the traditional one, since the need for compromise precluded support either for radical innovation or for strict Party oversight.

Although from about 1947 onwards the Communist Party-line did establish itself (due to changes in the larger power-political context), the atmosphere of a single cultural programme for all Germans lived on in the mind and dispositions of Becher, and in the influential and high-quality journal *Sinn und Form*, edited until 1962 by the poet of inner emigration, Peter Huchel. (*Die neue Rundschau* performed a similar tightrope act on behalf of serious high culture during the Third Reich.) It has been argued that literature right across the ideological spectrum in or around 1930 retreated to established positions, as a recoil, in the cultural sphere, from the proliferation of cultural modernisms. These were associated in people's minds with the crises of the 1920s, particularly the crash of 1929–30 (and, in our argument, with the founding crisis of the century: the First World War). This cultural reaction applied also, as we saw, to literature in the Third Reich, and in this there is another parallel between the two 'affirmative' literatures. They both have something of a conservative or museum-like attitude towards literature and its traditional genres. After the end of the DDR, the editor of the cultural journal *Merkur*, Karl Heinz Bohrer, referred to its literature as having been preserved as if in a 'cultural conservation area' ('Kulturschutzgebiet'), not only retaining the respectability literature had enjoyed in the bourgeois era but also protecting it artificially from the dominance of the technological media that, in the democratic capitalist sphere of publicity, removed literature from its position of privilege among practices of representation.

The importance of literature in relation to the establishment of the new consciousness (however that was to be understood) for the SED is clear from the official support authors received under the regime. Members of the Deutscher Schriftsteller Verband (Association of German Writers), founded in 1952, like members of the Nazi Reichskulturkammer but without quite the sinister threat behind the latter, were signed up to the collective political enterprise and received preferential treatment in housing and other areas (such as loans and bursaries and permission to travel abroad), and there was a substantial number of literary prizes and other official inducements to literary activity. The vocation of literary author, in this sense, was institutionalized, and this very institutionalization was conducive to a conservative construction of literature (and to the authors themselves developing a delusional sense of their own influence). It was exactly this that, in the 1980s, caused the western-inspired Prenzlauer Berg poets to ignore the official circuits of the artificial DDR public sphere altogether, reading and publishing only in unofficial formats.

There was another reason why the DDR looked to the past. The rejection of capitalism and embrace of communism was as fundamental a rebuttal of fascism as one could wish for, but it also involved pledging allegiance to an international revolutionary movement above narrow national concerns. This required a break with the bourgeois tradition and the espousal of a cultural policy for the labourers and peasants ('Arbeiter und Bauern') after whom the DDR named itself. In other words, given that the avant-garde, after a brief but glorious flowering in the first years of the Russian Revolution, had been murderously rooted out by the Soviet regime, it meant some version of the 'literature for and by the people' model. However, the parallel existence of a capitalist Germany in the form of the Federal Republic required the DDR to stake a strong claim to the German cultural heritage in order not to surrender it to the class enemy. This was all the more natural because, as we have seen, the line of thought that led to Stalin had begun in theoretical form in Germany.

Brecht argued that works from the German tradition, if they were creatively placed in their historical (that is, Marxist-Leninist) context would make it possible to bring out their true national, and therefore their international, meaning. He was talking about the quintessential German theme of Faust, which he took up in 1953 with a production of *Urfaust* at the Berliner Ensemble. Hanns Eisler too turned to the story of Faust in the early years of the DDR, publishing a libretto for an opera on the theme, in its pre-Goethean incarnation. They were both responding, like the serious artists they were, to exactly the challenge of providing the fledgling state with a distinctively German, yet also socialist, culture. However, Walter Ulbricht, the first leader of the DDR, averred that the Party would not permit the 'formalistic rape' of this national monument. On one hand, this illustrates the SED's fear of surrendering the German legacy to the capitalists in the West. On the other, it is a fine example of how non-dialectical, *dirigiste* and philistine the Party was.

Goethe (whose two-hundredth anniversary of his birth it was in 1949) was interpreted instead in such a way as to highlight his suitability as a forerunner of Socialist Realism. 'Formalist' was the communist equivalent of *entartet*, a scare word for modern art, held by both Nazis and communists to pose the threat of subversion to the ideological dominance of their respective parties. In 1953, Wilhelm Girnus produced an anthology of Goethe's classicist aesthetic statements, identifying him as 'the greatest realist in the German language' in order to establish the appropriate credentials. The preferred Faust was the hero of the rising middle class who had the vision, at the end of *Faust Zweiter Teil*, to see the post-feudal future and therefore prepare the way for the classless present. In this way, the reassuring figure of the classical Goethe was able to lend his authority and aura to the culture of the new German state.

Associated with the name of the Russian revolutionary author Maxim Gorki and enshrined in dogma since the early 1930s, 'Socialist Realism' was the practical solution found by the Soviets to how literature should serve Party interests. There were many famous and successful products of this aesthetic in the DDR. They start with the 1951 novel by Eduard Claudius (originally a bricklayer), *Menschen an unserer Seite* (*The People by our Side*) – which has something of the feel of a frontier Western about it – on the first heroic 'activist' of the DDR, Hans Garbe (Claudius makes a sheaf into an ear and calls him Hans Ähre), who achieved fame for an extraordinary feat of bricklaying in 1949. Erik Neutsch's later *Spur der Steine* (*Traces of Stones*, 1964), possibly the best-selling novel of the entire DDR, offered an analogous pioneer romance for the optimistic period of the early 1960s. The spectacularly popular *Nackt unter Wölfen* (*Naked among Wolves*, 1958) by Bruno Apitz is a shrewd blend of a Second World War escape story and a celebration of the pre-history of the DDR, set, amazingly, in Buchenwald. Hailed as a Socialist Realist classic, it may have owed something of its popularity to its deviation from the Socialist Realist tendency to depict an idealized contemporary DDR with formulaic monotony. Christa Wolf's *Der geteilte Himmel* (*Divided Sky*, 1963) and Erwin Strittmatter's *Ole Bienkopp* (1964) (like Neutsch's 1964 book), all from a time when optimism about the DDR's development had been refreshed by an economic upturn and the building of the Berlin Wall to stem the westward brain drain, are decent novels about processes of production and issues of management responsibility which successfully weave these mundane but real questions with stories about individuals. All of these novels contain examples of less-than-perfect heroes (although they are 'positive' heroes as the genre, like all popular genres, demanded), both good and bad Party officials, representatives of un- or only imperfectly reconstructed fascism and so on. The works by Wolf and Strittmatter cautiously open up space for a critique of ossified bureaucracy from the point of view of creative socialist individuals. The Party put a stop to this sort of development in 1965 in one of its recurrent clampdowns upon cultural developments they claimed in theory to encourage.

These products of the doctrine of Socialist Realism stand midway between our first possibility of socialist literature and our second. On one hand, they are descendants of the great nineteenth-century novels of Stendhal and Balzac, a connection forged particularly by Lukács in the 1930s in an attempt to keep his intellectual and his pragmatic positions more or less compatible with one another. But, on the other, Gorki was exemplary because he was a man of the people, or at least a man who had experienced deprivation and hardship, and spoke in his fiction (for instance, *The Mother* of 1907) for the Russian masses nearly liberated in 1904, and triumphant in 1917–1923.

This arranged marriage between the nineteenth-century form of the novel and the need to encourage individual readers to identify with the collective historical heroism of the working class produced what one might call 'popular naturalism' (which would describe all the novels mentioned above and many more from these first phases of the DDR). Lukács rejected Naturalism (that is to say, Zola et al.) for being superficial, which in the Marxist-Leninist vocabulary meant liberal or social-democratic. He argued instead for the aesthetic 'totality' of the earlier Realists, by which he meant that they constructed social reality not just as a description of circumstances but also as an embodiment of values (albeit bourgeois ones at that point in history). The new version of this 'totality' was proletarian and no longer bourgeois, so novel plots, characters and narrative techniques would reflect this (though Lukács never compromised his intellectual standards enough to express satisfaction with novels actually produced in the DDR). What less Party-bound communist intellectuals such as Brecht and Ernst Bloch disliked about this aesthetic conservatism was that the readers were held in a familiar and conventional, that is, unquestioning and passive, subject position by the style itself, regardless of the plot, story, tone of narrative and so on. On the other hand, this is exactly what appealed to the politicians, although they protested the opposite. As far as they were concerned, and as Lenin had taught, it was the Party that held historical agency on behalf of the proletariat, representing the institutionalized consciousness of humanity, and it was thus in its interests (exactly as it had been in Goebbels's) that art should reflect the objective 'laws of history' as they unrolled, and not encourage readers to think for themselves, become actively conscious or take historical agency into their own hands.

The DDR novels of the first decade or so are thus naturalist, with a small N, in that they are epistemologically unchallenging, but the obverse of this is that they are accessible (one of the criteria for Socialist Realism) and were enjoyed, and of course they do connect, or they did for a while, reading pleasure with a commitment to a common cause on the basis of a scientific worldview. This makes them aesthetically cognate with the kind of 1890s Naturalism we discussed in chapter 3, except that they made no claim to being aesthetically cutting-edge. On the contrary, what was modern now was the 'reality' itself, not the way it passed into fiction. Since there was no purely commercially driven literature on the DDR, and little popular literature in the western sense (it was hard, for instance, to devise plots for detective stories in a society claiming to have done away with the social roots of criminality), these novels offered a blend of entertainment and instruction which, from the point of view of the subjective reading experience, must have been rare since the eighteenth century. They also form part of the tradition of middle-brow serious popular naturalism that is usually invisible in literary histories of Germany (or only visible in the form of peaks such as Keller, Fontane and Raabe, all of whom were appreciated in the DDR). Some of them are not so far from the fiction of Böll in the West (whose work was actually published in the DDR until 1966 or so, when a hard line was laid down). A common ancestor is Hans Fallada (1893–1947), the Weimar social realist, inner emigrant and subsequent inhabitant of the Soviet Zone, about whom Christa Wolf wrote her student dissertation.

In 1959, at what became a famous literature conference held in the cultural palace of the Bitterfeld Electro-Chemical People's Collective, officers of the Party and the State, together with 300 worker authors ('schreibende Arbeiter') and 150 professional authors, made a commitment to increasing the involvement of workers in the production of literature and that of authors in the processes of production. This unusually constructive move by the authorities reflected dissatisfaction on their part at the failure of the bulk of Socialist Realist formula novels either to hold the interest of the reading public after the ideological honeymoon period or to produce literature that could show the DDR off in the West as the cultural and literary example it wished to be. They were neither as a rule good enough to qualify as heirs to the German cultural tradition, nor did they represent a genuine *rapprochement* between workers and authors because, although many novelists, such as Claudius, Apitz and Strittmatter were of proletarian origin, they were nevertheless professional writers. The entirely laudable, if utopian, objective was to overcome the division between artists and ordinary people, said to be entailed by capitalism (this was the 1960s when Joseph Beuys was declaring that everyone was an artist, and hundreds of thousands of people in Western European and US rock bands and art schools were proving it). The Bitterfeld initiative was indeed a measurable success, especially in encouraging workers to write collectively about their everyday experience in what were called *Brigadetagebücher* (team diaries) and writing circles. Novels like those of Strittmatter and Wolf (who went to work in a collective) are clearly influenced by what became known as the *Bitterfelder Weg*. The idea, then, of a dialectic between Party and people (and not only intellectuals) to progress socialism was alive in the DDR to this extent. On the other hand, it is entirely characteristic that by 1964 the authorities found it necessary to call a second Bitterfeld conference, at which it was explained that the point of view of the ordinary man and woman had been represented sufficiently, not to say to excess, and it was time to start producing texts which also gave the point of view of the responsible 'planners and leaders' of industry and agriculture.

The DDR lasted long enough to produce, in its middle years, at least two writers who in their creative maturity were of world stature, the dramatist Heiner Müller and the novelist Christa Wolf (born 1929). Müller and Wolf developed techniques of writing which belong to the third of our possibilities, namely an avant-garde literature for socialism.

Müller's remarkable aesthetic has already been dealt with under the heading of the Literature of Negation. The essence there was that, in his embrace of the dialectic of history, the moment of negation assumed special aesthetic and philosophical force. This went beyond any point that could credibly be thought useful in the construction of a real society. His potential significance for the development of a specific DDR consciousness, on the other hand, was as a powerful artistic corrective to Socialist Realism. In his dramas he tried to enliven its inert subservience to the official account of reality by remaining sensitive to the weight of actual historical circumstances. Hence his version of the true story, used by Claudius in his *Menschen an unserer Seite* of 1951, *Der Lohndrücker* (*The Scab*, 1956–7), takes account of the contradiction hidden by Claudius, namely that to perform prestigious feats of labour tends not just to glorify the new ethic but also to raise norms. This contradiction assumed concrete form in 1953 when the workers took to the streets precisely to protest at the attempt by the authorities to raise norms. Hans Garbe, upon whose exploit both Claudius and Müller based their works, was among them, his medal on his chest. The uprising spread across the DDR rapidly and could only be contained by force. Müller's play makes no attempt to smooth over the objective divergence of interest between workers and government but gives it dramatic form (that is, as you might say, makes it conscious), so that whatever lessons are learned from it for the progress of socialism will at least be real ones, even if they are not easy.

Müller's dramatization of scenes from Neutsch's massive best-seller *Spur der Steine, Der Bau* likewise addressed a problem Socialist Realism obscured. For Neutsch, as for the SED, the construction ('der Bau') of the Berlin Wall in 1961 was a measure intended to enable the state to consolidate itself, both in terms of improved economic development and of untroubled identification on the part of its citizens. For Müller, this new reality could not exclude the division of Germany upon which it was based. The contradiction was objectively given. The DDR was a construction site but also a site of containment. The unresolved question was whether the gains outweighed the losses.

With the maturing of the period of 'construction' in DDR literature into one of a developed self-consciousness in the 1960s and 1970s, Müller's writing deepened its engagement with the intransigence of actual history in the direction of the German past. Because it is a propaganda tool as much as an aesthetic, Socialist Realism has an interest in affirming the present and treating the problems of the past as if they were definitively overcome. The identity of the DDR depended upon the certainty that fascism had been overcome by the fulfilled project of the German socialist movement. Müller's work became truly probing when he developed theatrical and poetic means to suggest that it had not. It is not just contemporary circumstances and the survival of personal memories and attitudes of fascism that beset and test the socialist project but problems of the unsurmounted past within the very project itself. Another way of putting this would be to say that Müller takes the traumatic birth of the DDR seriously. Rather than the successful culmination of a series of bloody failed revolutions, the last of these as recent as 1918–19, the DDR, as *Germania Tod in Berlin* and *Die Schlacht (The Battle)* (both finished in the early to mid-1970s but originally dating back to the 1950s) suggest, is still struggling with an internalized authoritarian psyche that both caused the series of failures and informed the Third Reich.

With this move into the internalization of historical contradictions, together with a radical use of montage to bring it to an audience, Müller goes through and beyond the specifics of the historical situation of the DDR, and indeed during the 1980s he became part of the niche avant-garde performance scene in the West. Yet it is hard to believe that his experience of the violence of history upon the subject could have been so creatively suffered had he not struggled viscerally not only with the flawed socialist project of the DDR but also with his mentor Brecht who solved the problem of how serious art and political practice can be combined, only for his solution to be dissolved by the historical process. In order to remain true to Brecht one had to betray him, Müller famously claimed. He did both.

It may be an optical illusion produced by the western perspective, but more than any other author it is Christa Wolf who has come to personify the best possible spin that one can put upon the DDR. While never just servile, not even in her Socialist Realist period in the early 1960s, she represented a committed yet critical socialist consciousness throughout. More than once, she spoke up publicly and courageously against repressive measures, for instance at the 11 Plenum in 1965 when, in closed session, she was the only person to challenge Ulbricht, and then again in 1976, when she was a prominent protester, this time publicly, at the expatriation of the singer-songwriter Wolf Biermann. Like Müller, she remained in the DDR until the end, although, also like him, international recognition had given her the possibility of independence from it during the last decade of its existence. When the end did come, she, Müller and some others such as the poet and dramatist Volker Braun, were left exposed as utopians, one side of an abandoned dialectic, imagining briefly that the collapse of the old regime might be to the benefit of the ideals it had betrayed. Wolf's notorious (but actually insignificant) involvement with the *Stasi* in the late 1950s / early 1960s, whilst a perfect story for western publicity, in fact further exemplifies her representativeness as an intellectual torn between commitment to what was and to what might yet come to be. Her writing chronicles the increasing moral and psychological impossibility of such a dual allegiance.

In 1963, a conference on Kafka held, appropriately, in Prague, dared raise the issue of alienation under socialism. Kafka's work provided a reminder that there is an area of individual experience that will never be perfectly taken up into collective socialized identity, and that serious modern literature is called to address it. The thrust of the 1965 clampdown was to limit writers' freedom to explore the area of (inevitable) shortfall between lived individual experience and the aspirations of socialism, maintaining that the only problems that may occupy socialist literature are problems that it can hope to solve (like a sort of cultural engine oil). Ulbricht claimed that a true *Menschengemeinschaft* (this was the SED's version of the Nazis' *Volksgemeinschaft*) had been achieved, and there was therefore no longer any need to devote the public resource of literature to subjective experiences in tension with this assertion. On the contrary, to do so could only be subversive.

With *Nachdenken über Christa T* (*Reflections on Christa T*, 1968, Wolf verbalized exactly this area of experience. It is writing responding to the challenge posed by the falsehood of the position taken up by the Party. The probing, exploratory tone, in which a first-person narrator assembles a portrait of her dead friend from the information and partial knowledge available to her, unites Modernist sensitivity to language and to the complex construction of the subject with a clear moral agenda: to give form to the discrepancy between subjective aspiration and real possibility. The positive hero required by popular fiction and Socialist Realism alike is here pointedly withheld in favour of the opacity of individual singularity and suffering. The lack of fit between personal ideals and the fulfilments on offer, even in the socialist *Menschengemeinschaft*, turns exemplarity against itself: the story of Christa T's life and death is, as we read in chapter 5, a 'Beispiel, nicht beispielhaft' ('an example, not exemplary').

Sensitivity to language and to the complex construction of the subject also inform Wolf's most significant work, a novel that seems to stand at the point of intersection of every major twentieth-century German concern of substance, *Kindheitsmuster* (*Patterns of Childhood*, 1976). Wolf's distinctive contribution, like Müller's, is the potentially subversive one of reopening the fascist past. Her engagement this time is not with an opaque other but with the opaque self. Christa T, for all her problematic subjectivity, had been impeccably anti-fascist (and even a fan of Gorki). The empirical Christa, like all Germans of her generation, had on the contrary been socialized during the Third Reich. Wolf's novel finds technically sophisticated means to explore this difficult relationship between the adult socialist and the adolescent Nazi.

This substantial novel, Wolf's longest by some way, represents a direct confrontation between the Enlightenment moment of social hope that dwelt in the hearts of the best East Germans and the twentieth-century nightmare that is the condition of the Literature of Negation. Wolf's writing is Modernist not for the sake of being so but in order to acknowledge the depths of what threatens the utopia that would make an honest discourse of Socialist Realism. It expresses the central issue of the agency or otherwise of consciousness in terms of the relation between the individual subject and history. In order to validate the willed commitment expressed in Wolf's socialist convictions and, in its service, her art as a writer, it is necessary to plumb the past in which the wellsprings of responsibility and personality lie hidden.

This is from one perspective an anti-fascist undertaking because it involves coming to terms with the Nazi past. Although this had been out of bounds in the 1950s and 1960s, Erich Honecker had made a high-profile public declaration on succeeding Ulbricht in 1971 that, so long as an author's commitment to socialism was not in doubt, there were to be 'no taboos' for literature. In this sense, writing in 1974, Wolf was following the Party line. The 'patterns' of childhood in the case of Nelly – the name the novel's narrator gives to her childhood incarnation, who throughout is referred to in the third person – are certainly fascist ones, involving an internalization of anxiety, 'Angst', manifest in a feeling of self-alienation and characterized by the need to delete its traces in memory (chapter 10), which the narrative then painstakingly excavates.

Yet anxiety remains with the narrator as an adult, and the questions inevitably arise as to its meaning in the contemporary situation. Wolf's indefatigably civilized prose arrives at a perfect formulation of the question (which is not the same as an answer to it). The debilitating anxiety from which she suffers while engaged in the work of archaeology of the self can be one of two things: either no more than cowardice at facing the taboo of one's own Nazi past, and thus surmountable by the moral act of writing (sanctioned by the official cultural line of the Party), or else, and more worryingly, an existential anxiety ('Grundangst') at experiencing *too much*, and thus of entering a 'zone of discord' ('Nichtübereinstimmung') whose climate, she writes (chapter 17), 'you' (informal plural) have not yet learned how to tolerate.

The implication is that the self-alienation felt by Nelly as a girl is a pre-echo of the anxiety its recall occasions in the adult narrator. She too is self-estranged as she tries to adapt her authentic subjectivity, in all its unresolved and contradictory complexity, to the cultural needs of the people of the German socialist state.

By 1979, when Wolf wrote the *Erzählung*, *Was bleibt* (*What Remains*), she had become accustomed enough to the climate of discord to write about self-alienation in the DDR explicitly (although not yet publicly: the text was not published until 1990). In the 1976 novel, Wolf was still resolved to face down and overcome the anxiety set free by her honest return to the past. In the character of her daughter, Lenka, she embodies hope for a less alienated future subject of socialism (indeed there is a similar figure of hope in a young woman author in *Was bleibt*), and she finishes the novel not only by at last saying 'I', but enlisting the power of the imagination in the service of moral and social progress, promising not to rebel against the limits of the sayable ('die Grenzen des Sagbaren').

The complex literary apparatus of the text is thus finally pitched against negation and dedicated to the belief that the work of consciousness it exemplifies can loosen the dogma of the present and contribute to the socialist future. However, both the central importance in the text of the death of Ingeborg Bachmann (chapter 8), as a result of which a 'dark thread is woven into the weft of the pattern', and the handling of the historical trauma of displacement (especially the clinically traumatic moment in chapter 13 in which Nelly, helping refugees fleeing westwards, is handed a baby frozen to death, and blacks out) contribute to a composition which is by no means innocent of the moment of negation at the heart of Modernism. Wolf's text is moved by the inability of the language that she employs with such assiduousness to overcome this negation, and by awareness that under-structuring all traumatic loss is a constitutive disunity of the self that cannot be written out of history.

During the slow years of stagnation and decline, Wolf's writing took up global issues, subsuming the evident shortcomings of the regime in the DDR under a generalized technophobia and critique of patriarchy (*Kassandra* [1983], *Störfall* [*Accident*, 1987]). The text *Kein Ort. Nirgends* (*No Place. Nowhere*, 1979), fictionalizing the figures of Heinrich von Kleist and Karoline von Günderrode, reflected both the renewed interest, after 1971, in the whole range of the German legacy, and not just the politically correct Enlightenment socialist lineage that had been canonized in the DDR until that point, and the marginalization of intellectuals who from the later 1970s were less willing or able to collude in the fiction that they formed part of a genuine 'public sphere'.

It was in respect of Wolf Biermann that the relation between intellectuals and the state lost all realistic claim to being authentically dialectical. Biermann, the son of a Jewish communist father who had died in Auschwitz, came to the DDR voluntarily from Hamburg in 1953. He became notorious for his poems and songs of which this extract from 'Rücksichtslose Schimpferei' ('Ruthless Cursing') is a brief but characteristic example:

> If I were to smile mildly
> At each one of your fat lies
> You'd consider me smart

If I were to ignore injustice
Just as you ignore your wives
– you'd have long since
embraced me as one of your own (Biermann 1977, trans. Jack Zipes)

The authorities saw this as 'thinly veiled petty bourgeois, anarchistic socialism' and banned Biermann from performing or publishing his work in the DDR for ten years. Yet he was a committed pre-Stalinist Marxist, and he regarded his work as a contribution to a German state that never ceased to claim to be founded upon the ideal of anti-fascism. As a protest singer or *chansonnier*, there was something western about his brand of performance, and indeed he was celebrated in the West as a dissident (which is why he was a thorn in the festering side of the SED). Yet he offers a concrete example of our second type of possibility for literature under socialism, and in some ways combines all three. He saw himself as playing in respect of the DDR 'classic', Brecht, the role Heine (the champagne socialist of German literature and a hero in the DDR) had fulfilled in respect of Goethe, namely that of bringing classical language into the common parlance of ordinary people.

As we saw, when Honecker took office as the First Secretary of the Central Committee of the SED in 1971, it appeared for a moment that the cultural dialectic that had often seemed to become arrested under the old hardline Stalinist Ulbricht was going to begin to move once more. Honecker effectively called time on the doctrine of Socialist Realism. The *Bitterfelder Weg* (Mark II) was officially buried two years later. A prominent example of the relaxation of aesthetic dogma, as well as the new, productive, attitude to the classical legacy, was the spectacular multimedia success of *Die neuen Leiden des jungen W*. [*The New Sorrows of Young Werther*, 1972] by the film writer Ulrich Plenzdorf (1934–2007). Christa Wolf's *Nachdenken über Christa T*, which had been published in a very small edition in 1969 in order to minimize its critical impact, was now republished in a printing large enough to satisfy the actual public interest in her work.

Beneath the surface, however, coercion and lack of imagination on the part of the bureaucrats continued to hold sway. In 1976, Biermann was deprived of his citizenship while giving concerts in the West. This was the culmination of a conspiracy on the part of the SED to expatriate him that, as documents have since shown, went back as far as 1973. The measure backfired: not only was this a propaganda coup of huge proportions for the West but, more damagingly for the Party, all the most prominent writers of the DDR objected immediately and publicly (using the western media), which added to the PR disaster. Even worse, the affair initiated an unprecedented exodus of writers and artists from the DDR, which did not really stop until its final collapse, and from which the literary establishment in the East never recovered.

In exile, Biermann held to his belief in a dialectical brand of Marxism, associated with the name of Rosa Luxemburg, but his exclusion marked the end of any pretence that a genuinely progressive dialectic was possible in the 'real existing' DDR. A singer-songwriter with popular appeal was excluded, and the entire establishment of less populist, more nuanced and pragmatic Marxist authors (apart from the most died-in-the-wool Socialist Realists like Neutsch or writer-administrators like Hermann Kant) felt compelled to stand up and be counted in his support. It crystallized the sense that the DDR project had failed, even if some outstanding and authentic writers like Müller, Wolf and Braun remained in a kind of ideological limbo until self-deception became out of the question in 1989.

Although the DDR project certainly failed, history has yet to pronounce on the meaning of that failure. As Biermann remarked in 1974: 'I do not believe that Marxism is invincible because it is true [...] Truth can certainly be defeated, if the lie is well enough armed' (quoted in Gooch 1977: 7).

It remains to sketch briefly the story of the lyric, that aspect of DDR literature that Wolfgang Emmerich most wished to see rescued from reductive identification with a political regime, naming Erich Arendt, Karl Mickel, Richard Leising, Wulf Kirsten, Volker Braun, Bert Papenfuß-Gorek, Uwe Kolbe and Durs Grünbein in this cause. The story began with Becher and Huchel, both committed to the 'modern restoration' of bourgeois poetry, on one hand, and Brecht, as the representative of a commitment to literary modernization, on the other, while the Party wanted a lyric version of Socialist Realism, in other words an affirmative form of verse, stressing the collective at the expense of the individual. These older poets and others adapted as best they could to the task of construction but, once a younger generation had reached maturity in the DDR, it became possible for the lyric to come into its own for three specific reasons. First, the lyric is the most intense form of literature and, even in its bourgeois incarnation, linguistically creative and probing. Second, the DDR, as we have seen, was programmatically pro-literature and therefore at some level favourable to the composition of serious lyric poetry. Finally, the poets at the right age actually to experience themselves as part of an existing collective with a communal project for the future informed by the best ideals of mankind were at the same time by now able to write poetry of unique lived experience within it. In the traditional institution of the lyric,

Braun, Heinz Czechowski, Mickel, Reiner Kunze, Sarah and Rainer Kirsch and others pitched textually refined examples of raw consciousness against the collectivized consciousness claimed by the Party. At moments such as Stephan Hermlin's famous *Lyrik Abend* (Poetry Evening) of 1962 (at which Biermann made his debut, and for organizing which Hermlin lost his job), and in collections like *In diesem besseren Land* (*In This Better Country*), edited by Adolf Endler and Mickel in 1966, and *Saison für Lyrik* (*Season for Verse*), edited by Joachim Schreck in 1968, they provoked and tested the claim of the cultural functionaries to ownership of what Endler later called 'a planned literary history'.

The Party and its literature professors did their best to co-opt Brecht against what was (accurately) felt by them to be a resurgence of subjectivism. They used his distinction between 'profane' and 'pontifical' poetry to distinguish the socially useful lyric from metaphysical abstraction in the line of Hölderlin, which they claimed gave succour to the class enemy, and recommended instead the Heine tradition of folk song-inspired direct and accessible popular verse. We know how they responded when Wolf Biermann offered them exactly that. They recalled how Brecht had always insisted upon the authority of the author in relation to his subjective experience, reminding poets not to confuse the complex experiencing self with the lyrical self, the latter defined precisely by mastery over the former (just as they defined the mastery of the Party's consciousness by its priority over that of individual subjects).

In truth, this generation of poets (including Biermann) were the genuine heirs of Brecht in lyric poetry, as Müller became in the sphere of public dramatic representations. Brecht had briefly been in a position during the Weimar Republic to put Modernism or avant-gardism ('Formalism') into the service of the communist cause because anti-individualism, *Einverständnis*, was itself aesthetically and politically provocative (and thus engaged the pleasure of the reader or receiver). These poets retained the *Einverständnis*, and restored the provocation which had fallen away in the framework of a socialist state and without which there is no genuine dialectic, or, to put it another way, no real cultural pleasure, no 'Kunstgenuss' (as Endler wrote in 1972 in the course of a public debate on lyric poetry). They did this by reasserting subjective experience as intransigent (although not absolute). This was less affirmative, in the mechanical sense, and more resonant with the definition of 'affirmative culture' given by Marcuse in his famous essay of 1937 in the *Zeitschrift für Sozialforschung*, in which he argued that, in the condition of modernity, culture can be both gratifying and socially productive. Paradoxically, the theory and practice of the poets in the various lyric debates of the 1960s and early 1970s strategically deployed poetry, *das Gedicht*, as something which, by tradition, resists strategic deployment. These years represent a moment at which, as Emmerich argues, the profane and the pontifical, Brecht and Hölderlin, did cooperate.

Without exception, these poets became disillusioned, or masked their disillusion in self-delusion. In many cases, anything even resembling a belief in the active role of consciousness for history ceased when they fell silent or left the country. The new generation of disaffected post-modern poets associated with the Prenzlauer Berg district of East Berlin in the 1980s illustrates both the degree to which the DDR had failed and the overmastering influence of the West. The radical refusal of these poets to lend legitimacy to the official public sphere seals the fate of affirmative literature. This writing shades into the literature of democratic capitalism, to which we turn in the next chapter.

This story of lyric poetry in the DDR sums up this whole episode in the cultural history of German literature. Literature is taken extremely seriously (the bourgeois model) and supported and practised in the name of the people and the common cause (the proletarian option). It then comes, by virtue of a commitment to both those things and with the passing of historical time, to typify the best of DDR literature when it rediscovers for itself an authentic Modernism in the form of a cultural project that touches the limit of the human subject, without totalizing or dismissing either the subject or the limits. It posits the active role of consciousness in history, and then, as in Günter Kunert's poem 'Lagebericht' ('Update') already in 1970, seems to testify to the opposite in disillusion and delusion: consciousness of its own historical impotence.

The implicit claim by the western-influenced poets of the 1980s and commentators in the West after 1989 that their own critical consciousness is somehow located closer to the engine of history is suspect and tendentious. What we read from this hope and its dashing is the moving of the tectonic plates of history, and the merit of it is that at least the touch of this incommensurate motion upon real existing subjects is manifest in literature, and neither ludically disavowed nor commodified by it.

6

Literature in Democratic Capitalism

The literary field of democratic capitalism can be pictured as lying between the limit points with which the two previous chapters have been concerned. At one side is the Literature of Negation, turning away from the particulars of society and history in order to contribute to them as literature. At the other is the impact on literature of social revolution, which is the expression in terms of power and institutions of the imaginary constructions, dreams and visions with which literature is concerned. The whole field, in a creative ferment and variety only possible under the conditions of capitalist democracy, is warped, as it were, by the effects of the market.

If these conditions apply to all modern democratic societies, they clearly apply in a specific way to literature in German. Germany appeared in the nineteenth century to be heading towards leadership of the free world but became, in the subsequent century, a succession of traumatized rumps. The resonance of this was felt across the different Germanies, German-writing countries, exile communities and isolated individuals of the twentieth century.

The moment of negation, the proximity of actual historical events that could only be addressed by (and give substance to) forms of creative evasion, ran beneath the cultural ferment of the Weimar Republic (1918–1933), and virtually paralysed the literary creativity of the Federal Republic (1949–). And while Weimar was alive with revolutionary dreams, the Federal Republic found the energy to live with its necessary denial through dreams of utopia, some of which were supported in an ambiguous way by the DDR, the 'real existing' sibling and rival, a failed realization or 'stranded object', in Eric Santner's term, of the socialist dream of Weimar.

Peter Sloterdijk, in a major work of creative cultural criticism, *Kritik der zynischen Vernunft* (*Critique of Cynical Reason*, 1983), made the important link between Weimar and what was then the contemporary reality of the Federal Republic. He reasoned that the mentality – he called it 'enlightened false consciousness' – common to both was more vibrant and self-aware in the 1920s, more able to combat the top-down cynicism of modern political realities with a bottom-up subversive 'kynicism' associated by Sloterdijk with the figure of the Greek philosopher Diogenes. In order to understand ourselves, he argued, we need to understand Weimar, to whose level of consciousness the present can only aspire.

Sloterdijk observed that the most important rules guiding human behaviour concern not what to do but what to not do (Sloterdijk 1983: 939). In the world of enlightened false consciousness, a disabused modernity, without beliefs other than the conviction that there is nothing to believe in and no greater error than to submit to the thought that there might be, there is a paucity of guidance in relation to those areas of experience that require silence, respect, the admission of unknowing. On the other hand, there is no brake whatsoever upon activity, 'doing', amplified to unimaginable and literally terrifying dimensions by the hypertrophy of science and technology.

The democratic capitalist literary cultures of this period can be categorized as, on the side of 'not doing', a rising literary culture of 'the writing of experience': defensive listening out for, rather than imposition of, meaning. On the other side, that of 'doing', there are those manifestations of literary culture that formed hybrids in the new medial field. At the extreme they form alliances with that ultimate application of scientific technology, social revolution.

All these cultures, even as they tend at the extremes to imagine themselves (using 'imagine' in the strong sense appropriate to cultural history) free, are subject to a three-way pull: that of the market, that of the commitment to witness, and that of the commitment to social improvement.

From *Erlebnis* to *Erfahrung*

As we argued in chapter 4, the First World War and its revolutionary aftershocks in the interior of Germany did not provide art with a new topic to represent but invaded it with a new reality. One way of expressing this, in particular relation to the art of literature, is to say that 'experience' became a problematic category.

For Wilhelm Dilthey, author of *Das Erlebnis und die Dichtung* (*Poetry and Experience*, 1906), the link between experience and literature had been of central importance. *Erlebnis* was an integration point, allowing philosophical thought coherently to investigate the complexities of culture, on a basis as secure as that upon which the empirical sciences were conducted. As we suggested in chapter 2, his theory was instrumental in the academic elevation of 'literature' to the status of a privileged medium for access to the truth of cultural history, if not to metaphysical truth itself. Literature was a concretization of *Erlebnis*, a category in which human values and meaning fused with the historical realm of causality. Dilthey favoured the genres of the *Bildungsroman*, biography and autobiography, especially of historically significant individuals (Augustine, Rousseau and, above all, Goethe) because in the textual rendering of the individual life one could learn to see the truth of the complex interplay of historical forces refracted in the human spirit: a glimpse into the continuity of human meaning from the individually lived, recollected and interpreted life, to the sweep of history itself, the self-interpretation of the species.

Already with the outbreak of the war the Diltheyan compact between literature and experience was weakened in the sense that traditional literary standards were set aside in favour of the expression of experience in various loosely defined literary forms such as amateur lyric poetry, anthologies of letters from the Front, diary-like records and so on. The hope in 1914 was that the recording of this world-historical *Erlebnis*, although conceived in reaction to the shock of the historically new, would in time flow into a larger sense of historical meaning. With the actual course of the war, this form of literary activity, driven not by academic or aesthetic criteria but by the urgency of the moment, necessarily failed to deliver such a meaning.

The extreme strain under which Dilthey's category of *Erlebnis* came is clear from Ernst Jünger's use of the term in the title of a collection of essays published in 1922, *Der Kampf als inneres Erlebnis* (*Warfare as Inner Experience*). If Dilthey's *Erlebnis* was a meaningful fusion of human experience and history consummated in literature, the experience of the soldier on the Western Front was approximately the opposite. It objectified the individual subject and was not susceptible to traditional literary fashioning. Jünger's insistence upon *Erlebnis* is the exact measure of his unique position as we described it in chapter 4. He appears to have believed that only when men had indeed internalized what appeared irreducibly resistant, namely modern technology, and only when they had surrendered the old form of integral selfhood and identified themselves with the machinery that put them to the extreme test, could humanity be renewed and life itself regain a future-oriented meaning.

After the war, the need to attach meaning to individual experiences by way of autobiographical testimony took on a political turn. Generals Hindenburg and Ludendorff and Admiral von Tirpitz, for instance, quickly wrote memoirs in order to explain the defeat away by blaming it on others. Historically less prominent individuals, not only Ernst Jünger but also, for instance, conservative authors such as Hans Carossa (*Rumänisches Tagebuch* [*Rumanian Diary*], 1924) and Rudolf Binding (*Aus dem Krieg* [*From the War*], 1925), or the proto-fascist memoirists of the Freikorps studied by Klaus Theweleit, bore personal witness to the seismic movement in European history. Both during and after the war, pressure from censorship and other legal interventions ensured that this autobiographical-testimonial writing was predominantly nationalistic and militaristic in colour.

At the other end of the political spectrum, Ernst Toller addressed the issue of how to make sense of war experience in the idiom of Expressionist drama, pushing it to the point of a direct exhortation to revolutionary action. In *Die Wandlung* (*The Transformation*, 1919), he represented graphically the inability of conventional aesthetics to 'gestalten' (both 'depict' and 'fashion' or 'shape') the meaning of the war. Friedrich is an aspiring sculptor and is seen in the seventh tableau of the fourth episode labouring at a marble statue of a more than life-size figure of a naked man, 'all muscles, clenched fists outstretched', as the stage directions says. The meaning of this work of art, in whose stone Friedrich strives to infuse his own heart's blood, is to be 'The Victory of the Fatherland'. Confronted with the unmediated suffering of the war, his will to believe in and form ('gestalten') what had become an uncanny abstraction is broken. In a dramatic climax, he smashes the figure. This symbolizes the collapse of his sanity, whereupon his 'transformation' ensues. 'Conversion' is a topos in autobiography (in the *Confessions* of Augustine, or the Pietist autobiographies of the German eighteenth century) through which inner experience is suffused with more-than-individual significance. Friedrich is converted to the cause of all of humanity, not that of certain vested interests, whether nationalist or commercial, within it. The play ends on a call to revolution, upon which the subsequent historical turn of events offers ironic but poignant comment (Toller himself was actively involved in, and imprisoned as a result of, the ill-starred communist revolution in Munich in 1918–19).

If in the immediate post-war years personal experience of the historical trauma became culturally politicized on the right and aestheticized on the left (Toller's play was spectacularly produced by Expressionist director Karlheinz Martin in his Tribune theatre in Berlin in 1919; Georg Kaiser's stylized *Gas* plays are another example), the lasting effect it had on literature in German was to pave the way for a new cultural informality, an increased importance for authenticity and a diminished one for art. One might say that the violent incursion of technological modernity initiated a democratization of literature, a writing of individual experience.

In the new arena, the search for meaning is carried out in a kaleidoscopic profusion of testimony. The vision of personality as an integration point for modern European secular meaning, upon which Dilthey's *Geistes-geschichte* was founded, was no longer compelling, but in compensation there arose a discourse of self-interpretation in an informal modern litera-ture. Many autobiographies of significant individuals achieved popularity, not as literature in Dilthey's sense but as adumbrations of value systems, based on personal example, amid the moral kaleidoscope of post-war life. Examples are Henry Ford, *My Life and Work* (1922; German 1923), Albert Schweitzer, *Aus meinem Leben und Denken* (*Out of My Life and Thought*, 1931), Alexandra Kollontai, *Ziel und Wert meines Lebens* (*Aim and Value of My Life*, 1926), Erwin Piscator, *Das politische Theater* (*The Political Theatre*, 1929), Leo Trotzki, *Mein Leben* (*My Life*, 1930). Although Hitler was at the time not as significant an individual as he regrettably later became, *Mein Kampf* (*My Struggle*, 1925–6) could be seen as a point of convergence between books of this sort and the ontological blockbuster popular in German since the Wilhelmine era, such as *Rembrandt als Erzieher, Also sprach Zarathustra* or *Entartung* (see chapter 3) or Oswald Spengler's immediate post-war success *Der Untergang des Abendlandes* (*Decline of the West*, 1918 and 1922).

Travel writing was a particularly widespread variant of the writing of experience in the Weimar period. Richard Katz was a successful exponent of the genre whose books sold in their hundreds of thousands. He saw the travel writer as midway between poet and tour guide, and prided himself on having no fixed point of view. He regarded this as liberating. His pro-cedure in writing and publishing accounts of his travels all over the world was to inventorize moments in experience (*Erlebnisse*) like tesserae in a mosaic.

Walter Benjamin (1892–1940), a cultural theorist as characteristic of the democratic capitalist cultural environment as Dilthey had been of the Wilhelmine one, reflected upon what had become of 'experience' in this amplified and mediated profusion. He reread the birth of modernity in the nineteenth century from the perspective of the First World War and its aftershocks. For him, *Erlebnis* became the means by which the modern subject defends himself against the shocks of modernity (of which shell shock is the traumatic extreme). Richard Katz may have felt himself to be a free-wheeling modern individual unburdened by scientific and moral preconceptions, but Benjamin's analysis of his activity would have been that it was precisely as passive as Katz thought it was active. For Benjamin,

Katz is not creating new value systems but protecting himself from the fallout from the collapse of the older ones.

There are two words in German for the English word 'experience', *Erlebnis* and *Erfahrung*. Although in practice they are often used interchangeably, they do have distinctly different connotations. The former refers to certain inner events, or to the way outer events impact upon the mind and memory, while the latter refers to something that happens to you, from which lessons can be learned (as in: 'to learn from experience'). Dilthey thought that in culturally significant cases the first was more profound than the second. Benjamin differentiated between the inner events, 'Erlebnisse', which he understood, under the influence of Freud, as a sort of *Reizschutz*, or shield against (excessive) stimulus, and the 'Erfahrungen', to which he attached more value than Dilthey. For Benjamin, 'Erfahrung' was valuable because it referred not to an event confined to and helping to define one individual but to the sort of experience that serves as a basis for social organization.

Benjamin undertook an exploration of this complex distinction, which also required consideration of different types of memory, in a literary context. In a celebrated essay of 1936 called 'Der Erzähler' ('The Storyteller'), he argued that in modern society the capacity to exchange 'Erfahrungen' had been lost. It was specifically the First World War and its aftermath that prompted him to make this claim. There is a memorable formulation in the opening section: 'never before has experience [*Erfahrung*] been more radically given the lie than in the way strategic experience has been caught out by trench warfare, economic experience by inflation, physical experience by mechanized warfare, moral experience by those in power.' Benjamin goes on to picture the 'tiny, fragile, human body' beneath the open sky, and between body and sky there is no longer anything familiar at all, but instead 'a forcefield of destructive torrents and explosions'.

This is the individual in modernity who, to survive, protects himself by registering and remembering the stimuli to which he is subject, not in order to exchange the information in a traditional and collective accumulation of wisdom but as a sort of internalized, particularized inventory of information. As Benjamin wrote in a later study of Baudelaire: 'Perhaps the special achievement of shock defense may be seen in its function of assigning to an incident a precise point in time in consciousness *at the cost of the integrity of its contents*' (quoted in Wolin 1994: 229). Modern consciousness, in a sense, becomes self-defeating. In protecting itself, it vanishes entirely into the activity of self-defence, and loses real contact with the world of nature and other people.

In the 'Storyteller' essay, Benjamin contrasts the novel and its narrator to the storyteller whose stories, whether actually spoken or written down, are still close to the oral tradition and function within the shared memory of a community. The novelist's practice, on the other hand, is historically inseparable from the print medium (that is, technological mediation). The novel, for all the teeming life it represents, is composed in isolation, without reciprocal engagement in a living collective.

The multitude of writers who told their personal stories in print in the Weimar period and in the Federal Republic from the 1960s onwards were (more or less) democratically free to do so but simultaneously dependent upon the very techno-industrial energies that forced these stories from them. Their writing occupied a position on the border between literature in the pre-war sense, politics, journalism and advertising. They were not 'storytellers' at all in Benjamin's sense but, from his perspective, individuals caught in an unrelenting struggle to protect consciousness from disintegration.

Our introductory claim that the writing of experience belongs to the 'not doing' end of the spectrum refers, therefore, to the circumstance that the frenzied activity of writing about immediate experience seemed, to the best cultural theorists of the time, in fact passive. It was no more than a defensive strategy that left the basic need for meaning in abeyance, generating a false consciousness in its place. But this is only one aspect of the way in which 'experience' is reconceptualized. The sense that Benjamin shared with other intellectuals of the period, such as Siegfried Kracauer, that individual experience was no longer able properly to grasp the nature and effect of the conditions under which it came about (namely those of democratic capitalism) had as its corollary the search for the kind of *Erfahrungen* that can, in recollection, give access to the lived experience of the past that lies hidden within the defensive activity of *Erlebnisse* in consciousness. These are moments of fusion between subject and object which arise involuntarily in memory and are, as such, a function of 'not doing' and not of 'doing'. They are the living connection between subjective experience and objective history and thereby provide encouragement for those who believe in the possibility of achieving social progress by keeping the benefits of modern industrial technology, its potential to distribute wealth and security to all, while overcoming the amorality of capitalism.

This view of experience, at least in Benjamin's thinking, is essentially conformable with the Modernist position that experience is not personal at all (see chapter 3). For writers like Nietzsche, the Rilke of *Malte Laurids Brigge*, the Musil of *Der Mann ohne Eigenschaften* and, especially, Marcel

Proust, subjectivity is not coextensive with conscious identity or personality but open upon the conditions within which these things emerge and become consolidated. This is also the teaching of psychoanalysis, at least in its Freudian form, with its – to some contradictory – assertion that there is an unconscious mind.

Benjamin's useful and apposite distinction between this Modernist view of the refraction of experience and the profusion of life writing after the First World War is therefore that, while the latter is generated by modern consciousness in overdrive, the former arises spontaneously and unwilled, exposing levels upon which individuals are authentically connected to each other and to their own times. Before the Third Reich and the Second World War, the hope widely shared by intellectuals on the left was that the kind of authentic human experience, the shared *Erfahrungen* that conduce to the organization of a better life, could be consolidated and realized through Marxism. Particularly the unified *Erfahrungen* of the proletariat, even though predominantly negative ones, might provide the actual force by means of which social and political revolution would be achieved.

This all looked different from the perspective of the 1970s, but the difference and the perspective are significant. What makes Benjamin so important a writer for the period after the Second World War is that almost alone he had committed himself both to thinking about how to live well with technology, to 'doing', and to the spiritual reality of human experience, the moment of 'not doing', at which immemorial counsel can be discerned behind the noise of technological publicity. His poetic theorizing attempted to reconcile spirit and machine, in the service of an understanding of history conducive to social progress. He adopted Marxism (under the spell of Brecht), that is to say the doctrine that as a matter of historical necessity class antagonism will lead to a revolution in the relations of production, because it was the structure of hope available to his generation. At the same time, his cultural analysis was by no means exhausted by it. It was this combination of a profound melancholic cultural earnestness and rigorous orientation upon a better future that furnished resources to the post-Second World War democratic capitalist world.

From the perspective of the 1970s and 1980s, the difference between *Erlebnis* and *Erfahrung* seemed less categorical. Peter Sloterdijk, in *Literatur und Organisation von Lebenserfahrung* [*Literature and the Organization of Life Experience*, 1978], a study devoted to the life writing of the 1920s but clearly inspired by that of the 1970s, suggested that the new breeds of textual exploration of life experience captured and shaped the reaction of the subject at the point of its destabilization. To these moments of destabilization he gave the name 'Stör-Erfahrungen' (experiences of interruption). In an environment in which the liberal human subject in the Dilthey mould no longer functioned as an explanatory model of experience, subjective experience need not be entirely deprived of a claim to moral agency, so long as there is no longer the assumption that it might or should become entirely transparent upon itself. 'Stör-Erfahrungen' were moments of opacity that forced a subjective rewriting of the self. They were disruptions of a certain language of individual consciousness but also salutary reminders that consciousness is always embedded in a life practice that exceeds it, and with which it must continue to contend. One can imagine these interruptions on a spectrum from trauma to *Verfremdung*, that is to say, from experiences that exceed the capacity of consciousness to assimilate them to experiences that, in challenging it, alter and raise it. The reorganization of experience in language might issue in a scuttle back into safe ideological identification or else have the outcome of fostering the development of critical experience that can be deemed 'proto-political', to use Sloterdijk's neologism, that, in other words, keeps alive the hope of social progress. In this description of modern life writing, *Erlebnis*, the specifically individual experience, can either surrender to false consciousness or become *Erfahrung* itself, that is to say, not only public (in which form it risks alienation) but available to be shared and acted upon.

Sloterdijk's model is useful because it combines the high-literary Modernist sense that subjectivity is not personal with the empirical fact of the efflorescence of life writing, or what one can call personal or autobiographical fictions. While post-war German intellectuals, such as Alexander Kluge and Oskar Negt in their influential book *Öffentlichkeit und Erfahrung* (*The Public and Experience*, 1972), concentrated upon the social and political question of how social experience could become fruitful in practice despite its inevitable mediatedness, Sloterdijk's investigation depended upon the part that fell specifically to literature in the socialization of *Erfahrungen*.

The 'Stör-Erfahrungen' of the German twentieth century indubitably reached the condition of trauma in 1945 and thus by definition exceeded the ability of culture to assimilate them immediately, in an analogous way to the situation prevailing in 1919 but to a greater extent. At this later juncture, the political appropriation and interpretation of the events preceding the defeat of Germany was taken over by the victorious occupying powers. This left a cultural vacuum bounded on one side by legal depositions, as well as other forms of documentary record and, on the other, a self-conscious literary revival which, as we shall see, interposed an anachronistic 'literariness' between itself and those incommensurable events.

In this context, the Swiss writer Max Frisch (1911–1991) played an important linking role. His *Tagebücher* [*Diaries*] *1946–1949*, which were widely read and admired on their publication, are a model of the twentieth-century writing of experience (making their publication date of 1950, exactly mid-century, singularly appropriate). They combine the immediacy and informality of the diary format with travel writing, in which personal experience or experience of self happens in relation to exposure to new environments. What is new about the environment in which Frisch travels is less its exoticism than the unfamiliarity consequent upon historical rupture (essentially the reduction of parts of Germany to a pre-industrial level of existence). At the same time, Frisch is consciously in the tradition of the literary Modernism of Rilke and Proust, so that his personal testimony is enriched by a sophisticated grasp of the construction of subjectivity, and interested in serious literary ways of acknowledging it.

Frisch's text is in fact structured around the idea of *Erlebnis*. As a German-language author not directly implicated in the physical and moral collapse of the Germany that had briefly become the Third Reich ('als Verschonter', 'one who has been spared', as he says in the introductory note), he could write about his first-hand experience of post-catastrophe Germans with a mixture of empathy and distance accessible to neither damaged survivors nor appalled exiles.

He insists that his personal involvement as a writer has significance only in relation to his 'Zeitgenossenschaft', a word which conflates 'contemporary' (*Zeitgenosse*) and 'association / cooperative' or 'membership of an association / cooperative' (*Genossenschaft*) with a dash of socialist pathos (*Genosse*: 'comrade'). If this identifies this writing with the kind of writing spawned by the incommensurateness of the First World War, Frisch is also distinctly Modernist in his understanding of subjectivity in modernity: 'writing', he says very near the beginning, 'means reading oneself.' The pen becomes an instrument for the measurement of seismic movement: 'and in fact it is not we who write, we are being written.' This is a direct echo of *Malte* (see chapter 3), but now the force doing the writing is no longer anonymously metaphysical but identified with the seismic movements in history.

In the introductory note, Frisch asks the reader not to consume these diary entries as bite-size portions of 'experience', as *Erlebnisse* in Benjamin's sense, but to read the entire book since its value resides not in the discrete moments of writing of which it is made up but in the mosaic of their willed configuration. Frisch's introductory statement positions his discourse close to the Literature of Negation which we explored in chapter 5. In a section from May 1946 headed 'Zur Schriftstellerei' ('On the business of writing'), he describes his writing as a defence against a reality so chaotic that it either destroys you or demands transformation. He places himself squarely in the field described at the beginning of this chapter. The defensiveness of the writing of experience is acknowledged, while the remedy, though there must be one, is left imprecise since Frisch does not say whether the transformation to which he refers is the rebuilding of a broken civilization or the aesthetic formation ('the 'mosaic') of which he had spoken at the outset.

In the end, the *Diaries* provide two outcomes in relation to the value and meaning of *Erlebnis* in the immediate aftermath of the war. The culminating aesthetic-Modernist insight is the Kierkegaardian one Frisch went on to build into his fictions on the theme of the disparity between subjectivity and identity, such as *Stiller* (1954) and *Homo Faber* (1957). In the entry for July 1949, he writes: 'every experience (*Erlebnis*) will remain fundamentally unsayable, as long as we try to express it using the actual example that has befallen us.' Only literary art which constructs the appropriate fiction can do justice to personal experience. Frisch therefore offers the making of literature as the means by which *Erlebnis* can be turned into *Erfahrung*, that is, communicated and shared.

This is an aesthetic outcome, and one that in the democratic capitalist world is wide open to appropriation by the culture market, as Frisch's successful career as a novelist and author of popular parable plays went on to demonstrate. But there is also a political outcome in relation to *Erlebnis* in the diaries. In the entry for August 1949, Frisch defines and condemns the use of the word by surviving Germans as a moral defence. The fact of having experienced ('erlebt') so much is offered as a substitute for confronting what that experience might mean and what might be learned from it. He might have added that the 'we' implied by this shared experience is defined negatively and turned towards the past.

Between the time that Frisch published his first volume of diaries and that of the student unrest of the mid- to late 1960s, his criticism of the Germans' attitude to their recent past was valid, although there are important qualifications to which we shall return. Literature itself, including Frisch's own novels (although the same cannot be said of his plays), tended to define itself as independent of the contemporary political sphere and to thematize the past, and especially the Holocaust, only very tentatively. This attracted derision from the younger generation of student revolutionaries of the 1960s who preferred action to literature (they had this in common with the National Socialists) and who advocated rejection of the institution of art as a bourgeois aberration, acknowledging cultural activity only insofar as it contributed to the real overthrow of capitalism, which they conflated with fascism.

With the ebbing of the student movement at the beginning of the 1970s, German writing of experience came into its own. As the dominant contemporary variant of the ageing medium of literature, bound for good or ill to individuality but adapted to the century of shocks by means of a new informality, it proved its value as a social, psychological and political resource. The failure of the revolutionary moment of the late 1960s to issue in meaningful action exposed activism on the basis of strictly theoretical considerations as essentially random, not to say murderous. The untheorized practice of life proved resistant to direct intervention, however passionate or violent, resistant to what we call, using Sloterdijk's shorthand, 'doing'. The print medium of the written word was disclosed as the site of 'not doing', the medium in which deeper-than-personal conditions and circumstances appear within the language of the self and cause damage, facilitate renewal or do a mixture of both.

Three contrasting high-profile texts give a sense of the range of functions fulfilled by the 1970s writing of experience. They are Bernward Vesper's *Die Reise* (*The Trip*, completed in the late 1960s but published 1977), Karin Struck's *Klassenliebe* (*Class Love*, 1973) and Verena Stefan's *Häutungen* (*Shedding*, 1975).

Vesper's text reports from the heart of the radical student movement in the late 1960s. Yet Vesper was not only an extreme left-wing radical but also the son of an extreme right-wing father. Will Vesper, the Nazi poet who we mentioned briefly in the previous chapter, remained an unreconstructed fascist and Holocaust-denier after the war. The text recounts Bernward's militaristic upbringing. The third strand of the text reflects Vesper's experiences during an LSD 'trip' during which the hidden connections within him between his fascist socialization and his contemporary extremism are disclosed.

The representation of the drug experience was intended not only to lay bare a terrifying subterranean continuity between enslavement and liberation, but also to suggest an answer to it. It was a theoretical turn that owed something to Walter Benjamin's hopes for the future, based on the mind-expanding moments in Baudelaire and surrealism, and a lot to Herbert Marcuse, the highly popular émigré theorist who sought to conflate Marx and Freud into a hedonist overthrow of capitalism in ontological best-sellers like *Eros and Civilization* (1955; German 1965) and *One-Dimensional Man* (1964; German 1965).

The hope was that self-hatred might be turned outwards, in the form of violent political activism, and thus change society for the better. However, before the text was ready for publication in 1970, Vesper was admitted to a mental institution after an attempted arson attack, and committed suicide. When *Die Reise* did eventually come out in 1977, it was more a social memory of flawed utopianism than, as Vesper had hoped, a revolutionary intervention. Yet no other literary text could convey with more immediacy and power how the writing of subjectivity, especially in Germany, revealed layers of historical and personal trauma which were overwhelmingly resistant to facile resolution, although not, of course, to triumphant commercialization.

Karin Struck's *Klassenliebe*, written in a loose journal form which permits a blend of verisimilitude and stream of consciousness, presents itself as a process of self-exploration and intentionally positions itself between autobiography and fiction. What Struck takes from the intensely politicized period just passed is the assumption that the personal is indeed political. The aspect of her approach to self and world which made it so typical a text for this period was the conviction that general historical and political issues only made sense if they were taken together with their refraction in individual subjects.

Literature is a reality for Struck in two ways: first, as a tradition; and second, as a social environment in which she and her fictional shadow wish to establish themselves: as authors. In the face of *Erfahrungen* that are far from inwardly unifying, it is recurrently Struck / Karin's ambition to fashion herself as a writer that provides the 'proto-political' organization of life experience (to use Sloterdijk's term).

In *Klassenliebe*, and the many books like it, the writing of experience reaches its democratic outcome. Struck / Karin's Marxist intellectual lover tells her that she has already achieved her ambition to be an author because 'jeder Mensch ist ein Schriftsteller' ('Every person is an author') (Struck 1973: 121).

Struck's authenticity was not very good art and it was marketed as a reassuring 'new subjectivity' in relation to the frightening radicalism from which it came and which it denounced. Yet its cultural significance lies in the consolation it gave the many readers who recognized *Erfahrungen* in it with which they could identify, including disillusion with the revolutionary moment and the accompanying insight into deeper-lying historical traumas.

For the actual potential of the writing of experience to transform self-consciousness into social change, we need to turn to the classic of the West German feminist movement, Verena Stefan's *Häutungen* (*Shedding*).

If Struck's book was personal experience for the sake of literature, Stefan's was literature for the sake of personal experience. It addressed a new kind of *Öffentlichkeit*: radical feminism. It is a short, polemically focused text without the endless linguistic navel-gazing of Struck; it knows where it's going, and goes there with panache and conviction, but not without feeling, complexity, analytical insight or effective literary skill.

Coming like Struck from the milieu of the radical student movement, Stefan not only understood that 'subjectivity' was a problematic issue but also knew the reason and sensed the answer. The reason that experience was not personal was that men had stolen it. The feeling of exposure once you 'shed' the default identity that awaits you on going out into a man's world is recognizably Modernist. Though uncomfortable, it is welcomed. In the terms of Sloterdijk's 'doing' versus' leaving alone' alternative, once Stefan's protagonist-self has undone the unfortunate effects of being subordinated within the dispositions of men, other and new things can start to happen.

The clarity and force of Stefan's feminist and intimate-personal version of this Modernist configuration comes from the fact that it has sex as its focus. Sexuality is irreducibly personal and unavoidably interpersonal. It is spontaneously both literal and metaphorical. Hence in Stefan's book, the coercive effect of technology is concentrated into the penis as an instrument, imposing upon sexuality its own reductive function and direction. Whilst genital sexuality can both represent and actually be a way in which embodied subjectivity is coerced, Stefan is able to suggest what an alternative might look like by describing the path of her feelings for other women, in which sexuality and affect are mingled in less prescribed or homogenized ways.

Like Rilke, but in a much more straightforward way, she was able to imagine a form of relationship that was not subordinated to a third term or known language, but consisted in the touching of two subjects in a certain way. What defines the way they touch, literally and metaphorically, is a relationship to the self, and not first to an other. The body becomes a unique and changing site of colours, textures, a landscape of imperfection. Stefan describes bodily experiences to which no label is as yet attached, simply stirrings and discomforts which are hard to remember because they have no name. Between such bodies, 'a new language of skin words' ('hautworte'; Stefan 1975: 93) comes about. The most important relationship described by Stefan in the book is very slow to develop because it grows from within two people (the protagonist and her friend Fenna), who have no name for it. Here, too, the importance of leaving and of knowing when not to 'do' but to wait is shown to be productive in a concrete human situation.

Like Frisch, Stefan knows that skill in writing resides in fashioning an equivalent to the original experience. Unlike *Die Reise*, this is no agonized assault upon institutions inseparable from the personality structure of the person wishing to mount the assault, nor, unlike *Klassenliebe*, is it a shapeless and incoherent enactment of how insightful but directionless consciousness can be and usually is. *Häutungen* has a form, a *Gestalt*, because it is the formulation of a specific shape of life, a shape like that of the life writing of the 1920s in Sloterdijk's model: one language of consciousness is interrupted and the consequent textual engagement with this interruption takes on proto-political force in its contribution to thinking, feeling and being otherwise.

The disruption of ordinary social expectations leads to a release of energy through structures of thought once confined to the cultural sphere. It is applied Modernism. This release is inscribed in the literary text, a controlled experiment with lyric poetry and dream narrative, which conducts the energy charge outside itself into the network beyond, where, to echo Negt and Kluge, *Erfahrung* translates into *Öffentlichkeit*. *Häutungen* became a best-seller by word of mouth initially, and eventually its proceeds bought independence for the feminist *Frauenoffensive* publishing house (see Plowman 1998: 139).

The very popularity of *Häutungen*, one might say its legibility, attracted the disapproval of radical feminists and theorists alike. In terms of the cultural history of German literature under democratic capitalism, it was an unusual success and an inevitable failure; the passionate competence and precision of Stefan's assault upon stereotypes became a new stereotype. But it also contributed to the emancipation of women.

Old literature adapts to the new world

In 1919, a book appeared by a new author, Emil Sinclair, in which Sinclair gives a first-person account of his youth. It begins in a conventional Wilhelmine setting. This becomes first uncanny and is then transcended by experiences and encounters that discover new spiritual horizons within Sinclair. These resonate – somehow – with the outbreak of the war, in which the Wilhelmine reality itself disappeared. The text is an outcome of an impulse on the part of the author to give an account of his life. He has been wounded at the Front and is confident that he will die more easily when he has told his story. The book had spectacular success and public recognition, winning a literary prize for a first work in the year of its publication.

The reason why this book was not discussed under the heading of auto-biographical writing in the previous section is that the author of *Demian. Die Geschichte einer Jugend* (*Demian. A Young Man's Story*) turned out not to be a first-time author at all but a reinvented Hermann Hesse, who by that time, as we have seen in chapter 3, was already a famous writer (his author-ship of *Demian* became public knowledge in 1920). Though Hesse's life had undergone many profound changes, one thing that had not changed about him was his sense of himself as a literary author. *Demian*'s claim to being absolutely authentic, eloquently made in its Foreword, was part of the fiction.

The Foreword to *Demian* is a remarkable document. In just over two pages, addressing its readership directly, it resets the framework for litera-ture. It renounces the 'sweetness and harmony of invented stories' but claims that literature can, by dint of a new authenticity, re-establish itself in the new post-war world. Hesse co-opts for literary fiction the change in the value and significance of personal experience. It is unthinkable, Sinclair tells his readers, that mechanized slaughter may be permitted to cancel out the significance of a subjectivity since each subjectivity is unique. In the face of imminent extinction, the anonymous death on the battlefield, he relates the story in which the mysterious resources that lie within the self emerge to reveal something at once irreducibly individual and meaningful. The meaning, therefore, can only be revealed to the self, but the text is realized, formed into a symbolic *Gestalt*, so that each reader can understand that he must, and can, find his own meaning: 'Das Leben jedes Menschen ist ein Weg zu sich selber' ('every person's life is a journey to himself').

Literature in this new incarnation is less grand, omniscient, yet more accessible and of more use to its readers. It is at once socially legible (unlike avant-garde writing) and (like it) constructed upon acknowledgement of the schizophrenia inseparable from being honest with oneself. Hesse inte-grates into a fundamentally traditional discourse the Modernist knowledge about selfhood, namely the lack of fit between subjectivity and social identity. What *Demian* announces is a new sort of social identification, plural, various, self-made and facilitated by reading.

It was not only the war with its disruption on the macro-level of assump-tions about moral and historical meaning that enabled Hesse to shift the position of literature in this way, but the disruptions in his personal life that brought him into close contact with psychoanalysis, then in its early days. Hesse read the works of leading doctors in the field (Freud,

Jung, Adler) and underwent treatment himself during and after the war. Psychoanalysis provided the bridge from the 'sweet harmonious fictions' of the old order of personality to the new template of, to use the words of the foreword, nonsense, confusion, madness, dreams. These were now the material from which fiction could be made, for author and reader, just as psychoanalysts acknowledged the reality of subjectivity unable to fit the required social personality and tried to achieve an accommodation between them. Like psychoanalysis, Hesse democratized the 'outsider' of Dostoevsky, Nietzsche and Rilke. He adapted Modernism's complicity with madness to the needs of the mass market.

Der Steppenwolf (1927) shows more clearly and elaborately how Hesse's new branding of literature enabled identification with the outsider. In order to give an account of a reclusive, tormented but insightful protagonist, Hesse employs several narrative points of view and styles of discourse. An account of an eccentric lodger by a bourgeois narrator is followed by that lodger's own account of his experience, played out on the border between reality and fantasy, and culminates in a phantasmagorical 'Magic Theatre' in which the idea of personality is fundamentally reconfigured, prior to the sense that Haller, Hesse's grumpy hero, will return to his quotidian struggles, refreshed and confirmed in the ultimate truth behind his glimpses of a 'golden trace'.

Those who see a familiar Romantic device in this transition from the ordinary to the uncanny and fantastic are correct. Yet in 1927, as opposed to 1827, the address is less to a metaphysical referent than to the modern mass readership of the Weimar Republic. The different forms of discourse of Hesse's text are chosen to guide the reader between the dull conformity of the first narrator and the full-blown schizophrenia of the Magic Theatre. The modern metropolitan reader is addressed in his uniqueness: by reading, he occupies the space at which, in the midst of ordinary life, the advertisement for the Magic Theatre of the personality addresses him: 'not for everyone.'

This is not realism, or indeed really referential at all: it is advice. Alfred Adler's psychoanalytical notion of 'styles of life', first propounded in 1929, is taken by some to be the source of the advertising industry's term 'lifestyle' (though some attribute it to Max Weber), which profitably links the conduct of the self with consumerism. This would be entirely consistent with Hesse's achievement in which psychoanalysis meets advertising. As one of the Magic Theatre slogans reads: 'Instructions for the construction of personality. Success guaranteed.' 'Reality' is either problematic or incidental; what matters is the value of and the work on the self.

Hesse democratizes literature by negotiating an accommodation between familiar European culture (Goethe and Mozart, who make important guest appearances, and not least Hesse himself) and the capitalist democratic strangeness of the 1920s: jazz, radios, egregious philistinism, deviant, cynical attitudes and so on. All these things play their part in defining a liveable space for the modern reader between madness and conformity. Hesse's popularity in the 1920s and once more in the 1960s and 1970s is another indication of the cultural identity of the two periods. In both, the regulated hedonism of the market worked together with the utopian aspirations of the modern democratic subject.

Thomas Mann brought traditional literature to the post-war conditions brilliantly. Unlike the pacifist Hesse, who went into early exile in Switzerland in 1912 and had always been a non-conformist, Mann adapted a conservative Wilhemine identification to the Weimar Republic.

Mann had a taken an important step towards democratic-capitalist fiction in *Buddenbrooks* (see chapter 3). His great first novel can be read as the point at which the bourgeois realism of the modern novel is transformed into a commodity, in the sense that it denies its own socioeconomic origin. Where 'Thomas Mann' should be in the succession of his family, there is only Hanno, who, for all his artistic sensitivity, can hardly get out of bed in the morning, let alone write a 700-page novel. Thus the novel itself has the 'fetish' property of the commodity that it comes to the reader as if from nowhere, denying the conditions of its own production. The reader of *Buddenbrooks* is not, like the reader of Stendhal, Balzac or Fontane, reading about the world he or she is reading in. It is a confection (of the highest Lübeck quality) prepared for the reader's pleasure.

Der Zauberberg (*The Magic Mountain*, 1924), Mann's great novel of the Weimar period, refers to no world 'out there' at all but suggests instead that whatever the world is to be rests in the hands of the human subjects who have emerged in it and who have responsibility for it. Reading the novel, which is demanding and pleasurable as befits serious literature, is a lesson in assuming democratic responsibility after the collapse of the old imperial-colonial order.

Mann stages a contest between the competing forms of consciousness in relation to which he had been clearly partisan during the war, when he had sided against democracy for an honourable German form of irrationalism. The most famous such competition takes place between the figures of the progressive humanist, Settembrini, and the intellectual irrationalist, Naphta, but the scientific paradigm is also prominently represented by the doctors who run the sanatorium in which the hero, Hans Castorp, spends seven years, as are a plethora of other possible worldviews from hedonism to spiritualism.

He is lifted out of his 'ordinary' Wilhelmine existence by his stay on the Magic Mountain, where across the hundreds of pages of philosophical and cultural material, he is exposed fundamentally to one circumstance, namely that there is no single persuasive account of the world that responds to the 'empty silence' that he had received when, in an only half conscious sort of way, he had wondered about the meaning of life behind the automatic behaviour of everyday existence. There is no winner in the consciousness competition; there is just the competition itself.

As in *Demian* (and *Der Mann ohne Eigenschaften*), within the text of *Der Zauberberg* the First World War provides a horizon beyond which it can only be a matter of informed projection what moral shape the future will take. Whilst, as with Hesse, there are many ways in which Mann's novel can be placed within German literary tradition, not least its parody and renewal of the *Bildungsroman*, the point we stress here is that it brings this tradition, extremely consciously, into the new world, thereby asserting at least the possibility of meaning in the ontological vacuum left by the war. If, as Sloterdijk says, 'das Ich nach dem Krieg ist ein Erbe ohne Testament' ('the ego after the war is an heir without a will'; Sloterdijk 1983: 703), Mann, like Hesse and Musil, seeks remedies to the state of cultural intestacy.

In Hesse and Mann, the 'split' subject, already acknowledged and addressed by Freytag, Keller and Fontane in the division of imagination from pragmatism (see chapter 2), moves in the direction of the self-creating subject of modern capitalism. The commodity aspect of their novels is that, unlike the Modernist turn against immediate gratification ('sweet harmonious stories'), they recognize the role of pleasure as well as that of self-regulation and -denial in the self-creation of the modern subject. This recognition they share not unwillingly with the logic of modern mass readership. In their highly popular novels, something of the life force of capitalism takes up the semantic slack remaining after the best efforts of psychoanalysis (Hesse) or more-in-hope-than-in-anger humanism (Mann) to make sense of technological modernity.

A third example of a writer formed before the war but adapting and producing major work in its aftermath is Robert Musil. He shared with Mann, Hesse and many others the Nietzscheanism that provided a proleptic text for the collapse of civilized Europe but combined it with a more hard-nosed scientific attitude, as we mentioned in chapter 3. *Der Mann ohne Eigenschaften* is a huge, unfinished novel, the bulk of which was published in the early 1930s while the remaining unpublished fragments did not see the light of day until 1952. Set in 1913, it is a mixture of narrative and essay in which the pre-war atmosphere of Vienna is represented in a sophisticated historical parody, arranged around the preparations for a fictional celebration due to take place on the 70th anniversary of the Emperor Franz Joseph's accession to the throne, due in 1918. There is thus a structural irony underlying the entire extended representation of the campaign to mount the festivities, since the reader knows that 1914 will render it futile.

As we saw, Musil's novel shares the war as horizon or 'vanishing point' in David Midgley's term (Midgley 2000: 228–9), with Mann's *Zauberberg* and, like Mann, Musil is non-committal on how or even if the damage done to civilization by the war can be repaired. But the Musil text differs in two main ways from Hesse and Mann in the way the literary text proposes or embodies values which might help.

First, Musil opposes what he calls the 'dilettantism' that, while acknowledging and even welcoming the complexity, the 'competing consciousnesses', of the modern world, maintains an unexamined and unexplained confidence that the human soul can nevertheless guide us in respect of how to live well. This his hero 'without qualities', Ulrich, calls 'singing in the dark'. It is nothing but fear; fear of the scientific knowledge that will certainly falsify all hypotheses that such a soul actually exists. But this is no simplistic affirmation of scientific progress. In a more clear-sighted Nietzscheanism than anything to be found in either Mann or Hesse, Ulrich explains that, regardless of the devastation wrought upon moral order by scientific knowledge, it is impossible to not want to know.

Musil proposes a relativism that extends not only to the affirmation of rival forms of consciousness (as Hesse and Mann do too) but to the construction of the subject itself. Dismissing 'the ambition to be a complete person' as an anachronism, Ulrich redefines the entire subject–object relationship with the marvellous precise urbanity that characterizes Musil's prose: ('There is no longer a whole man confronting a whole world, but a human something floating about in a universal culture-medium' ['in einer allgemeinen Nährflüssigkeit']).

The conversation from which the previous two paragraphs derive their material occurs in the justly famous chapter 54 of Book Two of *Der Mann ohne Eigenschaften*. Musil, as a true Nietzschean, embeds thinking in the body. But the literary skill with which he does it displays a wit and wide-awake melancholy, seldom found in Nietzsche: 'The final result for all of them was wet feet, an irritation in the brain – as though the thin, bare branches of the trees, sparkling in the wintry sun, had been left behind like splinters on the retina – a base yearning for coffee, and a sense of human forlornness.'

The second way in which Musil differs from Hesse and Mann is that he does not write for a mass readership but for a literary audience that perhaps no longer really existed, or did not exist yet. He disdained popular writing (including that of Mann) because by definition it does not meet the challenge facing serious intellectual endeavour in the new real world, which is to work towards the ability to live without a unified meaning. He had no interest in pandering to the need for 'meaning', although he understood well enough that the need was real.

Notwithstanding his aversion to popular culture, Musil was an excellent theorist of democratic capitalism. It is curious that Nietzsche had a blind spot for the degree to which capitalism offered the historical embodiment of the will to power, but then he rarely if ever experienced urban modernity in its full magnificent awfulness. At all events, Musil was not subject to this blindness, writing soon after the war that capitalism has the advantage of recognizing the driven nature of human subjects, which makes it at once the most powerful and the most flexible form of socio-economic organization yet known to man. Although *Der Mann ohne Eigenschaften* is not directly concerned with politics, this view is implicit in it, as is the proposition that capitalism is compatible with a democratic form of government, once one acknowledges that it is necessary to be able to live with the simultaneous existence of different forms of consciousness (see Midgley 2000: 181–2).

Der Mann ohne Eigenschaften represents the glory and the tragedy of pure literature in the applied age. Musil was better able than perhaps anyone to understand the nature of the new world, to rid himself of nostalgia for the old one, to perceive and represent modernity as it really was (irreducibly perspectival, technical, specific, in process) and reflect upon what was needful for living in it. But he could not adapt to it in his writing as adeptly as Mann or Hesse. To say he was unwilling to compromise is to point up the tragic contradiction within his impassioned pragmatism. He could not want not to know and show.

Testimony, market, society

In Erich Maria Remarque and Erich Kästner, both born around the turn of the century and with some first-hand experience of the brutality of 1914–18, literature is divested of secure knowledge in relation either to what the world is or to what a person is. Yet this moral and ontological 'forlornness' (to recall the condition of Musil's interlocuters) is sustained by the sheer will to live and is mediated through a market alive to the need to bear witness and to pay heed to the social question.

Remarque's novel *Im Westen nichts Neues* was the most spectacular bestseller in the history of German literature. It is still read and remembered today for the immediacy with which it represents the extraordinary life of ordinary soldiers on the Western Front. It is literature as a modern mass medium. Its success was compounded by the US film version, *All Quiet on the Western Front*, directed by Lewis Milestone in 1930.

In a sense, *Im Westen nichts Neues* cynically exploited the atmosphere of and need for informal but genuine testimony generated by the First World War. Remarque was an advertising copywriter and sports journalist with serious literary aspirations. He later admitted that his novel was not drawn from personal experience although it was effectively written as though it was. He had only spent a few weeks at the Front before being wounded and had composed his fiction from the 'mouth-to-mouth' exchange of anecdotes. He was happy to go along with Ullstein, the publisher, when they said in their publicity that this sensational new book was the work of a novice ('not a professional author'; literally accurate, but in fact Remarque had already written three novels). As one promotional headline put it: 'Nur um sich zu befreien, hatte er seine Kriegserlebnisse gestaltet' ('He had found form for his war experiences simply as a means of freeing himself'; Howind 1988: 55).

In a celebrated prologue to *Im Westen*, Remarque had originally insisted that what he was about to put before the reader was above all *not* an *Erlebnis*, since death cannot be described as such for those who are confronted with it. This would seem to be in explicit differentiation from Jünger's 'Kampf als inneres Erlebnis' which was referred to in the previous section and which as said above was at some pains to represent exposure to modern technological warfare as meaningful. Remarque's important distinction was included when the novel was first published in serial form in the *Vossische Zeitung* but removed for the book publication. It has been thought that Ullstein edited the prologue in this way in order to maintain the illusion that the text was autobiographical. Yet Remarque's original formulation reveals an appeal deeper than the publicity team at Ullstein grasped. Far from the familiar term *Erlebnis*, which they employed for advertising purposes, it was the denial of meaningfulness, nevertheless couched in an aesthetic language, accessible to a wide readership, that distinguished Remarque's novel. It was public testimony to 'the old lie' that it is sweet to die for your country.

Walter Benjamin in his 'Storyteller' essay explicitly denied that the flood of war novels at about the time of *Im Westen nichts Neues* constituted the mouth-to-mouth exchange of socially meaningful 'Erfahrungen' that he maintained was no longer possible since (at the latest) the First World War. In writing his essay, Benjamin was much influenced by Georg Lukács's *Die Theorie des Romans* (*The Theory of the Novel*, 1916), in which Lukács, establishing the credentials of the novel as a literary genre, had constructed a dubious categorical distinction expressly to deny all meaning to the modern popular ('entertainment') novel, which he claimed was a caricature of the real novel; sometimes almost indistinguishable from it, but based on nothing and thus 'entirely meaningless' (Lukács 1978: 73). Neither he nor Benjamin, in other words, was willing to accord social significance to a novel like Remarque's.

Both Benjamin and Lukács were committed to establishing links of substance between metaphysical truth and social improvement (Lukács on his way from Hegelian Idealism to Marxism; Benjamin mediating between Marxism and mysticism) and had no interest in establishing social value in the literary products of contemporary capitalist democracy. The aspect of *Im Westen nichts Neues* that suggests that it had a real psycho-social function, despite the calculating marketing of authenticity that went into it, was the popular success that followed. The literary representation of meaninglessness did not seem meaningless to the millions of buyers of the book, not only in German but in the dozens of languages into which it was translated.

The first instalment of the text was published in the *Vossische Zeitung* ten years to the day after the armistice. Of course, this was in order to focus and increase interest in the product. Yet the trauma, both as it had been suffered by so many, and as an object of horrified fascination for many others, was addressed. This was part of a process of collective assimilation, a model of how the capitalist democratic process can contribute to the overcoming of collective trauma by the institutionalization of memory: in part a falsification, in part a naming; taken together, a memorial.

The event of Remarque's unique success had social and political substance. His novel was furiously contested by those with an interest in the end of the democratic capitalist Weimar regime. As we saw, right-inclined authors, such as Werner Beumelburg, Edwin Erich Dwinger and Franz Schauwecker, wrote 'völkisch' responses to Remarque's novel. In 1930, Goebbels organized demonstrations against showings of the film and it was an immediate selection for the students' bonfire list in 1933.

Erich Kästner's *Fabian. Geschichte eines Moralisten* (*Fabian. Story of a Moralist*, 1931) is, like *Im Westen*, a literary triumph based upon the absence of meaning. Kästner's text is an episodic, satirical, witty but bleak representation of 1920s Berlin in the period of recession. Here, too, it is perfectly clear that behind the 'broken compass' of the period lies the First World War. The protagonist suffers from the same 'Herzleiden' (meaning a weak heart, but also 'suffering of the heart'), originating in brutalization during military training, that afflicted his creator. The central episode of the book, the suicide of Fabian's friend Labude as the result of a cruel prank by an envious academic rival, has the arbitrariness of death on the battlefield. The usually passive Fabian, on establishing the identity of the abject individual accidentally responsible for his friend's death, becomes uncharacteristically active and savagely beats the culprit. The group of students who witness this act of blind revenge, and indeed readers too, are gripped by a delusory sense of just retribution. However, Fabian's attempt to make up for the meaningless death of his friend by venting his frustration upon its accidental cause is as far removed from making genuine sense as is the attempt to lend significance to one meaningless and horrifically destructive war by starting another one.

The text (like that of Remarque) has something of the melancholy of the writing of the second post-Second World War generation in the 1970s, born of the need to deal with the catastrophic failure of a parental generation. Fabian is a 'Melancholiker' because, to employ Kästner's bitterly apposite school imagery, the Wilhelmine curriculum of his parents' generation has been abandoned by its teachers, the timetable has disappeared and the entire continent has failed to make the grade. The moral chaos of Berlin is simply the historical result of the formalistic incompetence of the parental authorities.

This moral chaos, however, is also the scene of extraordinary energy. Kästner's scorn for the bankrupt generation responsible for the war is subordinate to the question posed by the present rather than the past, which is fundamentally: to what extent can the energy that inspired Fabian to attack Labude's resentful rival, or that animates the pervasive hedonism of the epoch – in a word, the force of life – to what extent can it identify itself with the dynamic cynicism of modern capitalism without becoming self-destructive? H. G. Wells (the most prominent historical Fabian) is quoted as saying that it was time that advertising extended its remit from soap and chewing gum to the dissemination of ideals. The text tests this Fabian rationality but remains non-committal, more interested in observing the overlaps or divergences between authentic feeling and social roles than in formulating a theoretical programme for their unification.

In chapter 11, Fabian muses that perhaps it is a sin to love life without having a serious relationship with it. This dawning moral consciousness, put in an aphoristic mixture of wit and insight characteristic of Kästner's prose, is not allowed to issue in a happy union between the reality and pleasure principles because Fabian recollects his dream of identifying himself (rounding his personality) with his job as an advertising copy-writer, only in the immediate aftermath of losing it.

At the end, Fabian dives into a lake in order to save a drowning child, only for the child to swim to the shore and for Fabian to drown. His affirmation of life is shown to be deficient in any practical effort on his part (he should have learned to swim), but then his humane gesture was based on a misunderstanding, just like Labude's suicide, and was meaningless in the first place.

Labude, whose need for moral clarity suits him ill for survival in Weimar Berlin, turns to Fabian as the 'Fachmann der Planlosigkeit' ('expert in getting by without a plan'). If Fabian is exemplary, a moralist, then it is in the fact that his passivity is not resignation. It is rather that he is unwilling to impose a shape on a future which he respects as unknown. Kästner's satirical humour, a kynical energy, to use Sloterdijk's phrase, a disruptive, pragmatic, disabused intelligence, is turned against the cynicism it recognizes in the 'humourlessness' of the advertising whizz-kid Zacharias, who, in chapter 15, is dismayed that Fabian has not got a proper return on his talent: 'if I were as talented as you I would be running the entire business by now!' The sardonic knowing jokes carry the immanent will to live, the affirmation of life, while refusing to bind them to a programme or imagining that in themselves they could deliver meaning.

Musil's theoretical advice that one must learn to live with different consciousnesses is here applied brilliantly in the sphere of popular literature. *Fabian* as a text, with its unmediated confrontation between cynicism and empathy, constructs a reader who can mediate between dynamic inauthenticity and authentic passivity.

Exile

The cultural history of German literature was interrupted by what in literary histories is sometimes treated under the heading of 'exile'. This is not a very satisfactory category for a type of literature but it illustrates once more how, in the twentieth century, literature ceased to function as a more or less stable cultural institution and was instead invaded, scattered and refracted by historical events. Exile is not really a category at all but the name for the results of political brutality which caused hardship, despair and, in many cases, suicide (for instance Ernst Toller and Walter Benjamin).

German authors who did not find themselves in sympathy with the new regime in 1933 sometimes found ways of staying in Germany and maintaining integrity (Kästner, for instance) but a large number of highly significant authors, among them Heinrich and Thomas Mann, Döblin, Brecht, and Anna Seghers, left the country. For many, there was no choice because they were Jewish or prominently identified with the left and would have lost their liberty; others, like Thomas Mann, agonized for a time, since for an author to lose his audience is no small loss.

Some writers wrote novels representing the condition of exiles, for instance Seghers's *Transit* (1944), Lion Feuchtwanger's *Exil* (1940: Feuchtwanger had written a novel too, also in a traditional realist mode, on the Weimar Republic, *Erfolg* [*Success*, 1930]) and Thomas Mann's eldest son Klaus Mann's *Der Vulkan* (1939). The task of bearing witness grew exponentially in practical urgency and became inseparable from political and social commitment. It was a matter of the utmost immediate importance to convey to those outside Germany how an entire national culture has been usurped.

A genuinely effective literary intervention from exile was Seghers's novel *Das siebte Kreuz*, a chapter of which was published in Moscow in 1939 and which was published, while Seghers was in Mexican exile, in English and in German in 1942. Opposition to the Nazis recommended it to a wide ideological spectrum. It was the story of escape from a concentration camp in pre-war Nazi Germany; the seventh cross of the title refers to the trees upon which the camp commandant vows to hang seven escapees when they are recaptured. One, Georg Heisler, evades capture with the help of fellow-communist resistance members and other Germans of good will. This novel is written in the spirit of Socialist Realism, in line with Seghers's political beliefs, and became a DDR classic. Yet it was selected as Book of the Month by American literary critics in October 1942 and made into a film with Spencer Tracy as (a now non-communist) Heisler in 1944. The US company of Little, Brown agreed to publish the translation because it was felt that it conveyed to the world outside Nazi Germany that there was a difference between Nazis and Germans. Seghers was much influenced by Benjamin's 'Storyteller' essay and strove in this novel as well as her exile novel *Transit* (which contains a kind of homage to him and his suicide for want of a transit visa) to put storytelling to good use again. The curious position in which her narrative found itself between Socialist Realism and Hollywood suggests again, after Remarque and *pace* Benjamin, that literary narrative, in conjunction with the more powerful and immediate modern media, contributes to real struggles.

Exile, by separating outstanding writers like Mann and Brecht from their immediate and natural cultural context, had benefits for the production of literature since words became a kind of home from home. It is hard to imagine that Mann's *Joseph* tetralogy (1933–1942), though begun during the Weimar years, would have become the mixture of myth and democratic humanism that it did become had it been finished there and not in the USA. And Brecht's exile, removing him from an unambiguous rhetorical-political position in relation to his public, forced him into a devising a more many-sided, differentiated and dramatically involving idiom than the one with which he had been working in the last Weimar years.

To conclude this section on vicissitudes of literature in exile, we turn to an example of exile suffered less by an author than by a remarkable novel. Elias Canetti was born in Bulgaria in 1905 (chronologically roughly the generation of Kästner and Remarque), left Austria in 1938 and spent the rest of his life in England and Switzerland. His novel *Die Blendung* was written in the early 1930s in Vienna, and first published there (with some difficulty, given Canetti's Jewish background and the not remotely *völkisch* nature of the book) in 1935. The German-speaking world was not in a state to receive it at that point (although it had *succès d'estime* and Thomas Mann and Musil read and appreciated it). In 1946, it was published in English translation under the title *Auto da fé* and in French in 1949 as *La tour de Babel*. Its 1948 German republication found no resonance, perhaps because conditions were not yet right for the reception of so uncompromisingly demanding and idiosyncratic a work. In this case once more, we find a link between the 1920s and 1960s: in 1963, once Kafka had been fully acknowledged as a modern master of German literature, Grass's grotesque and brilliant Modernist-related *Die Blechtrommel* (*The Tin Drum*) had had spectacular success, and Canetti's own *magnum opus* on the theory of crowd behaviour, *Masse und Macht* (*Crowds and Power*), had made his name, a third German edition of his novel was published by the prestigious Hanser Verlag and became world famous, contributing to the award of the Nobel Prize for literature to Canetti in 1981.

In a sense, that publishing history is all the story we wish to tell about this novel: a story of symbiosis. It is the story of a novel written in German by a writer whose first language was a Sephardic dialect of Spanish, known in translation before it registered in the German literary arena, defying place and time and existing as it were outside the categories that normally shape literary history. Yet it is a book that is profoundly literary, seriously engaged with the question of the place and meaning of books in the kind of world Canetti encountered, to his shock and fascination, in the Berlin of the late Weimar period. This novel, he explained later, was his attempt to be the Gogol or the Stendhal of the new world of dislocated consciousnesses.

Inspired by the asceticism of Karl Kraus in relation to the literary marketplace, and also by Kafka who had no conscious relation at all to the literary scene he came to dominate in the 1950s and 1960s, Canetti's book makes no concessions to public taste. It positions itself outside familiar cultural territory. Energy, the life force, is dissociated from all sorts of representations, most particularly from language itself. The main strand of the narrative concerns the relationship between the eminent sinologist, Peter Kien, and his books. This relationship is emphatically exclusive and makes living with the rest of the world, in which energy is not blocked within an obsessive-compulsive relation to a personal library, but is free to run around after sex, money and power, an impossible farce. In the end, Peter burns himself and his library.

The pathological rigidity that defines all the characters in the first two books of the novel is set against the remedy in the third of an unbounded flexibility in the matter of personal relations. Peter's brother Georges is a Parisian psychiatrist whose revolutionary method with psychotic patients is to take their delusions completely seriously. He was inspired to this brilliant method of treatment by making the acquaintance of a man turned into a gorilla who speaks his own gorilla language, entirely malleable and attuned to the movements of his body and appetites.

Critics disagree about whether or not the reader is invited to give his assent to the position embodied by Georges. But one way of reading the novel is to say that it positions itself and its implied reader outside both the book obsession of Peter and the unlikely, gorilla-inspired flexibility of his brother. If one wished to push the interpretation further, one might say that it places itself outside both the book culture of the old world (which ends up going up in flames) and the new, informal, psychoanalytical, lifestyle culture, which fails to prevent the *auto da fé*.

Canetti's novel differs from Musil's less in the depth of its cynicism about meaning than in that Canetti achieves powerful closure in it. Although the work has nothing of the urbane intelligence of Musil, it is finished. It has enough energy beyond good and evil to become complete and challenge the modern reader to endure the conflagration that consumes the old world, with no guarantee that anything to replace it will arise from the ashes.

The economic miracle

The experience of Germans who remained alive in the remnants of the National Socialist state in 1945 was more extreme than that of 1918–19. On this later occasion, the defeat was even more crushing, ending with occupation, the displacement of millions and the destruction of entire cities, bringing with it starvation and homelessness on a large scale. The shame of complicity in what became known as the Holocaust was morally crippling. These are experiences not easily overcome or reintegrated into civilized European discourse.

Elisabeth Langgässer, author and lyric poet whose life had been deeply marked by the Third Reich in a number of ways, wisely said in 1947: 'Vor allem gönne man der Sprache eine Zeit der Ruhe und des Schweigens' ('Above all we need to allow language a period of rest and silence'; quoted in Grimminger 1980: X, 222). Silence did not mean unmindfulness but was the adequate response to a set of conditions that exceeded the power of mind to organize them. If there was and remained for a time a core of silence in German literature, only the superficiality of modern public consciousness could confuse this with evasion. Indeed, as the examples adduced in chapter 4 suggest, creating the conditions for just such a silence amid the noise of publicity and the society of spectacle ('negation') is one of the important tasks of serious literature in modernity.

On the other hand, it is important to avoid the mythology of a 'zero hour'. Among surviving Germans, cunning, resourcefulness, duplicity, creativity, dishonesty, courage all reasserted themselves soon enough. 1945–7, like 1918–19, was a moment at which the sheer fact of survival gave rise to utopian thoughts. By 1947, the reality of Cold War alignments put a stop to these, and in 1948 the western allies reformed the currency in the zones they occupied, establishing the framework for economic recovery in what was to become in the following year the Federal Republic. Capitalist democratic society, especially in the US version but systemically in western societies, encourages all the human qualities listed above in some measure and in varying proportions. In the Federal Republic, its imposition or reimposition, as Alexander and Margarete Mitscherlich observed in their celebrated 1967 study *Die Unfähigkeit zu trauern* (*Inability to Mourn*), had the added function of deflecting the psychopathology of melancholy.

The disruption was by no means absolute. While there were urgent reasons for intellectuals not to identify themselves with the Weimar period, as we shall see in a moment, the publishers were keen to take up where they had left off in 1932 in terms of how their industry was to be organized. During the first post-war years, the most widely read authors were Christian writers of inner emigration, especially Ernst Wiechert (but there were many others). Gottfried Benn, who as we saw had actually supported the Nazis in 1933, although he later recanted, was cautiously reintroduced to the literary scene by a small Swiss publisher. His *Statische Gedichte* appeared with them in 1948, and throughout the 1950s Benn's name was revered as the greatest contemporary German lyric poet (he died in 1956).

Those, however, who were concerned to facilitate and contribute to a literature identified with the post-war moment and its possibilities found themselves between a rock and a hard place. Given the Third Reich, the freedom to write and read whatever you wished was the condition for any post-war writing ethos. *Sansibar oder der letzte Grund* (*Zanzibar or the Final Reason*, 1957) by Alfred Andersch (1914–1980) was constructed around an Ernst Barlach sculpture of a novice monk reading to make just this point. Yet the failure of Weimar Republic intellectuals to prevent moral and political meltdown confirmed the long-held conviction in German culture (going back at least to the 1830s) that *Geist* and *Macht* should never be segregated. This produced the obviously paradoxical outcome that only genuinely 'autonomous' art could be truly political.

In the conditions of democratic capitalism, this dilemma was refracted in two equally unsatisfactory ways. By the end of the 1950s, Böll realized that his own popular works, although critical of the subservience of the Adenauer government to the interests of the United States, were the perfect advertisement for the moral superiority of those interests. The existence and popularity of Böll's books provided evidence of freedom of expression and capitalism with a conscience, without having any more public influence than well-intentioned exile writing had had on the Nazi administration. They had autonomy foisted upon them. Böll examined this predicament in the effective but – for him – unusually introspective *Ansichten eines Clowns* (*Views of a Clown*) of 1960.

On the other hand, Günter Grass (born 1927) reminded his readers that poetic talent is not any kind of protection against political indoctrination. In *Kopfgeburten* (*Headbirths*, 1980) and also again in his controversial autobiography *Beim Häuten der Zwiebel* (*Skinning the Onion*) in 2006, he said that, had he been ten years older, his own writing drive and ability would initially have been put to the service of the Nazi regime (who needs autonomy when you are winning?) and then, after Stalingrad, adopted a more thoughtful, ambiguous tone. It is hard to imagine a more withering critique of 'autonomy' than the way Grass describes the kind of poetry he would have written: 'ortlose Trauer, verzweifelte Wortwahl, Dunkles, Vieldeutiges [...] *allzeit gültige* Verse' ('unlocalized mourning, despairing diction, darkness, ambiguity [...] *timeless* verse'; quoted in Neuhaus 1988: 38).

Grass recognized that autonomous literature is impossible with no ontological foundation. This is why Christian authors, who had such a foundation, were able to write and be read for a while, and indeed why Böll, who was an unorthodox Rhineland Catholic, could bring critical brio to bear upon the conservative restoration in the 1950s. Secular literary writing, that is to say 'literature' as understood in the post-Enlightenment world, will in democratic capitalism be pulled towards the ontological enigma, the vacuum that opened up for Grass and his generation when their National Socialist identification collapsed. At the same time, it is called to take social responsibility, affirming democratic institutions against the seductions of phoney ontological claims. The warping effect of capitalism is part of the pragmatic challenge, as well as a source of interest and energy. The threat of banality inseparable from the capitalist culture industry and journalism must be countered on its own terms. The only energy available to turn against it is its own. Böll's success with *Die verlorene Ehre der Katharina Blum* (*The Lost Honour of Katharina Blum*) demonstrates that by 1974 he had learned this lesson. Infuriated by the certainly capitalist, but less than democratic, way in which he had been treated by the *Bild-Zeitung*, Germany's leading tabloid newspaper, he shrewdly composed a narrative discourse so effectively damaging to the tabloid press that the publications of the Springer Press (publisher of *Bild*) refused to carry best-seller lists in which Böll's novel appeared.

The Gruppe 47 was the most influential literary grouping in the first decades of the Federal Republic. Its history exemplifies the quandary facing those who wished to re-establish a civilized German literature. It had its beginnings in the utopian post-war moment when Andersch and Hans Werner Richter founded a literary journal called *Der Ruf* (meaning something like 'the clarion call') in the cause of an independent democratic Germany. When the Americans closed it down, Andersch and Richter argued about how to continue the initiative. Andersch wanted to retain the political agenda; Richter took the view that only free, independent literature could be genuinely political (in other words, he embraced the paradox). He won, and the paradox became institutionalized.

Over twenty years, the majority of serious literary authors in the Federal Republic (and some from the Democratic Republic, for instance Günter Kunert and Johannes Bobrowski) attended meetings of the group. A small selection (in addition to Richter, Andersch, Böll and Grass) illustrates this: Bachmann, Celan, Hans Magnus Enzensberger, Peter Handke, Helmut Heißenbüttel, Uwe Johnson, Alexander Kluge, Siegfried Lenz, Peter Rühmkorf, Wolfdietrich Schnurre, Martin Walser, Peter Weiss and Gabriele Wohmann.

The group's history further typified something about cultural life in a modern democratic-capitalist media society. While it made it possible for a serious post-war German literature to be at the same time radical, in the sense of defiantly non-conformist, and autonomous, in the sense of putting the idea of literature as the preserve of independent creativity before all other considerations, this very mixture turned into a selling point. The meetings became media events, and the criticism that followed the actual readings passed from the hands of creative colleagues to those of uncreative pundits like Marcel Reich-Ranicki, who arrogated to themselves the right to say what was and what was not literature (Ranicki, interestingly, missed the point of *Die Blechtrommel*).

However, as Grass would be the first to affirm, this inevitable progression from informal workshop to marketing agency for the high-end culture industry by no means invalidated the group's achievement in the real world. Grass's 1979 story *Das Treffen in Telgte* (*The Meeting at Telgte*), a *roman à clef* about the group, was dedicated to Hans Werner Richter and celebrated what it achieved for and through literature in the aftermath of war. Grass did enter the public sphere by this portal and, once there, continued to fight the corner for genuinely creative art against all comers. Gruppe 47's very commitment to the craft and creativity of artists was what sold it to the educated reading public of the economic miracle and subsequently what caused the younger generation to reject it as apolitical. Curiously, this rejection was no more than a refreshment of the impetus which had inspired the founders of the group (who denied that it had ever been formally founded) in the first place.

In retrospect, one failing that can be laid at the door of the Group was that it was so committed to the future of German literature that by and large it avoided the Medusan glance backwards towards the Holocaust. At all events, its ethos did not encourage direct engagement with it. Once Richter had prevailed in the argument with Andersch, the group's commitment to literature carried silently within itself not only the paradoxical determination to remain outside immediate politics in order to make all the more effective a contribution to it but also the 'negation' of the recent political reality that had crossed the line into barbarism; a reality not, or certainly not immediately, susceptible to aesthetic treatment except, precisely, in silence and commitment to a better future. The dividing line between this silent acknowledgement and self-delusion or repression is very fine.

An exception was made by Schnurre, who in 1962 spoke unambiguously within the group for the importance of remembrance of the murdered, arguing that a *littérature engagée* in post-war Germany entailed recognition of Auschwitz. Yet the leading spokesman for the view that Auschwitz was the overriding question in aesthetic matters in those years was the Marxist social theorist and philosopher, T. W. Adorno. He returned to the Federal Republic from US exile in 1949. In an essay of that year (published 1951), he had said that to write poetry after Auschwitz was barbaric. Although experts disagree about the exact implications of what became more of a soundbite than an insight, there is no doubt that Adorno's theory is the purest and most stern version of 'negation' as an aesthetic absolute. Perhaps his extreme position can be described by recalling Freud's view from 'Zeitgemäßes über Krieg und Tod', quoted in chapter 4, that the illusion required for socialized existence can become counter-productive when the return of barbarism surprises the peoples of culture. At times like these, the disappointment threatens to become disabling. Here a dose of 'negation', that is reacquaintance with the reality of death, can help (see Santner 1990: 19–26). Adorno's disappointment (and he was hardly alone in this) at the return of barbarism was so great that he over-prescribed the dose. His view was that in the capitalist world (which for him was intrinsically undemocratic and complicit in the Holocaust), pervasive false consciousness could only be met and countered by absolute rejection of the sort only extreme hermetic Modernism can mount. He took the paradoxical position implied by the historical function and actuality of Gruppe 47 to its absolute theoretical limit, fusing the functions of witness and commitment to social improvement (only complete rejection of the way things are can provide a sense of how they might be otherwise) but, unlike the Group, blocked out the market completely – a theoretical luxury not available to practising poets and writers. Yet fundamentally his position was the same as theirs, namely that political and social criticism from literature should be immanent, and not explicit or instrumental.

Adorno was one of the panel of judges for a prize announced in 1957 by the literary journal *Texte und Zeichen* which challenged authors to write a novel couched in a form of realism adequate to the rhetorical demands of the day. They stressed that this had nothing to do with received stylistic notions of what constituted realism but should be as experimental as necessary to pierce the facade of what usually goes by the name of realism. Picking up Adorno's belief in the immanence of critique, it defied the impossible question about 'autonomy' by asserting that, as far as they were concerned, the phrase 'socially critical' and the word 'novel' were indivisible (see Scholl 1990: 35–6). None of the forty entries was judged by the committee to deserve the prize.

In 1958, Günter Grass read two chapters from the as yet unpublished manuscript of *Die Blechtrommel* at a meeting of the Gruppe 47. He was awarded the Group's prize and went on to become the most famous postwar author in German, receiving the Nobel Prize for literature in 1999.

One can't know whether he would have won the *Texte und Zeichen* prize as well but it is plain that he had indeed found a mimetic idiom in which to affirm the potency of literature as a medium in the particularly difficult rhetorical conditions of the Federal Republic. As Hans Magnus Enzensberger (born 1929), an occasional Gruppe 47 attendee and pupil of Adorno, said in a 1959 radio review and in defiance of the obviously fantastic elements of Grass's novel, 'Günter Grass ist ein Realist' (quoted in Neuhaus 1997: 120).

What distinguishes Grass's literary treatment of the Third Reich from the distanced tragic aesthetic of Thomas Mann in California – whose 1947 exile novel on the subject, *Doktor Faustus*, did not speak to but about contemporary Germans – was that Grass wrote from the subjectivity of a traumatized, ashamed, displaced but, despite all this, still living German.

Less sympathetic than Enzensberger, Günter Blöcker, the leading literary reviewer of the time, perceptively noted, also in 1959, that the novel met a hidden need of the Federal Republic for 'mortification' (Neuhaus 1997: 128). What he meant was that Grass's novel was a scurrilous affront to the aesthetic dignity proper to serious literature represented by such as Thomas Mann. Yet he was surely accurate in identifying this need as the result of the epoch's 'unassimilated past', its 'excess of guilt' and 'the arrogance with which it sought to disregard these things'.

Blöcker further disparaged both the Gruppe 47 for awarding its prize to Grass and Grass's publisher for the publicity attending the launch. This aversion to publicity seems perverse coming from a cultural journalist; it attests to a peculiar blindness to the cultural reality of the time. On the contrary, Grass's work is a rare, but not accidental or arbitrary, case of how artistic integrity and skill can not only live with the processes of the mass media but tap into the amoral energies of capitalism, even to the point of utilizing them not to evade trauma (it is always too late for that, by definition) but to engage with its effects.

Die Blechtrommel was a lesson, brilliantly conceived and executed, in living in history without moral or ontological absolutes and without the safety net of 'meaning' hidden in bourgeois subjecthood. This is why it is appropriate to see Grass's antecedents in the pre-bourgeois Grimmelshausen and the anti-bourgeois Döblin (of whom more below), as he himself did, in other words to see him as unambiguously post-Romantic and thus engaged with the dialectic of enlightened false consciousness that Sloterdijk identifies with Weimar. Attempts to see *Die Blechtrommel* in the tradition of the *Bildungsroman* (even assuming there is one) are in my view misleading (*pace* Enzensberger, who only made the connection in order to provoke those traditionalists who were shocked by it).

Die Blechtrommel affirms the embodied will to survive of the modern German subject, yet it simultaneously exposes the moral scars left upon him by history, scars which exceed the boundaries of individual personality. Through the device of the three-year-old drummer Oskar Matzerath, Grass entwines narrative drive with strands of cowardice, betrayal and homicidal inclinations in a whole carnival of life-affirming self-deception.

At the time of its first reception, silent acknowledgment-cum-repression of the Holocaust still obscured the degree to which the shame of it lived on as part of the moral reality of the Federal Republic. Blöcker's clear-sightedness mixed with aesthetic incomprehension is symptomatic: just naming the shame did not dispense with it.

Literary art can express shame without disavowing it. Grass knew perfectly well that he had no stable platform from which to regard the past as overcome since his own initial socialization as a Nazi could not be erased. This truth only took on headline properties when he revealed sixty years on that he had not served in the Wehrmacht, as he had consistently claimed, but as an infantryman in an SS regiment at the end of the war. But in fact Grass had been admitting the substance of his adolescent identification, both in encoded form in his fiction, in which the act of narrative is always associated with guilt, and explicitly as in the examples cited above, ever since he became famous, and ever more stridently. This slow-release reading of Grass is a measure of how gradually a sense of moral responsibility came into consciousness of the Federal Republic. And, of course, by the time it was established in the 1980s, it was already banalized by the logic of media society. Grass's great artistic achievements, especially with the Danzig Trilogy (apart from *Die Blechtrommel*, this includes *Katz und Maus* [*Cat and Mouse*, 1961] and *Hundejahre* [*Dog Years*, 1963]), is resistance mounted to this unedifying process from within the old institution of literature.

The 1980s was not a favourable decade for German writing. The preoccupation with the past entered ever more into public debate, producing a doubly negative effect from the perspective of literature: a peculiar historical distortion occurred according to which it seemed that post-war German writing had failed to respond to the issue of the past (as if Bachmann, Böll, Celan, Grass, Koeppen and others had never existed), but which simultaneously relieved literature of its function in this regard. Should literature (in the inherited sense) now confirm that it still had a conscience by addressing the big issues of the day, such as the threat to the ecology of the planet or the danger of nuclear war (as Grass himself did in novels like *Die Rättin* [*The Rat*, 1986]), or should it defend its 'specialness' as a privileged cultural practice cloistered by the traditional (and thus less vulgarized) print medium and the theatrical establishment (this was the position, for instance, of Botho Strauss [born 1944])? Two established survivors of the radical Modernist and avant-garde revival of the later 1960s, Enzensberger and Peter Handke (born 1942), were probably the most successful at steering a course between an adult respect for creative writing and a sense of the urgency of public affairs.

A remarkable symptom of how the Holocaust had now found a relatively unproblematic place in the old institution of 'literature' is provided by the programmatically traditional verse of Ulla Hahn (born 1946), the most widely sold lyric poet of the 1980s, who included in her best-selling collection of 1981, *Herz über Kopf* (*Heart over Head*), a poem entitled 'Television Image of a Jewish Woman in a Concentration Camp', concluding '... Bis ich/begriffen was dein Blick gemeint/und mich der Tränen schämte/ die ich um dich um euch nicht geweint' ('... Until/I had grasped what your gaze intended/and was ashamed of the tears/that I had not cried for you and yours').

The curse of a melancholy consciousness of impotence or irrelevance caused other writers like Wolfgang Hildesheimer (1916–1991) and (already in the 1960s) Koeppen to fall silent, while authors met to discuss if reading and writing had a future, as, for instance, in a symposium entitled 'Weiterschreiben' ('Continuing to Write'; papers published in *manuskripte,* issue 29, 1989) that took place in Styria, Austria, in 1989, at which the question was posed: does continuing to write (i.e. serious literature) represent complicity with the terrible truth, or does the terrible truth constitute the motive for continuing to write? One contributor, the literary critic, publicist and author Hubert Winkels, suggested that serious literature was now animated by an elegiac sense of its own redundancy and really only spoke to itself, author to author, while the new media occupied the space in the broad public mind that had once belonged to literature.

The resourcefulness and creativity of the capitalist 'warp' effect is once again demonstrated by the parallel circumstance that this debilitating sense of Modernist marginalization was triumphantly branded Post-Modernism by the culture industry. *Das Parfum* (1985), a novel by Patrick Süskind (born 1949), and a text conceding nothing to the Weimar Republic in enlightened false consciousness, became the most successful German novel since *Im Westen nichts Neues*. Constructed through a succession of reminiscences of former types of literary consciousness, it is ferociously literary (see Ryan 1990; it has this in common with *Die Blendung*). The central conceit, that of a subject who gives off no bodily smell but who has the olfactory equivalent of perfect pitch, situates the novel even more firmly in the post-Romantic world than Oskar had done for *Die Blechtrommel*. The idea that the extract of love can be distilled (as a perfume) and made to work on the masses without being mediated through the usual structures of personal identity and language conveys an uncanny sense of how Dionysus stalks the hedonistic market society of late capitalism. Süskind's book is like a *Blechtrommel* without its personal stake in history and only a brilliant pastiche of historical writing to put in its place.

In 1990, the publication of Christa Wolf's short text *Was bleibt* (see chapter 5) caused another of the regular journalistic debates about German identity that had preoccupied readers of the serious newspapers in the Federal Republic from the 1960s to the 1980s. This time the slow and difficult process of self-examination was quickened by historical events of global resonance, namely the breakup of the Soviet bloc and the consequent unexpected and unplanned reunification of Germany.

Christa Wolf, the one writer to enjoy equal prestige in both East and West, became the focus for the idea that post-war German literature, while in one sense divided by ideology and political reality, was in another united by language and tradition. It is worth mentioning in this connection that one of the specifically literary achievements of the period, in the anachronistic sense of a Thomas Mann or even a Musil, was rooted in a refusal to identify with either east or west, but rather in the impulse to explore the political and psychological implications of the division in the medium of Modernist prose. This was Uwe Johnson's *Mutmaßungen über Jakob* (*Speculations about Jakob*, 1959), written in the DDR but published by Suhrkamp in the Federal Republic where Johnson (1934–1984) soon moved, which is structured round the mysterious death of a railway official who has just returned to the East after a disillusioning visit to the West. It deals with a family group across both sides of the ideological divide, and the interface between two forms of consciousness. Johnson's major work, *Jahrestage* (*Anniversaries*, four volumes: 1970, 1971, 1973, 1983), rivalling in ambition the *Joseph* tetralogy or *Der Mann ohne Eigenschaften*, situates some of the characters from the earlier text, in a complex narrative framework, which, set in New York, puts the inner-German division into a global context. Another deeply literary author, the Modernist novelist and lyric poet Johannes Bobrowski (1917–1965), lived in the East but was published and read in the West where he was awarded the prize of the Gruppe 47 in 1962. He emphatically defined himself as a *German* author, and, like the Grass of *Hundejahre*, for instance, saw the current division between parts of Germany as simply another turn in a long history of such differences and accommodations.

However, this identification of a single German literature, honourably united and continuing the tradition of the nation of culture, going back to Herder, became in the debate about *Was bleibt* a stick with which to beat both post-war German literatures as failed projects to influence politics by writing. Wolf stood revealed as an ineffectual state author whose trust in the civilized literary discourse of 'subjective authenticity' to improve socialism had been manifestly misplaced. In an article of 2 October 1990, entitled 'Farewell to the Literature of the Federal Republic', Frank Schirrmacher, literary critic for the *Frankfurter Allgemeine Zeitung*, represented the whole thing in polemical simplification as a hapless leftist muddle. In this and other articles by him and by other influential voices, such as Ulrich Greiner in *Die Zeit*, the entire development of West German literature, beginning with the twenty-year regime of the Gruppe 47 and culminating in the discrediting of superannuated literary celebrities like Wolf and Grass, so evidently off the pace of actual historical change, was represented as the misguided attempt to place literature in the service of the correction of history.

The serious intellectual theory underpinning this assault upon what was called *Gesinnungsästhetik*, or the 'moralization of literature' (Bohrer 1991: 83), as Andreas Huyssen pointed out in a 1991 essay called 'After the Wall: The Failure of German Intellectuals' (Huyssen 1995: 37–66), was that of Karl Heinz Bohrer. Bohrer's aesthetic position, to use our terms, requires that literature remain faithful to the potential within it for negation. The deployment of literary Modernism in the service of a correction of history is a betrayal of the Nietzschean gaze into the heart of darkness that, it can be argued, dwells within Modernism proper. What we recognize here is an indictment of Richter's institutionalized paradox, according to which non-political literature and the shouldering of democratic responsibility are identical.

Bohrer's position is related to that version of the Modernist strategy of negation that is exemplified by Ernst Jünger (Bohrer wrote a lengthy study called *The Aesthetic of Terror* [1978] in which Jünger plays a central part). Bohrer, in a way, is a culturally nationalist Adorno (contradictory as that sounds), doggedly defending the distinction between aesthetics and (democratic) politics, and finding confirmation in the 1990 'crisis of the intellectuals' of his long-held opposition to the official confusion of serious aesthetic Modernism with a soft-focus leftist agenda.

This seems a dubious position for at least two reasons: first, it is at some level to wish for constant awareness of untempered historical catastrophe, which is as impossible as it is undesirable. Second, it denies aesthetic legitimacy to the capitalist-democratic determination of western literature in favour of a peculiar attachment to 'Romanticism'. Modern commercial literature is bound to engage with the past in German consciousness since, as we have argued and illustrated, that is the material to hand, material that throughout the twentieth century since the First World War has consisted of a peculiar and horrible drama. There is a place for the 'negation' that addresses the disappointment of civilized expectations, in Kafka and Jünger, Koeppen, Bachmann, Celan and of more recent authors, such as the impressive prose writer and lyricist Anne Duden (born 1942), but the fundamental mission of such death-related literature is still in the service of life, not death (as Bohrer would certainly concede), but thus also in the real world is bound to entwine with the rude life of capitalism and undergo the indignity of contamination as commodity.

While Bohrer's analysis does expose the systemic weakness in what were once unquestioned assumptions about art and politics, Schirrmacher's evident despair at the stagnation of West German literature in the 1980s, as Huyssen persuasively suggests, is caused at bottom not by the vitiation of literature by a lily-livered *Gesinnungsästhetik*, or confusion of aesthetic with moral criteria, but by the inexorable rise of the new technological media, against which literature in the West did not enjoy the official protection afforded to it in what Bohrer referred to as 'the cultural equivalent of a nature reserve' in the East.

Medial hybridity

While one has to mention (with melancholy if one loves it) that literature became marginal in the twentieth century, it is also clear that in many cases writing practices formed new kinds of hybrid with the new media, even where there was no interest whatsoever in the fate of the once great cultural institution (and often a political intention to replace it). The final section of this chapter therefore looks at that threshold area in which literature begins to blend into the media world, Debord's 'Society of the Spectacle'.

Many theorists and intellectuals, both during the Weimar period and in the Federal Republic, addressed the impact of new technological media upon culture. The most famous individual text on the subject is Benjamin's essay 'Das Kunstwerk im Zeitalter seiner technischen Reproduzierbarkeit' ('The Work of Art in the Age of Mechanical Reproduction', 1936). But many others, such as Siegfried Kracauer (in 'Das Ornament des Masse' ['The Mass Ornament'] and other essays), Hans Magnus Enzensberger ('Baukasten zu einer Theorie der Medien' ['Building Block for a Theory of the Media'], published in the journal edited by him in the 1960s and 1970s, *Kursbuch*), Alexander Kluge across a wide range of films, texts and theoretical contributions, Jochen Hörisch (for instance, *Ende der Vorstellung: Die Poesie der Medien* [*End of the Performance: The Poetry of the Media*, 1999]) and Friedrich Kittler (for instance, *Grammophon, Film, Typewriter*, 1986), not to mention the entire discipline of media studies (and the concomitant decline of literary studies), have reflected this systemic shift.

As we saw in chapter 3, Expressionism was a threshold case. It was multimedial from the beginning (important for both painting and literature, and particularly at home in the traditional hybrid medium of the theatre) and animated (or possibly just confused) by a dialectic between resistance to modernity and identification with it. The unprecedented manifestation of the dark side of technology through the war, and the sense of utopian political hope that followed, really outflanked the Expressionist style in both directions, although artists and publishers associated with it (Toller, for instance, or Franz Pfemfert's journal *Die Aktion*) addressed both the horror and the hope, expressing themselves artistically as well as politically. The rising dominance of the technological paradigm is suggested by the speed with which the first famous Expressionist film, *The Cabinet of Dr. Caligari*, came about (it was released after a cunning advertising campaign in 1919 and became a success in France and the US, as well as in Germany). By 1922, as a disparaging reference in Fritz Lang's *Dr. Mabuse: The Gambler* documents, Expressionism was seen as effete by comparison with the reality of the new world, the amorality of which was represented by Lang's eponymous Nietzschean hero. What the scene conveys – Mabuse glowering and singular in a refined salon full of chic primitive artefacts and Expressionist decor – is that the old aesthetic attitude is now in competition with one more commensurate with this medium, characterized by the will to power over others (hypnosis was also the theme of *Caligari*), exercised through greater impact and broader appeal.

The standard account of a development from Expressionism to *Neue Sachlichkeit* (variously translated as 'the new objectivity' or 'the new sobriety') somewhere in the mid-1920s in Weimar should be understood as the symptom of the culture industry catching up with and finding a brand name for the changing of the guard from a culture based on meaning (with Expressionism as its last gasp) to one based on the operation of technologies in capitalist democratic society.

Already in 1914, in a manifesto, 'The Berliner Programm', published in the Expressionist journal *Der Sturm*, Alfred Döblin had argued that literature traditionally understood was ageing, and in a lecture at Berlin University in 1928 he said something similar about the print medium in general: 'The book is the death of genuine speech.' He advocated the move away from the book ('los vom Buch') towards a new kind of stage or theatre ('Bühne'), by which he might well have meant film, or perhaps more likely radio (he was one of the first cultural contributors to German entertainment radio, inaugurated in 1924), rather than simply new experiments in old theatres.

At all events, the novel by which he is remembered (and which has been filmed twice for cinema or television, once soon after publication in 1931 and again, by Fassbinder, in the 1980s), *Berlin Alexanderplatz* (1929), is a hybrid cultural form in several ways. First, it is certainly written for a readership that brought to its reading the experience of the city, and of the cinema, both of which seemed to saturate, overload and fascinate the perception of individual subjects in modes of organization or disorganization that defied traditional narration.

Döblin's novel is also a medial hybrid in that it is composed of a montage of materials, some of them from 'found' material, such as medical textbooks, newspapers, refrains from poems and popular songs, advertisements, even pictorial reproductions of Berlin municipal logos; some of them mimicry of real speech, or different sorts of narrative or speech act, such as boxing commentary, fantasy, Biblical allusions, or phonetic transcriptions of noises. Nevertheless, there can be no doubt that this is a work of literature since the actual hero of the text is language itself, liberated from the various 'enchantments' by means of which it used to conjure up meaning. Döblin explicitly rejected the literary cliché that language (as a kind of crude technology) fails to convey the artistic thought at the origin of the work of art. Rather, he argued, it is indeed a species of technology or manufacture but a productive one that completes a process that begins in the mind of the author.

Released from the constraints of conventional realist mimesis, from narrators and characters, language can come from anywhere, exactly as real and exactly as artificial as the print medium and the empirical personality of the author. As Döblin had said in the 1914 manifesto, the epic text should not be (or pretend to be) 'spoken', it should be 'present' ('vorhanden'). At the same time, *Berlin Alexanderplatz* is unmistakably a reference to a real time and a real place, much as Grass's fantastic realism in the *Blechtrommel* would be. Grass made no secret of his debt to 'his teacher' Döblin. As such, the novel was also of necessity political in the sense that it made no categorical distinction between the material disposition, the constructions, of reality and the at once real and artificial saliency of politics in modernity.

The technological instrumentality of the modern world is not an individual affair, as the anti-story of Franz Biberkopf shows. Döblin's publisher had insisted the novel should be embellished with a subtitle naming a character and evoking the dimension of narrative: *Die Geschichte vom Franz Biberkopf*. But what happens to the proletarian and criminal protagonist of limited mental range is not really a story. It is the demonstration, rather, of the indifference of the world to his attempt to have one, in the sense of to try and take moral agency for himself and shape or *gestalten* his life into a meaningful form. Meanwhile, that world is seen as a construction site. It is a space of many-sided instrumentalization, building, scientific measuring and explaining. There is a leitmotif of the actual construction of the Alexanderplatz; there are the institutions, Tegel prison and the mental hospital Buch, that can 'read' Biberkopf as a criminal and a self-delusive sociopath respectively; there is the 'made' constitution of the text itself that evokes Döblin's formulation in the 1914 *Sturm* manifesto for the modern epic: 'you don't narrate, you construct' ('man erzählt nicht, sondern baut').

'Reality' is not situated within the individual psyche (not that anyone is denying that there is such a thing as the individual mind) but it is, first, a public, collective matter (as Döblin also, quite rightly, thought the modern epic should be) and, second, it is animated by a Dionysian *Machtseele*, an underlying violence, refracted and amplified by the machinery of the modern world. Biberkopf at one point is thrown from a speeding getaway car and loses an arm. This is the post-war world, in which the dispositions of civilization and the energies underlying society no longer securely map onto one another.

Döblin's aesthetic and indeed his politics consisted in the attempt to define a position for himself and the reader at a point between these dispositions and this violence. Between the unscientific haplessness of Biberkopf and the objective forces that determine him, from money through to language, all animated by life no less than he is himself, Döblin's writing identifies the need for a place of cooperation between the individual and the collective where social responsibility can arise.

As a doctor with a social conscience who himself worked in the working-class districts of Berlin, Döblin aspired to combine the scientific paradigm with social progress. The best metaphor for the kind of agency his practice suggests is the way in which he uses language: renouncing the Romantic mystical aura around words, he uses language's pre-existing shapes and dynamics as if he were flying a kite, a cooperation between human ingenuity and the forces of nature (or between doing and leaving alone, to use Sloterdijk's terms).

It is probably right that too many political kites were flown in the Weimar Republic, and it is true enough that at the end of Döblin's great city text aesthetic virtuosity fails before the political specifics it entails by engaging with the pragmatics of contemporary reality: exactly how is Biberkopf to remain true to himself and at the same time become part of a collective without continuing to be vulnerable to the pervasive and predatory clichés the text deploys so well?

There is a wide range of other examples of literary accommodations with the technological media in these periods. Arno Schmidt (1914–1979), for instance, was on the one hand committed to developing a kind of writing that took a scientific view of consciousness. His prose 'experiment' (for instance, *Das steinerne Herz* [*Heart of Stone*, 1956] or *KAFF auch Mare Crisium*, 1960), which achieved considerable *succès d'estime* in the 1960s, claimed to operate what he called a 'conformal representation' of different operations within human consciousness (conformal representation is a term taken from cartography to refer to the mathematical adjustments required to express the curved surface of the earth in two dimensions). On the other hand, this aggressively positivistic enterprise was profoundly literary: Schmidt wished less to explore the human brain than to add new prose forms to the existing stock of prose narrative techniques in German literature from Wieland onwards. What he really cared about was literature, but he was enough of an inhabitant of the twentieth century to recognize that the print medium and the practice of reading that went with it could only exist in opposition to the world around. Schmidt put up admirable opposition: translating popular works into German, giving many radio talks and writing essays about forgotten authors such as Wilhelm Friedrich Meyern, Heinrich Albert Oppermann and Leopold Schefer. His last books were actually medial hybrids in their very insistence upon their writtenness, and in the extraordinary challenge this posed to the reader to turn away from the world and become immersed in them. Of these, the most celebrated was *Zettel's Traum* (1970), 1,000 pages of facsimile typescript (which would have covered many thousands of conventional pages), in which a developed version of the earlier consciousness experiments became submerged in an ocean of quotation and montage of written (and some other sorts of) material, producing the very aura that technological reproduction dispelled, according to Benjamin, by the sheer eccentric excess of mediatednesss.

Another example of this paradoxical parading of literary mediality out of opposition to the effects of the media is the work of Rolf Dieter Brinkmann (1940–1975). Of a different generation to Schmidt, and from an urban rather than an aggressively rural base (Schmidt lived in the middle of the Lüneburger Heide near Celle and hardly spoke to anyone, while Brinkmann came from Cologne, and spent time in London and Rome), his extensive inter-medial work began in a mood of affirmation of 1960s pop culture, combining lyric poetry, photomontage, stream-of-consciousness prose (for instance, *Film in Worten*, 1969), and became, with the fading of the 1968 radical political challenge to the effects of the capitalist media, an affecting struggle against the deformation of modern consciousness. In *Rom, Blicke* [*Rome, Views*], published posthumously in 1979, a formless collage of found material – maps, postcards, letters, photographs – contrasts the contemporary ruins of *Erfahrung* with the achieved literary *Gestaltung* of Goethe's classical Rome *Erlebnis*. *Erkundungen für die Präzisierung des Gefühls für einen Aufstand* (*Enquiries in Relation to the Definition of Feeling for an Uprising*, also published posthumously in facsimile typescript with photographic material, in an edition prepared by his widow Maleen in 1987) elaborates the distress of the contemporary sense of self by the intrusion into consciousness of an explosion of electronic stimuli. Brinkmann had once, with MacLuhan, been ready to regard this revolution as an expansion of consciousness but, in trying to reassert an autonomous self, found there was nothing left to assert or do the asserting. Brinkmann's texts are more developed than Schmidt's in relation to the cross-contamination of media, less fervently literary, but display a similar cultural-literary extremism.

Although after the euphoria of 1968, it could seem as though the media had won (with what glee did journalists misrepresent Enzensberger to the effect that 'literature was dead' in order to prove him wrong when books continued to be published in the 1970s?), there were creative offshoots of that moment in which medial hybridity was affirmed. Examples are Klaus Theweleit's 1977 *Männerphantasien*, which employs profuse illustration in a highly creative way to expand the effect of the prose, or Negt and Kluge's 'Geschichte und Eigensinn' ['History and Obstinacy / "Sense of Oneself"'] of 1981, which diversifies the print medium into a gargantuan scrapbook in the service precisely of their positive campaign to meet the media on its own ground, taking up the Brechtian impulse to tack with the prevailing conditions, rather than wish that others prevailed.

Enzensberger, Negt and Kluge (as well as many others) are all the heirs of Bertolt Brecht in the Federal Republic. Brecht is the figure who towers above all the others when it comes to the new medial hybridity, revealing its essentially political aspect: literature becomes part of the applied technology that will bring about a humane society. Yet from today's perspective it is no longer Brecht's Marxism that defines him but, paradoxically, his quality as the quintessential author of democratic capitalism: hedonistic, cynical, materialist(ic) and opportunistic; above all entirely at home as an artist in technological modernity. As he put it in his account of the trial concerning the film version of the *Dreigroschenoper*, an account which is itself one of the best examples of his indefatigable practical combativeness: 'the mechanization of literary production cannot be thrown into reverse.'

Brecht was not evasive on the subject of whether art should be understood as technical or organic. What every author knows, he makes explicit: you steal, adapt, and revise; you make for an occasion. Text and their effects are material for intervention in social reality. Moreover, what every dramaturge or director knows, Brecht also rendered explicit: theatre is collective. He unblocked for German culture the traditional hybrid medium from its dependency upon text dating back to the *Sturm und Drang*. Wedekind was an acknowledged forerunner. Brecht opposed the division between the new media and the products of the older media. He argued that the new media should not be dismissed just because they came into existence on the back of the preoccupations of individual inventors and immediate appropriation by the profit motive. His point was, and this was precisely what Benjamin and Kracauer also tried to envisage theoretically, that they should be wrested from capitalism in order to serve the broad interests of human progress.

If the metaphor to describe Döblin's method was kite-flying, then the equivalent in the case of Brecht is 'tacking' ('lavieren' as Sloterdijk says), the mobility of the yachtsman in relation to prevailing conditions. As we saw in chapter 5, Marxism, especially as expounded by Lukács, provides theoretically for interchange between consciousness and history, but the historical examples of Stalinist USSR and the DDR rapidly became rigid dictatorships. In contrast, capitalism and democracy, albeit in different and incompatible ways, enshrine perpetual change in their constitutions. The incompatibility adds to the randomness of the outcome. The essence of Brecht's unique contribution was that he put together the idea from the Russian Formalist literary theorists (devised to counter the tired profundity of European Symbolism, and rapidly suppressed in the USSR) that art should refresh perception, defamiliarize ('Verfremden'), with the essentially pragmatic, political idea that the world can only meaningfully be apprehended as changeable.

Brecht's impact falls into stages, moving from a poetically rich engagement with amoral hedonism (*Baal* [1918], *Im Dickicht der Städte* [*In the Jungle of the Cities*, 1923]), with which he made his debut on the stage of the early Weimar years, to the highly self-conscious signature plays written in a pared down deadpan impersonal style, like *Mann ist Mann* (1926), in which the parallel between the construction of personal identity and that of a motor car is conveyed with enthusiastic cynicism, to the spectacular popular success of the *Dreigroschenoper*, which made him famous. Then there are the learning plays (like *Die Maßnahme*), radio experiments (*Der Flug der Lindberghs* [*The Flight of the Lindberghs*]) and film (*Kuhle Wampe*) of the later 1920s and early 1930s, more politically charged than the earlier subversive entertainments and explicitly communist (athough, as we argued in chapter 4, there is more to be said about a piece like *Die Maß-nahme*). This multimedial involvement in the cultural and political life of society was curtailed by exile, in which anti-fascism became the more pressing practical concern (too late). In Scandinavia and later in the US, Brecht worked on quite traditional theatre plays like *Mutter Courage* (1938–9) which made him internationally famous after the war, especially when he could supervise touring productions of them, as became possible once he was installed in the DDR with his own theatre company (The Berliner Ensemble).

What all this work has in common is, first, that it is not finished, indeed is constitutionally unfinishable because inseparable from its immediate context. And this leads on to the second factor that unites it, namely, that it is all context-specific. While this certainly relates to the political context within which Brecht fought his communist corner, the broader point is that he never worked without reflecting upon the mediality (if I may put it like that) of his practice and that of his associates. He didn't work within this or that medium; he worked on the media (this includes the broad range of types of lyric poetry he produced throughout his creative career). It is not what you say or even how you say it, so much as where, when and through which medium or media you say it. Brecht anticipated McLuhan and information theory in this.

The Hitler–Stalin non-aggression pact of 1939 demonstrated that the cynicism of the times exceeded by a gigantic factor the ludic, aesthetic cynicism, the freedom to practise which Brecht and his collaborators had enjoyed during the Weimar Republic (what Sloterdijk calls the kynicism, in the subversive tradition of Diogenes). His 'tacking' took him from Scandinavia at the last possible moment right across the Soviet Union to Vladivostok to the United States and thence (once marked out by the anti-communist US House Un-American Activities Committee) to the new DDR. Neither Brecht nor his reputation ever really recovered from the stain of association with Stalinism. Since 1989, his statue has been toppled like that of some dictator by the likes of John Fuegi, who published a compelling 1,000-page character assassination in 1994, and bourgeois theatre critics have at last been able to vent their resentment at Brecht's influence, like the *Times*'s Bernard Levin who wrote a piece in 1995 saying how pleased he was that Brecht had gone the way of Tito, Brezhnev and Mao.

However, it is impossible to exaggerate how important the example of Brecht was in the 1960s and 1970s. During the 1950s, he had become one of the three or four most performed playwrights in the world, to the extent that the Cold War West was forced to construct him as a kind of modern Shakespeare, transcending his unfortunate association with the other side. Once the atmosphere in the Federal Republic had found again something of the Weimar cultural-political edge in the late 1960s and especially in the melancholy aftermath of that surge of utopianism which, as Sloterdijk argued, approaches the mindset of Weimar even more closely, Brecht's uniquely intelligent and – vitally – practical combination of aesthetics and politics was the one existing universally recognized example of an anti-capitalist but creative use of the new media to which those on the left could point. Thus despite the (often facile) reaction against Brecht since the end of the Soviet Union, it is the French philosopher, Alain Badiou, summing up the twentieth century, who offered the balanced judgment in 2005: 'Without doubt, Brecht is the most universal and most indisputable among those artists who explicitly link their existence and creativity to so-called communist politics' (Badiou 2007: 43).

It is in the area of what can be labelled 'documentary' that literature merged with other media to the greatest extent, and this development is, again, common to both Weimar and the Federal Republic. When literature calls itself documentary, it clearly enters a demarcation grey zone between itself, journalism and politics. The documentary writing of the 1920s and 1960s was related to both. There is a strong line of documentary prose that arose during Weimar, for instance in the reportage of the communist Egon Erwin Kisch (*Der rasende Reporter* [*The Raging Reporter*, 1924). It was taken up again by anti-literary elements of the radical student generation, at which time, for instance, Erika Runge, a television documentary maker, published *Bottroper Protokolle* (1968), interviews with a cross-section of the inhabitants of the town in the Ruhrgebiet reflecting the repercussions of a pit closure, with hardly any commentary. In Ursula Trauberg's *Vorleben* (*Previous Life*, 1968), a young convict gave in her own words an account of her life until the point at which she committed the act for which she was convicted of murder. Both these projects, as well as other similar ones, had the imprimatur of the established novelist Martin Walser (born 1927), as if to say that this kind of informative text is contiguous with, or an extension of, the social concerns of literature. At the extreme edge of what can traditionally be called literature, but nevertheless a prominent part of BRD culture, was the investigative journalism of Günter Walraff (born 1942), for instance *13 Unerwünschte Reportagen* (*13 Undesirable Reports*, 1969), or *Ganz Unten* (*Rock Bottom*, 1985), on the plight of Turkish workers beneath the Federal Republic's welfare radar. The latter was one of the outstanding best-sellers of the 1980s.

The revival of documentary as a kind of rebuttal of *belles lettres* in the post-war period began not in prose but in the theatre. There was a direct line back to Weimar in the person of Erwin Piscator (see chapter 4) who, after Brecht, had been the most prominent man of the theatre on the communist left. His productions, for instance Ernst Toller's *Hoppla, wir leben!* (*Hey, We're Alive!*), with which Piscator opened his own Berlin theatre in 1927, were celebrated and deplored for the high-profile use of various kinds of engineering, particularly the projection of film, revolves, front and back gauzes, escalators and elevators, and so forth. Piscator's position was emphatically anti-literary. He wished to use the institution of the theatre as a means to effect political change. Technology was, first, the adequate means of expression of the age, and, second, the means by which that same technology should be wrested from the hands of those who had so signally abused it (that is, the bourgeoisie).

Individual action was to be contextualized historically by showing film and finding theatrical means to represent the class structure of society beyond the immediate subjective experience of individuals (for instance, in the production of *Hoppla* there was a structure housing six separate mini-stages, conveying the sense of simultaneous parts of the social structure in their interdependency). Theatrical performance was not an aesthetic but a political event. The artistic intentions of individual authors could not have been of less concern to Piscator (the same could be said of Brecht, with the exception of his own). Toller's carefully constructed and ambiguous, thoughtful, individualist drama *Hoppla!* was changed, for instance, into an unambiguous call for revolutionary solidarity. (Toller's text described the change from idealism to cynicism: the Piscator–Bühne production wished to change it back.)

Piscator spent four years of his exile in the USSR where he learned enough about Stalin to resist requests to join Brecht in the DDR after the war. He might have stayed in the US had it not been for his communist background, and he found himself in the Federal Republic in the early 1950s. In the 1960s, he directed a series of performances in which his experimental anti-literary theatricality reached its culmination in his production, and professional backing, of Peter Weiss's *Die Ermittlung* (*The Inquiry*, 1965). This was a remarkable use of the institution of the theatre to undertake a historical and moral task on behalf of the public: Weiss simply transposed ('documentary'-style) material from the Frankfurt Auschwitz trials of the early 1960s into the shape of a theatrical presentation in which the words of those immediately involved in the Holocaust described it. Significantly, the original plan to use projections of actual documentary material from the camps was dropped in the course of production. Political drama, as with Brecht and Müller (see chapter 4), reaches the point of negation but this time via documentary and technological, anti-literary theatre: not, however, providing information, nor explaining (although there is an anti-capitalist implication) nor ultimately doing propaganda (although there were outraged accusations of this from the press) but permitting a glimpse into the darkness for the enhancement of the light.

Another of the documentary plays staged by Piscator in the Federal Republic, Heinar Kipphardt's *In der Sache J. Robert Oppenheimer* (*The Case of J. Robert Oppenheimer*, 1964), together with Brecht's much-revised play *Leben des Galilei* (*Galileo*, originally 1938–9, revised in 1945–7; Brecht was working on a Berliner Ensemble production [1957] when he died in 1956), can serve as the endpoint to this treatment of the 'instrumental' life of literature under capitalist democracy. Brecht's play was written in Danish exile and revised with Charles Laughton in Hollywood, while the Piscator production took place in the BRD. They are both about the question of the meaning of technology for civilization as it was posed by the dropping of the atomic bomb by the Americans on Hiroshima on 6 August 1945: Kipphardt's play deals with it directly through use of documentary material concerning Oppenheimer's withdrawal from the US nuclear programme; Brecht's historical drama indirectly reflected the impact of the bomb in the later revision.

Both these plays deal with the question of the responsibility of the scientist. They are politically motivated, in that they examine the morality of technology, and conclude or imply that it is not safe in the hands of political authorities guided by interests other than those of broad humanity. The problem is that neither radical man of the theatre, although still culturally driven by the spirit of critique that had animated them during the Weimar period, was in a position to believe any longer that such a political authority might be on the horizon. What comes apart in these two texts, despite efforts to maintain a clear political focus, is the belief that the technological paradigm, in art and in politics, the pursuit of 'doing', will converge in a humane society, making it possible once more to make apolitical art and write poems about trees. What comes about are forms of representation at home in the capitalist democratic media, such as the parable play (like Friedrich Dürrenmatt's entertaining but apolitical *Die Physiker* [*The Physicists*, 1963], on the same theme), or the journalistic media documentary (Kipphardt's text was first broadcast on the radio). These make entertainment out of estrangement (*Verfremdung*), staging or posing imponderables that make you think, but in relation to which there is nothing very cheering to think about but an endless supply of further distractions to stop you realizing.

Conclusion: The End of the Age

According to the historian E. J. Hobsbawm in his book *Age of Extremes: The Short Twentieth Century 1914–1991*, the Golden Age of the twentieth century lasted from 1947 until 1973 or thereabouts. These were the years when capitalism and social responsibility held each other in check on both the international and the national level. They were, in the singer's words from the final chorus of Brecht's *Der kaukasische Kreidekreis* (*The Caucasian Chalk Circle*, 1948) '[die] kurze / Goldene Zeit beinah der Gerechtigkeit' ('[the] short, Golden age almost of justice'). In our model, the cultural potential for this fertile mix of capitalist 'will to power' and Enlightenment rationality was trialled for Europe in Germany in the Weimar period. The mood of anti-climax with which my account of the literature of democratic capitalism finishes reflects the sense of stagnation between the end of the Golden Age (the time at which the 'operations of capitalism had become uncontrollable': Hobsbawm 1994: 408) and the emergence of the effects of this in the reality of political and economic institutions. The same stagnation was felt in the DDR, as I reported in chapter 5, where, after a moment of productive optimism around 1970, there was a long slow realization that the economic and social models of the East were failing. In 1989–90 they did fail, at which point 'the collapse of one part of the world revealed the malaise of the rest' (10).

For German literature as has been suggested above (for instance, in the case of Heiner Müller), there was a convergence between the writing of the West and the East during these years of cultural stagnation. But clearly in terms of public discourse, in which we include the discourses of literature, 1989–90 was momentous for the Germans of the BRD and the DDR.

In this sense, although it may be a superficial one, our conclusion can strike a positive note to balance the downbeat fading of the previous two chapters. With the new historical turn – the sense that history still happened to Germans – there is no doubt that German writing received a powerful new impetus. This is reflected most obviously in works of more or less traditional literary fiction, such as Thomas Brussig's *Helden wie wir*

(*Heroes Like Us*, 1998, a *Blechtrommel* for the *Wende*), and Uwe Tellkamp's novel *Der Turm* (*The Tower*, 2008), a family saga of the 1980s DDR, which is structured to culminate in the drama of reunification.

Moreover, what we defined as 'the writing of experience' in the previous chapter took on a broad and liberating range, entering into the mainstream once dominated by the remnants of traditional literature. This took two main forms.

First, German writers, especially those who grew up in the DDR, could write from their own immediate experience about the intersection within the individual subjects of psychology and history. This discourse had in the 'unified' German public a natural target audience of genuinely interested readers. At the same time, it provided the 'writing of experience' with a topic less Medusan than the First World War or the Nazi legacy, but no less historically objective and, at least on the headline level, positive rather than calamitous. This new layer of historical-personal experience also released engagements with the Nazi past which had been frozen in the ideological oversimplification of the preceding forty years. Examples are the texts of Monika Maron (born 1941), such as *Pawels Briefe* (*Pawel's Letters*, 1999), or the more recent work of Uwe Timm (born 1940), for instance, *Am Beispiel meines Bruders* (*The Example of my Brother*, 2003), but there are dozens of others (of which accounts may be found in secondary works listed under Further Reading at the end of this book).

The new unified discourse of German literature was more open to the globalization that had begun decades earlier, but only now broke unmediated upon the national consciousness. In these terms, it seems reasonable to speak of a 'normalization' in Germans' sense of themselves as a nation within the European Union, important but not alone, identified with the global culture within which the experience of being German is a reassuringly familiar irritant rather than an historical disgrace.

The second major contemporary development of the writing of experience is that it grew to include an astonishing range of social and ethnic diversity: the global within, as it were, became explicit. This is surely a token of the ability to engage seriously with cultural difference and to acknowledge the existence of intractable social problems, as well, of course, as an effect of diversification in the market-driven sense. Writers in German whose subjective experience and discourse is formed by ethnic and social difference, as in the case of the many distinguished writers of Turkish origin such as Emine Sevgi Özdamar (born 1946) or Feridun Zaimoğlu (born 1964), or authors from remnants of German-speaking lands outside Germany, such as Herta Müller (born 1953) from the

Romanian Banat region and her ex-husband Richard Wagner (born 1952), or the Hungarian-German Terézia Mora (born 1971), now occupy a prominent position on the contemporary German literary scene. Mora's first novel, *Alle Tage* (*Every Day*, 2004), for instance, won literary prizes from Berlin and Leipzig, while in 2009 the Nobel Prize for literature itself was awarded to Müller.

It is too soon to say which elements of this great diversity, which includes a flourishing element of experimentalism (see, for instance, Kemal Kurt's *Ja, sagt Molly* [*Yes, Says Molly*, 1998] or Georg Klein's *Libidissi*, 1999) and countless other literary productions of all possible varieties, will survive. We are not in a position to say whether the great diversity and vigour of the contemporary German literary scene is one of superficial excitation or profound renewal. Yet, since this book is, as was said right at the start, as much about literature as about Germany, it seems fitting to end on a literary achievement which is not superficial.

The voluntary exile W. G. Sebald, who worked as an academic in England until his accidental death in 2001, quietly produced a body of writing in German (but also superbly translated into English) that renews the Literature of Negation for the age of prosthetic electronic consciousness. An essayist and poet as well as a writer of prose texts (for instance, *Die Ausgewanderten* [*The Emigrants*, 1992], *Die Ringe des Saturn*, 1995, and *Austerlitz*, 2001), he belongs in a tradition of aesthetic prose, with roots in the works of Swiss author Robert Walser and the Austrian writing of Stifter and Thomas Bernhard, but also in ahistorical dialogue with Kafka, Benjamin, Celan and many others (not only German: one thinks of Sir Thomas Browne and Jorge Luis Borges). His writing is pitched against the excessive noise and perpetual acceleration of the new world, slowing language down, rediscovering the possibility of literary narrative that is not banal or merely personal, opening his readers' ears to the murmur of the dead, yet siding by this very solidarity with real life. What characterizes his books is the estranging inclusion of photographs in the body of the text (in this he is not alone) and a drifting style of presentation that moves through chains of association, delicately held together by attribution to a writing consciousness. By these means, which are only inadequately expounded here, he redeems both the false meaningfulness that attaches to information in the computer age and the false authenticity that attaches to the representations of the world mediated through technology. In his work, one glimpses the possibility that the *Erlebnis* of existing in the fallen world might indeed again become, if treated with the appropriate aesthetic and cultural respect, the kind of *Erfahrung* that makes survival in it valuable.

References

This list contains only those books and articles that are specifically referred to in the text using the author–date system. Further reading is listed in a separate section below.

Badiou, A. (2007) *The Century*, trans. A. Toscano. Cambridge: Polity.

Baird, J. (2008) *Hitler's War Poets: Literature and Politics in the Third Reich*. Cambridge: Cambridge University Press.

Bathrick, D. (1995) *The Powers of Speech: The Politics of Culture in the GDR*. Lincoln and London: University of Nebraska Press.

Becker, E. (1996) 'Literaturverbreitung', in E. McInnes and G. Plumpe (eds), *Bürgerlicher Realismus und Gründerzeit 1848–1890, Hansers Sozialgeschichte der deutschen Literatur vom 16. Jahrhundert bis zur Gegenwart*, vol. VI. Munich: Hanser, pp. 108–43.

Benjamin, W. (1979) 'Theories of Fascism'. *New German Critique* 17: 120–8.

Berend, E. (1974) 'Jean Paul: Der meistgelesene Schriftsteller seiner Zeit?' in U. Schweikert (ed.), *Jean Paul*. Darmstadt: WBG, pp. 155–69.

Berlin, I. (1994) *The Magus of the North: J. G. Hamann and the Origins of Modern Irrationalism*. London: Fontana.

Berlin, I. (1999) *The Roots of Romanticism*. London: Pimlico.

Berman, R. (1986) *The Rise of the Modern German Novel: Crisis and Charisma*. Cambridge, MA and London: Harvard University Press.

Beutin, W. et al. (1993) *A History of German Literature: From the Beginnings to the Present Day*, trans. C. Krojzl. London and New York: Routledge.

Biermann, W. (1977) 'Ruthless Cursing', trans. Jack Zipes. *New German Critic*: 10: 7–8.

Bohrer, K. (1991) 'Why We are Not a Nation – and Why We Should Become One'. *New German Critique* 52: 72–83.

Cooper, I. (2008) *The Near and Distant God: Poetry, Idealism and Religious Thought from Hölderlin to Eliot*. London: Legenda.

Debord, G. (1967) *La societé du spectacle*. Paris: Buchet-Chastel.

Eichberg, H. (1977) 'The Nazi *Thingspiel*: Theatre for the Masses in Fascism and Proletarian Culture'. *New German Critique* 11: 133–50.

Eksteins, M. (1989) *Rites of Spring: The Great War and the Birth of the Modern Age*. London: Bantam Press.

Felstiner, J. (1995) *Paul Celan: Poet, Survivor, Jew*. New Haven and London: Yale University Press.

Geuss, R. and Speirs, R. (eds) (1999) *Nietzsche: The Birth of Tragedy and Other Writings*, trans. R. Speirs. Cambridge: Cambridge University Press.

Goetzinger, G. (1998) 'Die Situation der Autorinnen und Autoren', in G. Sautermeister and U. Schmid (eds), *Zwischen Restauration und Revolution 1815–1848, Hansers Sozialgeschichte der deutschen Literatur vom 16. Jahrhundert bis zur Gegenwart*, vol. V. Munich: Hanser, pp. 38–59.

Gooch, S. (trans.) (1977) *Wolf Biermann: Poems and Ballads*. London: Pluto.

Grimminger, R. (1980) 'Roman', in R. Grimminger (ed.), *Deutsche Aufklärung bis zur Französischen Revolution 1680–1789, Hansers Sozialgeschichte der deutschen Literatur vom 16. Jahrhundert bis zur Gegenwart*, vol. III. Munich: Hanser, pp. 635–715.

Habermas, J. (1987) *The Philosophical Discourse of Modernity*, trans. F. Lawrence. Cambridge: Polity.

Hamburger, M. (ed. and trans.) (1981) *An Unofficial Rilke*. London: Anvil Press.

Helmstetter, R. (1998) *Die Geburt des Realismus aus dem Dunst des Familienblattes: Fontane und die öffentlichkeitsgeschichtlichen Rahmenbedingungen des poetischen Realismus*. Munich: Fink.

Hobsbawm, E. (1994) *Age of Extremes. The Short Twentieth Century 1914–1991*. London: Michael Joseph.

Howind, A. (1988) 'Ein Antikriegsroman als Bestseller. Die Vermarktung von *Im Westen nichts Neues* 1928 bis 1930', in T. Westphalen (ed.), *Erich Maria Remarque 1898–1970*. Bramsche: Rasch Verlag, pp. 55–64.

Huyssen, A. (1986) 'Adorno in Reverse: From Hollywood to Richard Wagner', in *After the Great Divide*. Bloomington and Indianapolis: Indiana University Press, pp. 16–43.

Huyssen, A. (1995) *Twilight Memories: Marking Time in a Culture of Amnesia*. New York and London: Routledge.

Janouch, G. (1951) *Gespräche mit Kafka. Erinnerungen und Aufzeichnungen*. Frankfurt am Main: Fischer.

Jordan, L. (1981) 'Zum Verhältnis von traditioneller und innovativer Elemente in der Kriegslyrik August Stramms', in J. Drews (ed.), *Das Tempo dieser Zeit ist keine Kleinigkeit. Zur Literatur von 1918*. Munich: Text + Kritik, pp. 112–27.

Knight, D. (1990) 'Romanticism and the Sciences', in A. Cunningham and N. Jardine (eds), *Romanticism and the Sciences*. Cambridge: Cambridge University Press, pp. 13–24.

Köhler, J. (2000) *Wagner's Hitler*, trans. R. Taylor. Cambridge: Polity.

LaCapra, D. (1994) *Representing the Holocaust: History, Theory, Trauma*. Ithaca and London: Cornell University Press.

Lovejoy, A. O. (1948) 'The Meaning of "Romantic" in Early German Romanticism', in A. O. Lovejoy, *Essays in the History of Ideas*. Baltimore: Johns Hopkins, pp. 183–206.

Lukács, G. (1978) *The Theory of the Novel*, trans. A. Bostock. Manchester: Merlin Press.

Mann, T. (1990) 'Leiden und Größe Richard Wagners', in *Thomas Mann Gesammelte Werke*, vol. IX. Frankfurt am Main: Fischer, pp. 363–426.

Meinecke, F. (1946) *Die Entstehung des Historismus*, 2nd edn. Munich: Leibniz Verlag.

Middleton, C. (ed. and trans.) (1972) *Friedrich Hölderlin, Eduard Mörike: Selected Poems*. Chicago and London: University of Chicago Press.

Midgley, D. (2000) *Writing Weimar: Critical Realism in German Literature 1918–1933*. Oxford: Oxford University Press.

Müller, H. (1976) *Mauser*, trans. H. Fehervary and M. Silberman. *New German Critique* 8: 122–49.

Müller, H. (1982) *Rotwelsch*. Berlin: Merve.

Natter, W. (1999) *Literature at War 1914–1940. Representing the 'Time of Greatness' in Germany*. New Haven and London: Yale University Press.

Naumann, U. (1979) *Adalbert Stifter*. Stuttgart: Metzler.

Neuhaus, V. (1988) *Günter Grass*: Die Blechtrommel. Munich: Oldenbourg.

Neuhaus, V. (1997) *Günter Grass*. Die Blechtrommel. *Erläuterungen und Dokumente*. Stuttgart: Reclam.

Newman, E. (1933) *The Life of Richard Wagner*, 4 vols, I, *1813–1848*. London: Cassell.

Parker, S., Davies, P. and Philpotts, M. (2004) *The Modern Restoration: Rethinking German Literary History 1930–1960*. Berlin and New York: Walter de Gruyter.

Plowman, A. (1998) *The Radical Subject: Social Change and the Self in Recent German Autobiography*. Bern: Peter Lang.

Ryan, J. (1990) 'The Problem of Pastiche: Patrick Süskind's *Das Parfum*'. *The German Quarterly* 63: 396–403.

Santner, E. (1990) *Stranded Objects: Mourning, Memory, and Film in Postwar Germany*. Ithaca and London: Cornell University Press.

Schings, H.-J. (1983) 'Wilhelm Meisters Geselle Laertes'. *Euphorion* 77: 419–37.

Schneider, T. (2004) 'Bestseller im Dritten Reich'. *Vierteljahreshefte für Zeitgeschichte* 52: 77–92.

Schoeps, K.-H. (2004) *Literature and Film in the Third Reich*, trans. Kathleen M. Dell'Orto. Rochester and Woodbridge: Camden House.

Scholl, J. (1990) *In der Gemeinsamkeit des Erzählers. Studien zur Restitution des Epischen im deutschen Gegenwartsroman*. Heidelberg: Carl Winter.

Sengle, F. (1971) *Biedermeierzeit. Deutsche Literatur zwischen Restauration und Revolution 1815–1848*, vol. I, *Allgemeine Voraussetzungen. Richtungen. Darstellungsmittel*. Stuttgart: Metzler.

Simmel, G. (1950) 'The Metropolis and Mental Life', in K. Wolff (ed. and trans.), *The Sociology of Georg Simmel.* Glencoe: The Free Press, pp. 409–24.

Sloterdijk, P. (1978) *Literatur und Organisation von Lebenserfahrung. Autobiographien der Zwanziger Jahre.* Munich: Carl Hanser.

Sloterdijk, P. (1983) *Kritik der zynischen Vernunft,* 2 vols. Frankfurt am Main: Suhrkamp.

Stefan, V. (1975) *Häutungen. Autobiografische Aufzeichnungen: Gedichte, Träume, Analysen.* Munich: Verlag Frauenoffensive.

Steinberg, M. (2004) *Listening to Reason: Culture, Subjectivity, and Nineteenth-Century Music.* Princeton: Princeton University Press.

Steinweg, R. (1972a) *Das Lehrstück. Brechts Theorie einer ästhetischen Erziehung.* Stuttgart: Metzler.

Steinweg, R. (ed.) (1972b) *Bertolt Brecht. Die Maßnahme. Kritische Ausgabe.* Frankfurt am Main: Suhrkamp.

Stern, F. (1961) *The Politics of Cultural Despair: A Study in the Rise of Germanic Ideology.* Berkeley: University of California Press.

Stern, J. (1953) *Ernst Jünger.* Cambridge: Bowes & Bowes.

Struck, K. (1973) *Klassenliebe.* Frankfurt am Main: Suhrkamp.

Theweleit, K. (1977–8) *Männerphantasien,* 2 vols. Frankfurt: Roter Stern.

Timms, E. (1986) *Karl Kraus: Apocalyptic Satirist: Culture and Catastrophe in Habsburg Vienna.* New Haven and London: Yale University Press.

Vaget, H. R. (1970) 'Das Bild vom Dilettanten bei Moritz, Schiller und Goethe'. *Jahrbuch des freien deutschen Hochstifts:* 1–31.

von Molnár, G. (1987) *Romantic Vision, Ethical Context: Novalis and Artistic Autonomy.* Minneapolis: University of Minnesota Press.

Waldmann, G. (1982) 'Trivial- und Unterhaltungsromane', in F. Trommler (ed.), *Jahrhundertwende: Vom Naturalismus zum Expressionismus 1880–1918, Deutsche Literatur. Eine Sozialgeschichte,* ed. H. Glaser, vol. VIII. Reinbek bei Hamburg: Rowohlt, pp. 124–39.

Webber, A. (1993) 'Reality as Pretext. Robert Musil, "Die Verwirrungen des jungen Törleß"', in D. Midgley (ed.), *The German Novel in the Twentieth Century: Beyond Realism.* Edinburgh: Edinburgh University Press, pp. 30–44.

Weigel, S. (1999) *Ingeborg Bachmann. Hinterlassenschaften unter Wahrung des Briefgeheimnisses.* Vienna: Paul Zsolnay.

Wiedemann, B. (ed.) (2003) *Paul Celan. Die Gedichte. Kommentierte Ausgabe in einem Band.* Frankfurt am Main: Suhrkamp.

Williams, R. (1988) 'Theatre as a Political Forum', in E. Timms and P. Collier (eds), *Visions and Blueprints: Avant-garde Culture and Radical Politics in Early Twentieth-Century Europe.* Manchester: Manchester University Press, pp. 307–20.

Wolin, R. (1994) *Walter Benjamin: An Aesthetic of Redemption.* Berkeley: University of California Press.

Wright, E. (1989) *Postmodern Brecht: A Re-Presentation.* London and New York: Routledge.

Further reading

The following list includes books that provide stimulation or information or both. The emphasis is on works in English with broad relevance to themes discussed in the text. They often provide extensive and up-to-date bibliographies.

HISTORICAL SURVEYS AND REFERENCE WORKS

Batts, M. (1993) *A History of Histories of German Literature 1835–1914*. Montreal and Kingston: McGill-Queen's University Press.

Boyle, N. (2008) *German Literature: A Very Short Introduction*. Oxford: Oxford University Press.

Camden House History of German Literature (2001–) 10 vols. Rochester and Woodbridge: Camden House.

Fulbrook, M. (1990) *A Concise History of Germany*. Cambridge: Cambridge University Press.

Glaser, H. (1980–1982) *Deutsche Literatur. Eine Sozialgeschichte*, 10 vols. Reinbek bei Hamburg: Rowohlt.

Grimminger, R. et al. (eds) (1980–2009) *Hansers Sozialgeschichte der deutschen Literatur vom 16. Jahrhundert bis zur Gegenwart*, 12 vols. Munich: Hanser.

Schlaffer, H. (2002) *Die kurze Geschichte der deutschen Literatur*. Munich: Hanser.

Watanabe-O'Kelly, H. (ed.) (1997) *The Cambridge History of German Literature*. Cambridge: Cambridge University Press.

Wellbery, D. (ed.) (2004) *A New History of German Literature*. Cambridge, MA and London: Harvard University Press.

CULTURAL HISTORY AND THEORY

Anderson, B. (1983) *Imagined Communities: Reflections on the Origin and Spread of Nationalism*. London: Verso.

Blackall, E. (1959) *The Emergence of German as a Literary Language*. London and New York: Cambridge University Press.

Bovenschen, S. (1979) *Die imaginierte Weiblichkeit. Exemplarische Untersuchungen zu kulturgeschichtlichen und literarischen Präsentationsformen des Weiblichen*. Frankfurt am Main: Suhrkamp.

Bruford, W. (1935) *Germany in the Eighteenth Century: The Social Background of the Literary Revival*. London and New York: Cambridge University Press.

Bürger, P. (1984) *Theory of the Avant-Garde*, trans. M. Shaw. Minneapolis: University of Minnesota Press.

François, E. and Schulze, H. (eds) (2001) *Deutsche Erinnerungsorte*, 3 vols. Munich: Beck.

Hohendahl, P. (1989) *Building a National Literature: The Case of Germany 1830–1870*, trans. R. Franciscono. Ithaca and London: Cornell University Press.

Kittler, F. (1990) *Discourse Networks 1800/1900*, trans. M. Metteer. Stanford: Stanford University Press.

Lepenies, W. (2006) *The Seduction of Culture in German History*. Princeton and Oxford: Princeton University Press.

Marcus, G. (1989) *Lipstick Traces: A Secret History of the Twentieth Century*. London: Secker & Warburg.

Marcus, L. (1994) *Auto/biographical Discourses: Criticism, Theory, Practice*. Manchester and New York: Manchester University Press.

Moretti, F. (1996) *Modern Epic: The World System from Goethe to García Márquez*, trans. Q. Hoare. London: Verso.

Robson-Scott, W. (1965) *The Literary Background of the Gothic Revival in Germany*. Oxford: Clarendon Press.

Ward, A. (1974) *Book Production, Fiction and the German Reading Public 1740–1800*. Oxford: Oxford University Press.

Weigel, S. (1987) *Die Stimme der Medusa. Schreibweisen in der Gegenwartsliteratur von Frauen*. Dülmen-Hiddingsel: Tende.

Williams, R. (1958) *Culture and Society 1780–1950*. London: Chatto & Windus.

Woodmansee, M. (1994) *The Author, Art, and The Market: Rereading the History of Aesthetics*. New York: Columbia University Press.

INDIVIDUALS AND TOPICS

Baldwin, C. (2002) *The Emergence of the Modern German Novel: Christoph Martin Wieland, Sophie von La Roche, and Maria Anna Sagar*. Rochester and Woodbridge: Camden House.

Barner, W. (ed.) (1994) *Geschichte der deutschen Literatur von 1945 bis zur Gegenwart*. Munich: Beck.

Boa, E. (1987) *The Sexual Circus: Wedekind's Theatre of Subversion*. Oxford: Basil Blackwell.

Boa, E. and Palfreyman, R. (2000) *Heimat – A German Dream: Regional Loyalties and National Identity in German Culture 1890–1990*. Oxford: Oxford University Press.

Boyle, N. (1991) *Goethe: The Poet and the Age*, vol. 1, *The Poetry of Desire (1749–1790)*. Oxford: Clarendon Press.

Boyle, N. (2000) *Goethe: The Poet and the Age*, vol. 2, *Revolution and Renunciation (1790–1803)*. Oxford: Clarendon Press.

Bridge, H. (2002) *Women's Writing and Historiography in the GDR*. Oxford: Oxford University Press.

Burns, R. (1995) *German Cultural Studies: An Introduction*. Oxford: Oxford University Press.

Catling, J. (ed.) (2000) *A History of Women's Writing in Germany, Austria and Switzerland*. Cambridge: Cambridge University Press.

Emmerich, W. (1996) *Kleine Literaturgeschichte der DDR. Erweiterte Neuausgabe*. Leipzig: Kiepenhauer.

Frieden, S. (1983) *Self into Form. German-language Autobiographical Writings of the 1970s.* New York: P. Lang.

Herf, J. (1984) *Reactionary Modernism: Technology, Culture and Politics in Weimar and the Third Reich.* Cambridge: Cambridge University Press.

Kaes, A., Jay, M. and Dimendberg, E. (1994) *The Weimar Republic Sourcebook.* Berkeley: University of California Press.

Kolinsky, E. and van der Will, W. (1998) *The Cambridge Companion to Modern German Culture.* Cambridge: Cambridge University Press.

McInnes, E. (1983) *Das deutsche Drama des 19. Jahrhunderts.* Berlin: Erich Schmidt.

Newman, E. (1933–46) *The Life of Richard Wagner,* 4 vols. London: Cassell.

Nisbet, H. (2008) *Lessing: Eine Biografie.* Munich: Beck.

Norton, R. (2002) *Secret Germany: Stefan George and his Circle.* Ithaca and London: Cornell University Press.

Pascal, R. (1953) *The German Sturm und Drang.* Manchester: Manchester University Press.

Pascal, R. (1973) *From Naturalism to Expressionism: German Literature and Society 1880–1918.* London: Weidenfeld & Nicholson.

Paulin, R. (1985) *The Brief Compass: The Nineteenth-century German Novelle.* Oxford: Clarendon Press.

Perraudin, M. (2000) *Literature, the Volk and the Revolution in Mid-Nineteenth Century Germany.* New York and Oxford: Berghahn.

Reed, T. (1996) *Thomas Mann: The Uses of Tradition,* 2nd edn. Oxford: Clarendon Press.

Robertson, R. (2001) *The 'Jewish Question' in German Literature 1749–1939.* Oxford: Oxford University Press.

Robertson, R. (2004) *Kafka: A Very Short Introduction.* Oxford: Oxford University Press.

Saul, N. (ed.) (2002) *Philosophy and German Literature: 1700–1990.* Cambridge: Cambridge University Press.

Saul, N. (ed.) (2009) *The Cambridge Companion to German Romanticism.* Cambridge: Cambridge University Press.

Schlant, E. (1999) *The Language of Silence: West German Literature and the Holocaust.* New York and London: Routledge.

Sengle, F. (1971–1980) *Biedermeierzeit,* 3 vols. Stuttgart: Metzler.

Taberner, S. (2005) *German Literature of the 1990s and Beyond: Normalization and the Berlin Republic.* Rochester and Woodbridge: Camden House.

Taberner, S. (ed.) (2007) *Contemporary German Fiction: Writing in the Berlin Republic.* Cambridge: Cambridge University Press.

Index